SISTERS
ON SCREEN

SIBLINGS IN

CONTEMPORARY

CINEMA

Eva Rueschmann

 Temple University Press
PHILADELPHIA

Temple University Press, Philadelphia 19122
Copyright © 2000 by Temple University
All rights reserved
Published 2000
Printed in the United States of America

∞ The paper used in this publication meets the requirements of the American
National Standard for Information Sciences—Permanence of Paper for Printed
Library Materials, ANSI Z39.48-1984

Library of Congress Cataloging-in-Publication Data

Rueschmann, Eva, 1962–
   Sisters on screen : siblings in contemporary cinema / Eva Rueschmann.
      p.   cm. -- (Culture and the moving image)
   Filmography: p.
   Includes bibliographical references and index.
   ISBN 1-56639-746-4 (cloth : alk. paper) -- ISBN 1-56639-747-2 (pbk. :
alk. paper)
   1. Sisters in motion pictures. 2. Family in motion pictures. I. Title.
II. Series.

PN1995.9.S55 R84 2000
791.43´652045--dc21   99-051317

The lines from "Sibling Mysteries" (p. 137, herein) from THE DREAM OF A
COMMON LANGUAGE: Poems 1974–1977 by Adrienne Rich. Copyright ©
1978 by W. W. Norton & Company, Inc. Reprinted by permission of the author
and W. W. Norton & Company, Inc.

To my sister Anja
and my parents

Contents

Photographs follow page 116

Acknowledgments

A book is, in the end, always the product of more than its author, and many people have generously contributed to this work in different ways. First and foremost, I would like to express my deep gratitude and affection to my teacher and mentor, Catherine Portuges, whose tremendous professional support and friendship over the years have made this project and many others possible. Professor Portuges's original and provocative scholarship on the intersections of psychoanalysis, cinema, and gender studies has greatly influenced and enriched my own scholarship, and I feel very privileged to have worked with her as a student and colleague. I thank the members of my original dissertation committee, David Lenson, Richard Noland, and Lee Edwards at the University of Massachusetts, Amherst, who each in their own fashion contributed to improving the arguments in this book through their insightful and astute comments on an earlier version.

I am greatly indebted to my husband, Matthew Schmidt, without whom *Sisters on Screen* would not appear in its present form. He accompanied me with good cheer and helpful advice through the good and bad times of writing, and lived with this project for a long time. His superb editorial skills have helped me make this book more accessible and appealing to both academic and general audiences interested in the representation of sisters in cinema.

Margarethe von Trotta, whose oeuvre I discuss at length in this book, generously agreed to an extended interview in the summer of 1992, during which she candidly and in great detail spoke to me about her films, her life, and women in world cinema. I will always be thankful for this opportunity to exchange ideas with one of the great women directors of German and indeed international cinema. Her comments and insights have significantly enhanced my reading of her films about sisters, a viewing of which first inspired me to think and write about the subject.

My sincere thanks to Mary Corliss, curator of the Film Stills Archive at the Museum of Modern Art, for providing me from MoMA's collection the splendid film stills in this book.

To all my colleagues at Hampshire College I am deeply appreciative for their support, friendly collegiality, and intellectual companionship. In particular, Mary Russo, dean of Humanities, Arts, and Cultural Studies, provided the unfailing encouragement and confidence in my scholarship and teaching that have made it possible for me to bring this project to a successful conclusion. I would also like to thank the many wonderful and smart students I have taught at Hampshire College over the years. Their infectious enthusiasm and creative insights into film have continually renewed and deepened my scholarly interest in and passion for cinema.

I am grateful to my editor at Temple University Press, Janet Francendese, for recognizing the project's potential from its very inception and for her patience and congenial assistance during the completion of the manuscript. To Professor Robert Sklar, series editor for "Culture and the Moving Image" at Temple, I would like to express my appreciation for the special interest he took in this topic. Janet Greenwood and Bobbe Needham deserve particular mention for their incisive and careful copyediting of the manuscript.

I wish to thank Martha Yoder and Mona Heinze-Barreca, whose encouragement and longtime friendship I value greatly.

Finally, this book is dedicated to my family—my parents, Klaus and Traudi Rüschmann, whose love and support have always sustained me and who have taken pride in all my efforts; and to Anja, the very best of sisters and a very talented artist, who I hope will enjoy this book as much as I took pleasure in writing it.

SISTERS ON SCREEN

Introduction

Sisterhood is a love-hate roundelay, with iridescent levels of attachment. Laced with love, fraught with ambiguity, tainted with envy, the relationship is elastic and enduring. Because [sisters] view the same events at the same time from different perspectives, we are able to help one another remember, interpret, invent and even reinvent family history.

Emily Gwathmey and Ellen Stern, *Sister Sets: Sisters Whose Togetherness Sets Them Apart*

M y subject is the rendering of biological sisters and their psychological relationships in modern world cinema.[1] Although sisters in cinema is a topic that has been almost entirely ignored in the critical literature devoted to film, I join a number of contemporary scholars in the fields of feminist theory, literary criticism, and psychology who are examining the significance of the psychosocial relationship between biological sisters.[2] As the quotation from Emily Gwathmey and Ellen Stern reveals, the sister relationship is one of the most vital, emotionally complex, and lasting attachments between women. Indeed, for many women, a sister is a part of the personal identity they carry around inside, as indelible to their sense of self as their mothers and fathers. Throughout their lives sisters weave between them intricate and complicated patterns of psychological intimacy. During the formative years of childhood and adolescence, sisters often play pivotal roles in each other's self-definition. Friends and confidantes, rivals and antagonists, sisters claim mutual likenesses and assert individual differences through their relationship. In adulthood, too, the emotional intensity and depth of the sororal bond are frequently sustained, as sisters remain entangled in a common tapestry of mutual experience and remembrance, family and history.

The modern feature films I discuss in this book were chosen precisely because they concern themselves with the powerful emotional dynamics between biological sisters. Significantly, all are products of the modern era of cinema, dating from the 1960s into the 1990s, and all offer original, female-centered visions of women's lives and subjectivities. Sisters, of course, have appeared as characters in motion pictures since the silent-film era. The real-life sisters Dorothy and Lillian Gish, two of D. W. Griffith's favorite actresses, played twins in his famous melodrama *Orphans of the Storm* in 1921. And a whole subgenre of female twin melodramas was produced by Hollywood in the 1940s.[3] However, because these popular films almost always articulated male views of women, they rarely suggested the complicated social textures of biological sisterhood or the psychological desires that bind sisters to one another and the tensions that at times drive them apart. In contrast, the contemporary feature films I discuss here display far greater insight into women's intersubjective relationships. Although cinematic fictions, their sensitive and nuanced observation of women's emotional experiences and social interactions complement what psychoanalytic theory can tell us about the sister bond.

The sister films covered in these pages belong to a wider group of revisionist works about women, contemporary films largely, if not exclusively, the creation of a post-1960s generation of women writers and directors, most of whom have been aesthetically influenced by the modernist cinema movements of the 1960s. As film historians so often note, the advent of innovative film movements such as the French New Wave, Italian post-neorealism, and the New German Cinema in the 1960s, no less than the institutional collapse of the old Hollywood studio system and other technological and cultural changes in global filmmaking during the same time period, represented a crucial development in the medium's manifold responses to postwar transformations in cultural life, society, and politics.[4] For my purposes, these alternative cinema movements serve as a valuable frame of historical reference and a critical point of departure for appreciating the aesthetic strategies through which post-1960s cinema has attempted to redefine female screen identities. Stressing the centrality of feminine attachments for women's

identities, contemporary women directors and screenwriters have produced works that are unorthodox in subject matter, eclectic in narrative
form, and revisionary in their handling of mise-en-scène and point of
view as means to privilege women's interrelationships and perceptions.
Furthermore, many filmmakers working in the modernist vein have self-
reflexively scrutinized women as screen subjects in their works, thereby
acknowledging the artistic dimensions of rendering in cinematic terms
the psychological complexities of female subjectivity. This is particularly
true of the sister films prominent in this book, with their acute focus on
the psychosocial interactions between women—Margarethe von Trotta's
Sisters, or The Balance of Happiness (1979), Diane Kurys's *Peppermint Soda*
(1977), Jane Campion's *An Angel at My Table* (1990), Gillian Armstrong's
The Last Days of Chez Nous (1990), Allison Anders's *Gas Food Lodging*
(1992), Nancy Meckler's *Sister My Sister* (1995), and Kasi Lemmons's
Eve's Bayou (1997), among others. These post-1960s films, along with
a number of selected works by iconoclastic male directors, stand at the
heart of my analysis of sisters on screen.

The impetus for this work goes back to the late 1980s when I viewed
in tandem two feature films about sisters produced in the 1970s: Swedish
director Ingmar Bergman's *Cries and Whispers* (1972) and German filmmaker Margarethe von Trotta's *Sisters, or The Balance of Happiness*.[5] Powerful and provocative, the images of female subjectivity in these films
pivot on biological sisters bound together in love and hate. So psychologically astute and cinematically unique were Bergman's and von
Trotta's portraits of sororal passions, I found myself searching out what
had been written about these works and their directors. To my surprise,
I discovered that Bergman's *Cries and Whispers* had been much maligned
by feminist critics in the 1970s, who decried its supposedly negative
images of women.[6] Less surprising was my discovery that Margarethe
von Trotta—one of the most serious and energetic women directors of
the New German Cinema of the 1970s—had been inspired by
Bergman's work (an impression that von Trotta would confirm in my
1992 interview with her).[7]

Not often appreciated about Bergman's films of the 1960s is their
unusual engagement with the psychodynamics of female attachment.
Cries and Whispers and Bergman's earlier work about adult sisters, *The
Silence* (1963), are psychological portraits of sisters whose feelings of
love and friendship are mixed with disappointment and jealousy, rage
and envy.

In *Cries and Whispers* Bergman elucidates the childhood origins of these tangled feelings, tracing the ambivalent emotions between the sisters to the preoedipal world of the mother-child bond. The affluent Victorian manor where the action is set and the turn-of-the-century time frame of the drama establish the oppressive cultural atmosphere within which the upper-class sisters and their status-conscious mother define their social positions as women. But it is the film's "mindscreen" (to borrow Bruce Kawin's term) of dream, fantasy, and memory that gives structure and density to the intersubjective struggles between the sisters.[8] As Margarethe von Trotta had recognized earlier, Bergman's modernist rendering of female subjectivity captured a repressed layer of women's experiences in a patriarchally structured family and society. Taking into consideration theoretical concerns of feminist scholars in the 1980s and 1990s, we can now see that Bergman was posing prescient questions about the unconscious attractions and fears, idealizations and disenchantments, that attend women's most important childhood attachments—their bond with their mother and their ties to their sisters.

Since the 1970s Bergman's controversial portrayal of sisters' relationships in *Cries and Whispers* has been amplified and revised by women directors concerned with the sister bond. His stylistic and thematic influence is certainly apparent in von Trotta's *Sisters*, one in a trilogy of sister films by the German director that draw important connections between European women's psychological relationships and the cultural and historical forces that impact their postwar social identities.

The representations of sisters in these films by Bergman and von Trotta are far more psychologically intricate than the conventionalized images of women's relationships appearing in most Hollywood entertainments and, for that matter, in much of world cinema. As the extensive literature by feminist scholars on the history of women's film images has so convincingly demonstrated, the common portrait of feminine relationships in feature films and television has usually been framed by women's relationships to men. The narrative destinies of women characters has almost invariably revolved around the social dictates of heterosexual romance, love, and marriage.

This generic pattern is apparent even in the films of a modern director such as Woody Allen, whose work has often emulated Bergman's and who is sometimes regarded as being unusually sensitive to women's unique emotional and social realities. Lori Hope Lefkovitz, in one of the few critical works devoted to sisters in cinema, offers an insightful deconstructive feminist analysis of Woody Allen's *Hannah and Her Sisters* as a modern version of an old patriarchal fantasy.[9] The film borrows from the story of Rachel and Leah in Genesis. Allen's shlemiel character, Lefkovitz writes, represents "a relatively weak hero [who] overcomes his self-doubts and becomes potent by triumphantly sleeping with his wife's sister. . . . The traditional plot of the hero who sleeps with his wife's sister allays an anxiety about female intimacies as the plot reasserts male control over female relationships."[10] Lefkovitz identifies a recurrent plot pattern in narrative films of sisters competing for a man—father, husband, brother, or son—a pattern that implies that "women, no matter how close, principally feel envy for one another, and that this envy may be sexually exploited to ensure male mastery over sorority."[11] Feminist critic Louise Bernikow also identifies this recurring male fantasy in her 1980 book, *Among Women:* "These sisters do each other no good, . . . if the stories are to be believed. One would be better off without them. In this masculine vision, all women would be better off without other women, for the women alone—motherless, sisterless, friendless—can fix their eyes solely on father, brother, lover."[12]

Lefkovitz's reading of *Hannah and Her Sisters* is a perceptive analysis of a male construction of women's images, revealing how the cultural codes and generic conventions through which Hollywood and other national cinemas have so persistently misrepresented women's psychology are reproduced in the celebrated work of a major contemporary director. Yet, Lefkowitz's approach has limited value for analyzing the sister films that I discuss in these pages, all of which resist the plot formulae of male control and female dependency so ubiquitous in the works of male directors.

More relevant is Lucy Fischer's influential essay, "Sisters: The Divided Self," the only significant critical study of screen sisters besides Lefkowitz's. Fischer attempts to identify women filmmakers' critical subversion of classic Hollywood cinema, specifically by comparing the representation of the good/evil sister split in the subgenre of female twin melodramas of the 1940s with a feminist "countercinema" represented by Laura Mulvey's *The Bad Sister* (1983) and Margarethe von Trotta's *Sisters*. Fischer argues that these films revise the social ideology underpinning the dichotomous sibling relationships that fuel the plots of earlier Hollywood melodramas such as *Cobra Woman* (1944), *The Dark Mirror* (1946), and *A Stolen Life* (1946). Citing the Romantic or Gothic trope of the double or split self in narrative film, Fischer analyzes how the use of female twin sisters in these Hollywood melodramas reflected a division in social attitudes toward femininity and female roles in U.S. culture, validating the characteristics of the more "feminine" sister (with whom the spectator is invited to identify) and villainizing the more "masculine" sibling (the ambitious, destructive, and manipulative woman). Mulvey's avant-garde film *The Bad Sister* valorizes the sister who takes on masculine-coded roles of power and revenge, thereby exposing the ideological underpinnings of conventional film narratives about good and evil sisters. Fischer extends her reading of Mulvey's film as a feminist text belonging to a countercinema to von Trotta's *Sisters*. In a close analysis of that film, she emphasizes the psychological power dynamics between the sisters in relation to their status as women in West German capitalist society and highlights the ways in which they represent "male" and "female" poles of identity. In Fischer's view, von Trotta deconstructs this opposition in order to dramatize "a synthesis of gender identification in human life."[13]

I do not attempt in this book to identify a paradigm of the sister relationship in cinema. Fischer's discussion of sororal differences tends to reflect a common preoccupation in psychoanalytic feminist criticism with the ways in which traditional gender categories articulate differences between women in terms of "femininity" and "masculinity."[14] Although these gender categories are certainly sustained in the stereotypical portraits of women so common in Hollywood filmmaking, I am skeptical of readings that tend to universalize this particular ideological construction of gender differences throughout world cinema, even if the critic's objective is to identify the methods through which women filmmakers may attempt to subvert traditional forms of representation.[15] For instance, Fischer's interpretation of the two sisters in von Trotta's film as masculine and feminine versions of the self is initially persuasive, but on closer examination it fails to appreciate von Trotta's deep and sustained interest in sisters' actual psychological dynamics. Moreover, as a German filmmaker von Trotta has her own unique national and cultural orientation to women's cinematic representation, one not easily subsumed within an Anglo American model of feminist film practice.

This book is a critique of the varied ways in which modern filmmakers have dramatized the sister bond rather than a theoretical treatise on women in cinema. However, my discussions of sisters in modern cinema implicitly press the case for alternative psychoanalytic approaches in film criticism that move beyond the dominant models relied upon by feminist scholars such as Fischer and others who employ Freudian and Lacanian models of sexual difference and its construction in cinema. Following the lead of Laura Mulvey's seminal 1975 article, "Visual Pleasure and Narrative Cinema," feminist film scholars discern in the classical Hollywood cinematic apparatus the workings of patriarchal gender relations.[16] The female image, according to this account, is structured as an object of the voyeuristic and fetishistic male gaze, making impossible the female spectator's active pleasure and desire: she must either narcissistically identify with her image on screen or adopt, as in Mulvey's revised model of female spectatorship, a transgender identification that moves between the masculine and feminine.

Although Mulvey's theory of the male gaze has had an enormous impact on studies of gender in cinema, other feminist film theorists in the last several decades have reconceptualized the female spectator's relationship to women's cinematic images. For example, in a 1982 essay Mary Ann Doane argued for a concept of female masquerade wherein femininity is arrayed as a performance that implies a critical distance between female spectators and their own images. And Elizabeth Cowie, in her 1997 book *Representing the Woman: Cinema and Psychoanalysis*, makes a case for the spectator's positioning across gender lines, asserting that film as a scene of primal or unconscious fantasy opens up an imaginary space that allows spectators to assume a number of positions in the scenario.[17]

For my purposes, however, object relations theory offers the most promising frame of analysis for evaluating cinematic representations of women's intersubjectivity. For example, Janice Mouton's 1995 essay on von Trotta's *Sisters* moves beyond the Freudian model and the traditional masculine and feminine positionings in film narrative; it corresponds to my own use of object relations theory in the analysis of sisters in literature and film.[18] Inspired by psychoanalyst D. W. Winnicott's concept of creative play as an integral facet of childhood development, Mouton convincingly argues that von Trotta's films center on female identity formation and analyzes how her works explore the relational space between sisters—the psychosocial space in which two subjectivities creatively interact and negotiate a relationship of mutuality and difference.

Catherine Portuges has argued that cinema itself and the relationship between filmmaker, film, and spectator can be conceptualized as a "transitional space," appropriating "Winnicott's term for a hypothetical zone where self-actualizing creativity is said to take place." Winnicott's term refers to the period when the infant gradually emerges from the mother-child dyad and learns to symbolically represent its internal object-world in creative ways. Portuges contends that the extension of the object relations theory of creativity into the realm of imagination and cultural experience "holds as yet unrealized possibilities for elaborating the intersections of autobiography, gender and film theory."[19] The object relations approach to creativity and works of art, which has largely been conceived in terms of parent-child relationships, can be profitably expanded and amended to include sibling bonds. Siblings, as psychoanalysts are beginning to realize, are cathected both in relation to and independently of the parental oedipal and preoedipal bonds.[20]

Jackie Stacey's *Stargazing: Hollywood Cinema and Female Spectatorship* (1994) is another recent work of feminist scholarship that draws on object relations theory and expands the psychoanalytic discourse on female relationships within narrative cinema. Stacey contends that feminist scholars have failed to recognize the forms of pleasure and desire *between* women on and off screen. Her critique raises questions left unanswered in Fischer's and Lefkovitz's discussions of sister representations in cinema: What happens when sisters fix their eyes upon each other in cinema? What can we say of films in which sisters are presented as desiring subjects? And what of the female viewer's complicated identifications with her specular sister(s) in cinema?

Analyzing female spectators' relationship to their images, Stacey argues that object relations theory provides a framework for seeing women's complex interactions with one another as modes of negotiating their identities with other potential selves. In her study she deploys Jessica Benjamin's idea of "intersubjective dynamics"—a psychoanalytic approach to subject formation that takes into account the significance of the active role taken by another subject in the individual's struggle to creatively construct an identity. Indeed, Stacey asserts that the part played by intersubjectivity in identity formation is especially relevant "to films concerning one woman's obsessive fascination with another, since the dynamic between the two female characters on screen reproduces that between women film stars and female spectators: a fascination with an idealized other which could not be reduced to male desire or female identification within the available psychoanalytic dichotomies, but rather necessitated a rethinking of the specificities of forms of female attachment."[21]

Hence, Stacey turns aside from the theoretical cul-de-sac represented in Laura Mulvey's earlier conception of women's fixed subject positions within a cinematic apparatus construed as male, a conception structured in psychoanalytic terms around narcissism and masochistic feminine identification. Instead, Stacey demonstrates how Benjamin's research on intersubjective relationships between self and other and the desire for recognition underlies many object relations, including that between female star and spectator. Benjamin, in *The Bonds of Love* (1988) and in *Like Subjects, Love Objects* (1996), revises object relations, maintaining that the self grows not only through relations with its *internalized* objects but also through the relationship with another *subject*. Benjamin thus joins other post-Freudian object relations theorists such as Daniel Stern who suggest that the psychoanalytic process unfolds between two subjectivities, each with its own constellation of internal relations, who encounter each other and build a new relation between them. Benjamin's intersubjective view conceptualizes self and other as "distinct but interrelated beings" who are engaged in an complex matrix of assertion of self and recognition of the other.[22]

I believe Stacey's application of Benjamin's theory of intersubjective dynamics—a concept of impressive explanatory power—points the way to a better understanding of the psychosocial complexities of sister relationships and their representations in the modern films that I explore in this book. As I discuss in the next section, classic psychoanalytic studies of sibling relationships have focused on sibling dynamics as a mere reflection of their relationship to the parents, with little or no regard to the independent sibling interactions. However, Benjamin's revised model of object relations recognizes women's need for mutual recognition as subjects and the constant tension between connection and separation in female relationships—dynamics that in fact inform the sister films in this study. Her approach lends itself to a better understanding of the emotional ambivalence that often characterizes the bonds between sisters and their quest to integrate loving and hating affects toward each other.

I analyze the ways in which modern filmmakers have envisioned sister relationships and used the sister trope as a vehicle for women's quest for self-knowledge through their siblings. As Jackie Stacey's work shows, object relations theory can profitably lend itself to examining how, in cinematic texts, women negotiate their identities with other potential selves. Most directors featured in this book, such as Diane Kurys, Gillian Armstrong, Jane Campion, and Margarethe von Trotta, have moved well beyond one-dimensional representations of sisters as mere plot devices, idealized projections, or allegories of a split self. The films of these and other filmmakers convey women's unique subjectivities and life experiences through the psychological insights they bring to bear on biological sisters.

In the psychoanalytic view, the cinema has long been associated with the realms of fantasy and dream, allowing for imaginative play with gender identities, sexuality, and familial relationships. As far back as German film expressionism in the 1920s, the cinema's remarkable capacity to visualize the psychological enigmas of subjectivity and the paradoxes of identity has fascinated a large group of filmmakers. This fascination is most prominently reflected in the modernist art cinema of the 1960s, especially in the experimental works of Bergman, Alain Resnais, Luis Buñuel, Michelangelo Antonioni, and Federico Fellini. A large body of critical literature is devoted to the directorial careers of these male auteurs, their uses of the film as a medium of autobiographical or cultural exploration, and the psychoanalytic and ideological implications of their works. Today, however, film scholarship is recognizing *women's* use of cinema as a creative space for self-exploration and social critique, examining the works of earlier women directors such as Maya Deren, Sally Potter, Agnes Varda, Marguerite Duras among others.

In one of the few recent reevaluations of modernism in the postwar European film, *Cinema and Modernity* (1994), John Orr discusses modernist—or what he calls "neo-modern" cinema—in light of its inheritance of the legacies of early twentieth-century modernism. He cites modernist architecture and its redefinition of space, the death of tragedy, the inward turn of expressionist painting, and the psychological turn of narrative. He identifies the emergence of neomodern cinema with the genesis of the French New Wave and subsequent European new waves in the late 1950s into the 1970s, interpreting these movements as forms of aesthetic resistance to bourgeois certainties. He notes, for example, their critical stance toward romantic conceptions of love and marriage as fruitful forms of intimacy. The growing crisis of sexual identities and fixed points of experience also implies, according to Orr, a challenge to the conventions of perception. Neomodern cinema's response to the fragmentation of postwar society and the crisis of values is related to "the inherent ambiguity of the visual field of perception," where "all human subjects, filmmakers, actors and spectators alike, are both subject and object, viewed and viewing, looked upon and looking."[23]

An early example is Eric Rohmer's *Claire's Knee* (1977), in which the protagonist's fetishistic obsession with a young girl's knee is visually and narratively examined in self-reflexive ways as an ambiguous failure in his quest for self-knowledge and self-definition. Orr cites Anthony Giddens, who claims that "the reflexive culture of modernity is one in which the searches for self-discovery, for new ways of seeing ourselves in the process of seeing have all increased over the last thirty years as the certainties of absolute knowledge decline." Noting the frequency of doubles in modern cinema, Orr argues that a splitting of the bourgeois self poses complex questions about the identity of self on screen. Moreover, the split self destabilizes the spectator's acts of identification: "If the screen 'persona' is the absent other of the spectator, the screen character can project an 'other' version of self, or even multiple versions of potential personality, all of which become potential doubles. What the spectator sees here is often like a set of mirrors reflecting to infinity."[24] This expanded conception of the gaze and perception as intersubjective and self-reflexive counters conventional conceptions of the Romantic double. In Romanticism the figure of the double or alter ego characteristically reflects the self's search for organic wholeness, for psychic integration through union with an other.

Modernism introduces a more dialectical vision of intersubjectivity in which mirroring selves never completely coincide. Modern narratives in film and literature are no longer exclusively structured around the father and the oedipal complex. Though Orr does not explicitly address a gendered view of perception and the gaze, his ideas hold promise for a theory of the cinematic gaze that pushes into new territory. In modern cinema, the gaze is not exclusively a form of masculine control and mastery of difference (although it *can* be that); rather, the eye ("I") of the camera can serve as a locus for women's questioning and inquiring encounters with a multiplicity of female selves.

Modern cinema's attention to the psychic interior and its analytic dissection of the domestic world and its moral structures open the way to a more nuanced exploration of sibling relations in narrative filmmaking. Sisterhood is a permanent, lifelong, and changing relationship that, in the mercurial climate of modern cultural life, assumes special psychic value. Sisters usually play pivotal roles in each other's social and psychological growth during childhood and adolescence. Initially drawn together through their crisscrossing orbits around their parents, young sisters as they grow up soon rotate around one another through the mutual attraction of play and fantasy. The pattern of interaction they create becomes more involved and elaborated in adolescence, when they must assert their individuality in relation to the social universe beyond the family. Furthermore, because of the intimate nature of the relationship, sisters can come to embody for one another a unique source of familial identity. In a modern world "where all that is solid melts into air," where subjects struggle to make themselves at home in a constantly changing environment, sisters intimately mirror and challenge the self through time.[25] Witnesses to one another's youthful passages into worldly experience and mature self-knowledge, sisters in adulthood often remain bound together through time and memory under the spell of their likenesses and their differences.

Sisters' very importance to one another makes them more subject to scrutiny in the context of modern social relations. The sister bond, like all other kinds of intimate relationships in the modernist cinema, has fallen under the probing lens of the camera. As the films in this study show, that bond is multifaceted, characterized by pleasure and discord, fascination and anxiety. In this sense of paradox and contradiction, the sister bond is perhaps indicative of modernism's examination of the wider ambiguities in our social and psychological existence. In modernism the unmooring from tradition, authority, ancestral bonds, philosophical certainties—indeed, the waning of the oedipus complex itself—opens up a space of anxiety but also of possibilities for new self-definitions and explorations. In an arbitrary and contingent world, the loss of faith in traditional social structures and authorities may well be accompanied by the enhanced importance of our most intimate familial relationships as a space for creating our identities. As "a matrix through and against which women work out or fail to work out their differences," the sister bond thereby takes on heightened significance.[26]

This book is divided into three major parts, each of which begins with a thematic or topical overview that introduces key issues relevant to the films in that section. The first part establishes the presence of sisters in late twentieth-century cinema by juxtaposing two nearly contemporaneous films that both adapt literary (auto)biographies about sisterhood: the nostalgic feminist romance *Little Women* (1994) and the more modern, elliptical *An Angel at My Table* (1990). The striking contrasts in these two films' portrayals of the woman writer's rite of passage into adulthood and the meaning of her sororal affiliations are what makes these two cinematic versions of the *Künstlerroman*, or artist's novel, especially fascinating.

Female coming of age is the unifying motif for the narrative films in the second part of the book, all of which focus on how sisters negotiate sameness and difference during adolescence and postadolescence, critical life stages for identity formation. Each of these coming-of-age stories, very much like the two films in part one, examines different and often contradictory family stories through the eyes of female siblings. Their uses of multiple or conflicting points of view are also important in the films by Ingmar Bergman and Margarethe von Trotta discussed in the third part of the book. In Bergman's *The Silence* and *Cries and Whispers* and von Trotta's sister trilogy, adult sisters' unresolved conflicts herald a return to the emotional ghosts of the past; memories, dreams, and fantasies disclose the unconscious roles the sisters have played in each other's lives.

Altogether, these films display the eclectic range of film styles, story forms, ideological concerns, and cultural contexts so characteristic of women's cinema in the modern period. They demonstrate the elasticity and elusiveness of modern film practices, and the pitfalls of attempting to define a modernist paradigm within contemporary cinema in purely formal terms. Some films in this study, such as Allison Anders's *Gas Food Lodging* or Kasi Lemmons's *Eve's Bayou*, blur the boundaries between "art" film and "popular" film, fusing the traditions of melodrama with the open-endedness and ambiguity associated with neorealism. Others, such as Mina Shum's *Double Happiness* or Todd Solondz's *Welcome to the Dollhouse*, playfully rework comedic conventions, employing the satirical or ironic vignette as a central narrative device. Aesthetically, what counted most in my selection of sister films was their creative transformation of the forms and techniques they inherited from both classical filmmaking and the modernist new waves of the 1960s, their revisioning of post-1960s women's narrative cinema for their own artistic and ideological ends.

PART I

Sisters as Artists in the Cinematic *Künstlerroman*

As a rule there is only one person an English girl hates more than she hates her eldest sister, and that's her mother.

George Bernard Shaw, *Man and Superman*

Reengagement with the actual sister of our early years is only the beginning; it leads to an exploration of the ongoing meaning of that relationship throughout our lives, toward an understanding of how it reappears, transformed, in many of our friendships and love affairs, and to a deeply challenging revisioning of our innermost self. . . . It is the interactions among sisters that instigate the heroine's journey toward self, toward psyche.

Christine Downing, *Psyche's Sisters*

lways aware of the poet's intuitive understanding of psychoanalytic propositions, Sigmund Freud quoted this passage from Shaw's *Man and Superman* in his lecture "The Archaic Features and Infantilism of Dreams" to illustrate the often intense and prolonged rivalry between siblings for parental love, common possessions, and living space within the family.[1] Although Freud stressed the sexual rivalry between siblings of the same gender, he did not analyze the sister relationship in particular, perhaps because—like the mother-daughter bond—it was too "foreign" to him, a "dark continent." In contrast, Christine Downing's neo-Jungian reevaluation of the sister bond in her 1988 book, *Psyche's Sisters: Re-Imagining the Meaning of Sisterhood*, which describes the lifelong maturational role played by the sister relationship in women's inner lives and development, argues that "our sisterly relationships challenge and nurture us, even as we sometimes disappoint and betray one another."[2] These two views of the psychological significance of sisters—that of rivals versus developmental guides—reflect the contradictory "narratives" of sibling relationships found generally in psychoanalytic theory.[3]

Perhaps not surprisingly, these opposing perspectives also inform cultural representations of sisters and critical discourse on sisterhood. On the level of popular culture, as Lucy Fischer has pointed out, the Freudian model of oedipal competition between siblings underpinned the Hollywood sister melodramas of the 1940s, a genre that always involved good and evil twins vying with each other for male love and attention.[4] This formulaic scenario of romantic and sexual competition between sisters and female characters generally is, of course, still ubiquitous in Hollywood cinema, television, and romance literature. Since the 1980s, however, a new wave of women's cinema has surfaced in popular culture that challenges the old formula. Films such as *Beaches* (1988), *Steel Magnolias* (1989), *Fried Green Tomatoes* (1991), *How To Make an American Quilt* (1995), *Boys on the Side* (1995), and *The First Wives Club* (1996) offer images that accentuate the nurturing and supportive roles played by women in each other's lives as they confront male domination and exploitation or as they deal with changing social expectations and emotional needs. In effect, these popular works cast into metaphorical terms the developmental perspective Christine Downing articulated in respect to biological sisters, but in many cases they also sentimentalize the sisterly bonds between female friends, and to some degree carry into the cultural mainstream the utopian fantasies of sisterhood that arose in U.S. feminism during the 1970s.[5]

My discussion of Australian director Gillian Armstrong's 1994 film version of *Little Women* considers this idealistic strand of post-1960s women's cinema. A neoromantic rendering of Louisa May Alcott's novel, the film merges the narrative traditions of sentimental fiction informing Alcott's 1868 novel with the melodramatic conventions of the classic woman's film (a longstanding Hollywood genre partly derived from the nineteenth-century sentimental novel). But Armstrong and screenwriter Robin Swicord also update *Little Women* to appeal to a new generation of U.S. moviegoers. The film foregrounds the "tomboyish" Jo March, focusing on her growth as a female writer and her emotional struggle to come to terms with the death of her closest sister.

Since the silent film era, writers, painters, sculptors, musicians, actors, and other artists have served as popular cinematic subjects. However, the vast majority of films that focus on the lives of artistic women, such as *Camille Claudel* (1990), *Artemesia* (1998), or Gillian Armstrong's own earlier film about Australian writer Miles Franklin, *My Brilliant Career* (1979), have depicted female artists struggling to assert themselves in a traditionally male-dominated realm. In *Little Women*, Armstrong associates Jo's artistic growth with her social and emotional affiliation with a close-knit community of women. This is also true of director Jane Campion's *An Angel at My Table* (1990), adapted from the 1989 autobiography of New Zealand writer Janet Frame. Indeed, as cinematic versions of the female *Künstlerroman*, Armstrong's *Little Women* and Campion's *An Angel at My Table* are thematically and situationally linked: both explore the experiences of women writers in a homosocial context, treating the powerful intersubjective role of sisters in shaping the identities of their central protagonists.[6] In this respect, both works align themselves, if not with a larger biographical genre of female-artist films, then with a different vein of post-1960s filmmaking—women's cinematic autobiographies.

In autobiographical films such as Michelle Citron's *Daughter-Rite*, Diane Kurys's *Entre Nous*, and Nadia Trintignant's *Next Summer*, Catherine Portuges identifies "a tendency to situate the female protagonists in a scenario that highlights links among people rather than the isolated heroine surveying her world," which "suggests a sensibility at once more attuned to and more embedded within a social world than those of their male counterparts."[7] Although *Little Women* and *Angel at My Table* are hardly as experimental as these autobiographies, the films are nonetheless based on literary works by women that also stress the social connections informing the actions and consciousness of female protagonists. Much like the contemporary coming-of-age films about sisters that I treat in part 2, *Little Women* and *An Angel at My Table* embody a female-centered account of women's self-definition and development, realizing in the cinema what feminist literary scholars have defined as a "relational self" in women's writing: "Women characters, more psychologically embedded in relationships, sometimes share the formative voyage [of psychological maturation] with friends, sisters, or mothers, who assume equal status as protagonists."[8] Feminist critics, in their analysis of women's narrative self-representations, have drawn widely on this interrelational model of female development. Whereas traditional initiation stories centering on males have often stressed the hero's psychological need to separate from the parent, feminist theorists have emphasized the importance of the social, intersubjective world in young women's journeys toward adult identities.

Unfortunately, feminist critics have primarily discussed the relational self in women's narratives only in connection to the daughter's lifelong entanglement and ambivalent attachment to the mother, relying heavily on the concept of the preoedipal mother-daughter bond.[9] Often overlooked is the horizontal, intragenerational relationship between sisters that impacts so many women's lives, as the sister films I treat in these pages reveal.

In the films *Little Women* and *An Angel at My Table* the influence of sisters on women's identity formation is framed by the theme of creativity. Bound together in childhood worlds of play and fantasy, sisters in these two films assume the psychological function that D. W. Winnicott has characterized as a maternal mirroring face, an intimate other sensitively attuned to the emotional experience of her sibling.[10] Moreover, in both films sisters serve as alternate selves, questioning or challenging their sibling's values and beliefs.

The nature of the sisters' influence on the female artist is more profoundly problematized by Jane Campion in *An Angel at My Table* than by Gillian Armstrong in *Little Women*. *Little Women* is essentially nostalgic in its rendering of sisters' symbiotic relationships, while Campion's film explores the shifting and ambivalent emotions that lie below the surface of the sister bond. While Jo March's sisters inspire her development as a writer, Campion's film presents as antiromantic the complicated and painful process by which Janet Frame extricates herself from the social conventions of femininity her sisters embodied for her. Although the portrayals of sisterhood in both films bear out Jackie Stacey's assertion that women on-screen and off define themselves actively rather than passively through a female other, Campion's film reveals that the intersubjective relationship between sisters involves identifications arising not only from commonalities but also from differences.[11]

Both Armstrong and Campion play upon a broad tonal scale of emotion to convey the paradoxes of feeling that exist in familial relationships. The visual "consumption" of the sister as an idealized other and as a desired self is a major thread of Alcott's original story, and Armstrong's film honors *Little Women*'s inherent romanticism through its nostalgic vision of the period and melodramatic structure, which facilitates a smooth and unproblematic identification between spectators and the loving sisters on screen. Indeed, Armstrong is a brilliant orchestrator of the melodramatic mode, skillfully moving her audience along the film's emotional arc from the sisters' happy childhood to their shared grief over the death of sister Beth. Campion's approach in *An Angel at My Table*, however, owes a lot to modern tragicomedy, with its unexpected mix of pain and humor, and few episodes or even individual scenes in the film express a single mood or dramatic effect. Unlike *Little Women*, Campion's film provokes a range of emotional reactions by subtly maintaining a dual narrative perspective on its artist-protagonist. The film's episodic structure (so unlike the smooth arc of melodrama) and its sometimes ironic scene juxtaposition complicate our view of Frame's own self-perceptions and make us understand more completely the nature of Janet Frame's conflicted identifications with her sisters and the larger society.

At base, however, even if the films differ in how the sister bond affects the life of the female artist, *An Angel at My Table* and *Little Women* share a common premise: sisters serve as deeply important and often enduring objects of emotional attachment.

The Romance of Sisterhood
Little Women *and Popular Nostalgia in Contemporary Women's Cinema*

or more than a century, Louisa May Alcott's *Little Women* has stood as the quintessential portrait of sisters in American fiction. A semiautobiographical evocation of the loving and supportive bonds between Alcott (1832–88) and her three sisters in nineteenth-century New England, *Little Women* tells the story of Jo March and her sisters Meg, Beth, and Amy, who grow up under the loving care of their mother, Marmee, while their father is away during the Civil War. A perennial favorite of children, the book has never gone out of print since its publication in 1868.

Given *Little Women*'s sustained popularity, it is not surprising that four Hollywood feature films have been based on it. What is ironic is that, after the third adaptation appeared in 1949, Hollywood took more than forty years to produce the fourth.[1] Studio executives apparently failed to see how a novel so intimately focused on nineteenth-century women's identities and friendships could speak powerfully to contemporary women. Yet its central theme of unity, support, and love between sisters evokes the spirit of female solidarity and community that captured the imaginations of multitudes of American women during the feminist revolution of the 1960s and 1970s.

This is also the theme that drew Australian director Gillian Armstrong to remake Alcott's story for 1990s audiences.[2]

Released in 1994, her version of *Little Women*, with Winona Ryder in the lead role of Jo March, is a truly contemporary rendering of Alcott's romance of sisterhood. The film offers a brilliant and skillful synthesis of the sentimental conventions of Alcott's Victorian storytelling with the melodramatic traditions of the Hollywood woman's film. On the one hand, Armstrong preserves much of the Romantic period flavor of Alcott's novel. Nostalgic, lushly photographed, but with a psychologically observant script and naturalistic acting performances by the principal cast members, *Little Women* is an exquisite cinematic visualization of what historian Caroll Smith-Rosenberg has termed "the female world of love and ritual" of women's domestic life in nineteenth-century America.[3] On the other hand, Armstrong teases from the novel what many literary critics have identified as its proto-feminist themes, discarding its concerns with the social education and moral improvement of the Victorian girl. In this respect, her adaptation anticipates other recent feature films that attempt to contemporize eighteenth- and nineteenth-century novels centering on women, such as Pen Densham's 1996 version of Daniel Defoe's *Moll Flanders*, Ang Lee's and Emma Thompson's 1995 adaptation of Jane Austen's *Sense and Sensibility*, or Jane Campion's 1996 adaptation of Henry James's *Portrait of a Lady*.[4] In stressing the virtues of sisterly love and unity in light of modern feminism, Armstrong's *Little Women* puts a decidedly contemporary spin on Alcott's story and characters.

Armstrong's film, like the 1933 and 1949 versions of Alcott's novel, downplays the book's Victorian morality to meet the narrative expectations of modern film audiences. As Anne Hollander has observed, Armstrong's film and the previous adaptations of *Little Women* all offer period-specific views of prevailing tastes in "American movie good girls."[5] As with historical or biographical films that ostensibly deal with the past but "provide for the ideological needs of the present," each adaptation of the novel has more to say about the sociohistorical context in which the film was conceived and the audiences it was intended to address than it does about Alcott's story and its nineteenth-century milieu.[6]

Director George Cukor's 1933 version of *Little Women*, with Katherine Hepburn in the lead role of Jo March, exploits the novel's rhetoric and spirit to indirectly comment on American life during the peak years of the Great Depression. His film emphasizes the March daughters' moral and social development in the face of poverty and want (a major theme, in fact, of

Alcott's story), drawing from the novel an object lesson for Depression-era audiences coping with the grim realities of economic hardship and social upheaval. Although the March sisters grow up in genteel poverty, Cukor stresses the close-knit fabric of the March family, the sisters' pleasures in simple, homespun pastimes, and the cohesiveness of their village community during the Civil War.

Mervyn LeRoy's 1949 version abandons this theme and instead celebrates, as Hollander remarks, "the fresh postwar pleasure of acquiring sleek new possessions," to better reflect the nation's mood during the economic resurgence following World War II.[7] Moving the historical time period of Alcott's novel forward to the Gilded Age of the 1880s, LeRoy transforms the March sisters into "little consumers," showcasing the production's richly appointed period costumes and decor in Technicolor.

The 1994 adaptation of *Little Women* again reinterprets Alcott's text, refurbishing its idealized portrayal of a female utopian community for a new audience of contemporary women. Elizabeth Francis aptly describes the film as a shrewd merger of realism and sentiment that appeals to post-1960s notions of female creativity, feminist politics, and the self-sufficient female household, while still managing to evoke popular cultural conceptions of romantic love.[8] A key figure here is Marmee, who heads the all-female household while her husband is away at war. Played in the film by Susan Sarandon, Marmee articulates a philosophy of social compassion that in spirit echoes that of Louisa May Alcott's own mother, Abigail Alcott, whose championing of women's suffrage, temperance, abolition, and social work typified the politics of progressive women in the mid-1800s. (Sarandon's star persona underscores this liberal political subtext, since her outspoken political activism is well-known to many 1990s filmgoers.) Emphasizing Marmee's compassionate views toward human suffering in conjunction with the spirit of harmony and love that exists between mother and daughters, this latest version of *Little Women* encourages viewers to nostalgically "return" to the idyllic matriarchal world of Alcott's novel.

Jackie Stacey's analysis of the female spectator's consumption of idealized femininity in *Stargazing: Hollywood Cinema and Female Spectatorship* is highly apropos of the romantic images of sisterhood in Armstrong's film.[9] The warmly inviting home of the March family in nineteenth-century Concord, Massachusetts, allows the viewer to luxuriate in "the visual enactment of sentimentality, domesticity, and the bonds between women as loving, ritualistic, and powerful"—a fantasy facilitated by a classical Hollywood style that effortlessly sutures the viewer to the narrative.[10] The film's neoclassical studio style and lovingly detailed mise-en-scène encourage our consumption of feminism as it supposedly existed at an earlier time.

One especially important cinematic device Armstrong uses repeatedly to create a nostalgic mood is the window as a frame. The March sisters are shown frequently throughout the film gazing through the window glass as they imagine their futures as adult women or as they speculate among themselves about the activities of their young, handsome, and wealthy neighbor Laurie (who also gazes wistfully out his window at the March girls). Perhaps more importantly, the spectator often looks *into* the March home through a window, witnessing domestic scenes around the hearth that, like a fifth sister, she longs to join. Armstrong also employs the window frame as a kind of portal to the past, rendering Marmee and her four daughters in a family tableau reminiscent of old frontispieces of the published novel. Shirley Marchalonis notes that the film "is visually beautiful, with authentic clothing and sets, there are many long camera shots and less 'action,' and the predominant browns throughout create an effect of coziness and warmth."[11] This affectionate visualization of the sisters' domestic unity is enhanced by the film's many allusions to the turmoil and death occurring on Civil War battlefields, far from the sanctuary of the March home.

The film's often witty, modern perspective on nineteenth-century gender roles also contributes toward making Alcott's world a hospitable imaginative space for contemporary audiences. Screenwriter Robin Swicord's script, for instance, incorporates moments of gentle satire directed at the March sisters' neighbor Laurie—humorously capitalizing on his feminine name, he is once mistaken for a girl, and on several occasions teasingly referred to as the honorary "fifth sister." With Laurie, Swicord also undermines longstanding stereotypes of the male as the stronger and the female as the weaker of the sexes. At the opening of the film he is visually framed as a captive in his family's manor house, staring longingly through his window at the snowy village landscape where the March sisters tumble playfully together in the cold with the kind of free-spiritedness more customarily associated with adventurous boys. The film's doleful picture of Laurie as a lonely prisoner of his wealthy but class-bound upbringing cleverly reverses similar images of the genteel Victorian woman as a psychological victim of the suffocating nineteenth-century household—images that reoccur in such British and American novels of the period as Charlotte Brontë's *Jane Eyre* and Charlotte Perkins Gilman's *The Yellow Wallpaper.*[12]

Far more important to Armstrong's and Swicord's update of the book, however, is the pivotal role of the film's artist-heroine. Alcott's central character, Jo March, is her most memorable literary creation and the most popular of the novel's cast of sisters. Tomboyish, self-assertive, and often rebellious, she is a charismatic character with strong appeal for contemporary women. Tellingly, the post–World War II generation of feminist writers and critics, from Simone de Beauvoir to Carolyn Heilbrun, tended to see themselves mirrored in Jo, largely because her inquiring and independent mind prefigured modern women's rejection of Victorian ideals of passive femininity. As Heilbrun comments, Jo "may have been the single female model continuously available after 1860 to girls dreaming beyond the confines of their restrictions to independence." Indeed, some feminist literary critics have found Jo March so inspiring that they have described *Little Women* as a "militant version of permanent sisterhood."[13]

In Armstrong's film, Jo's significance is even greater than in Alcott's novel. The director renews here her own interest in the figure of the female artist, which dates back to her 1979 debut as a feature filmmaker with *My Brilliant Career* and appears again in her 1990 film *The Last Days of Chez Nous.*[14] Indeed, for those who know Armstrong's previous films, it is apparent that her adaptation of *Little Women* is as much concerned with the making of Jo March as a writer as with the interactions between the March sisters. However, what makes *Little Women* exceptional in Armstrong's oeuvre is her engagement with the roles played by sisters in fostering female creativity. She makes it impossible to separate the two main strands of the film—Jo's artistic development and the March sisters' collective tale—highlighting the active influence of Meg, Beth, and Amy as inspiration for the young writer's flights of fantasy and imagination.

In *My Brilliant Career*, adapted from the 1901 autobiographical novel by Australian writer Miles Franklin, Armstrong touched on the subject of a female artist's creative development but concentrated on a young woman's struggle to embark on an artistic career against the objections of her family and friends. The film is set in the tradition-bound bush country of turn-of-the-century Australia, when "respectable" women were largely discouraged from professionally putting pen to paper, a theme Armstrong reintroduces in *Little Women*. But at the heart of the later film lies the story of how the female artist's nurturing relationships with her sisters prepare her for the world of writing.

In contrast to this affirmative vision, Armstrong's other artist film, *The Last Days of Chez Nous*, fixes on a middle-aged woman writer whose bourgeois existence is thrown into tumult and crisis when her impetuous and destructive younger sister interferes in her marriage. Dramatizing the psychological interplay of sibling rivalry, sexual anxiety, and writer's block, the film dissects the unresolved emotional conflicts that lie beneath a woman writer's unfulfilled creative and spiritual needs in modern-day Sydney.

In *Little Women*, Armstrong's direction is at its best in scenes that recreate the March sisters' elaborate playacting and fantasy games. One of the great strengths of Alcott's novel is its affinity for the artistic lives of children, and Armstrong shows how the March girls speak a common language of art that transcends each sister's adoption of a different artistic medium. Beth is the musician, Meg the actress, Amy a budding painter, and Jo the writer. Stressing the sisters' creative interrelationship, Armstrong repeatedly frames the siblings in their cocoonlike, light-suffused attic playroom, where they collaboratively compose their newspaper, "The Pickwick Papers," or enact fanciful roles in Jo's melodramatic "blood-and-thunder plays." Armstrong's direction in these scenes suggests how adolescent siblings employ fantasy as a vehicle of self-exploration, self-expression, and self-control. Indeed, Armstrong conveys how these intersubjective fantasies allow the March sisters to rehearse through play a range of social roles that help them to master their fears and anxieties while preparing them for adult life.[15]

As Armstrong presents it, this creative camaraderie is key to understanding Jo March's development into a writer. Jo discovers her first willing and adoring audience in her younger siblings, whose participation in her fantasy world assists her in the maturational process of learning how to "dramatize the self" to the eyes of others.[16] An essential learning rite for any child, and especially for a young woman who dreams of becoming a writer, the capacity to play different roles is facilitated by siblings who bring to life potential selves through the imaginative stories of childhood play. Jo's sisters also afford her some imaginative control over her relational world. For instance, Jo commands Meg, Beth, and Amy to perform in her turbulent melodramas, an assertion of authority that assumes special psychological coloration in light of her underlying need to alleviate her anxiety about losing her siblings to other heroes, to other loves, to the inevitable separations of adult life. Much later in the film, after Beth dies and Meg and Amy marry, Jo's memories of the sisters' lost childhood—evoked in a 360-degree pan around the dusty, empty attic—inspires Jo to recapture the past by creating the very novel that Alcott herself would write and call *Little Women*.

Armstrong's self-conscious merger of Alcott's fiction and personal journal represents a feminist interpretation of *Little Women* that regards Jo as a thinly disguised alter ego for the author herself. The film greatly embellishes the novel's portrait of her as fledgling writer by transposing selected facets of Alcott's life into the film. Swicord radically alters the novel's original dialogue passages to include entries from Alcott's private journal, which are read in voice-over by Winona Ryder as Jo.[17] This and other key narrative revisions transform Jo March into an artist-heroine whose professional ambitions and sororal relationships speak to women's expectations in the 1990s.

Although the film obviously draws on background research into the Alcott family and the period of New England Transcendentalism, Swicord's screenplay expunges from the March sisters' story the socio-religious morality so central to Alcott's novel and the genteel tastes of her readers. Written for Victorian girls, Alcott's *Little Women* is overtly concerned with young women's moral quest for self-improvement through learning the Christian virtues of self-denial and self-sacrifice. Yet Armstrong's and Swicord's adaptation, as Shirley Marchalonis points out, "presents young women who are all but perfect—they already know everything the novel shows them learning. The great strength of the film is its successful portrayal of family love and closeness among the five women—love that reaches out to include others."[18]

By the end of Alcott's novel, Jo March and her sisters have grown up to become "little women" in accordance with nineteenth-century expectations: having learned to suppress their anger and govern their impulses, the girls achieve the moral knowledge and temperamental self-control that enable them finally to make wise marriages.[19] Amy goes abroad and marries their rich neighbor Laurie, while Meg becomes engaged to John Brooke, Laurie's childhood tutor. Even Jo ultimately succumbs to marriage—to an older man, Professor Bhaer. After Beth's death from scarlet fever, Bhaer becomes the central figure in Jo's life and the censor of her lurid, gothic thrillers. Eventually, even Jo abandons her artistic aspirations and ceases to write.

Armstrong and Swicord smoothly resolve what contemporary readers and feminist critics have identified as the novel's most bothersome contradiction: its celebration of female solidarity on the one hand and on the other the siblings' willingness to leave behind their artistic ambitions and separate from each other to marry. In the film, the March sisters do not suppress their desires and ambitions to wed. And at its conclusion, all family members and the sisters' husbands are united (except of course for Beth, who serves as the film's melodramatic sacrifice and thus becomes—in accordance with sentimental convention—the quintessential "angel in the house," dying in her youth). Amy, now Laurie's wife, avows that "the relations of sisters is more important than marriage"—a serious rewrite in Swicord's screenplay of the sorrowful breakup of the sisters in Alcott's original tale.

In the novel, when Jo March hears the news of the wedding engagement of her sister Meg to young John Brooke and foresees Meg's inevitable departure from the family, she laments:

> I just wish I could marry Meg myself, and keep her safe in the family . . . she'll go and fall in love, and there's an end of peace and fun, and cozy times together. I see it all! They'll go lovering around the house, and we shall have to dodge; Meg will be absorbed, and no good to me anymore; Brooke will scratch up a fortune somehow, carry her off, and make a hole in the family; and I shall break my heart, and everything will be abominably uncomfortable. Oh dear me! Why weren't we all boys, then there wouldn't be any bother.[20]

Jo's attachment to her sisters in the novel is so deep and so passionate that she perceives Meg's impending marriage as a kind of "death." She anticipates it creating "a hole in the family" as large and almost as painful as that created by the loss of her sister Beth to scarlet fever.

The "bother" Jo March feels over the rending of the sisters' bonds is rather muted in Armstrong's film. And, curiously, Robin Swicord's screenplay refuses to treat Jo's own marriage as a serious obstacle to her ambitions to write. Where in the novel the married Jo puts aside her plans to become a writer, the film portrays her husband, Bhaer, as more respectful and approving of Jo's writing, and we assume she will find fame and creative fulfillment as the author of *Little Women* (the film's self-conscious announcement of its merger of autobiography and fiction). Armstrong's decision to invest the relationship between Jo and Professor Bhaer with greater marital equality is rather unexpected, given that the feminist theme of her earlier *My Brilliant Career* sprang from a young woman's choice *not* to marry for the sake of preserving her writing career from spousal intrusions. Furthermore, Jo's choice of a husband in the film is dictated not merely by her desire to wed a man who will allow her to write, but by romantic longings, too. Whereas Alcott portrays the paternal Bhaer as much older than Jo, sketching him as a slightly ridiculous, caring, but also domineering, mentor, the film casts in the part the comparatively youthful and ruggedly handsome actor Gabriel Byrne, who personifies both intellectual compatibility *and* romantic charm—the ideal of the modern husband for companionate marriage in a postfeminist era.

Armstrong's and Swicord's revisions to the novel's conclusion effectively sidestep the questions that have perplexed and divided feminist critics. Does Alcott's *Little Women* champion romance at the expense of sisterhood, and propose marriage as an emblem of adulthood achieved— an ideal and social expectation that shaped most women's lives through the 1960s? Madelon Bedell, for one, writes that in the end Jo "betrays herself, the reader, and the bright promise she showed at the beginning of the legend." Or is the novel's dominant narrative pattern of marriage and motherhood countered by the images of female fulfillment within a sororal community that occupy the core of Jo's story? Nina Auerbach claims that Jo develops into "a cosmic mother—the greatest power available in her domestic world."[21]

The critics' debate over the novel's ambiguities and contradictions is, in my view, rather misleading. Alcott's *Little Women* displays what Sandra Gilbert and Susan Gubar have termed the palimpsestic quality of much nineteenth-century women's writing: the tension between a surface conformity to social norms of female development and an underlying resistance to those norms coupled with subterranean anger toward them.[22] Certainly, Alcott's portrayal of Jo March's creative endeavors and deep affection for her sisters expressed the author's own quiet rebellion against conventional images of women as submissive wives and mothers, as well as some of the social dichotomies of being a female writer in a culture where women's lives were still largely defined by marriage. *Little Women* celebrates young women's emotional bonds, but the novel's structure of feeling remains tied to the vexed sentimental genre from which it sprang. The traditional male hero of the nineteenth-century bildungsroman almost invariably undergoes a physical and social separation from home and family, which serves as the catalyst of a youthful journey toward his practical understanding of the larger world, his moral awareness of the self's relationship to the broader society, and finally a sense of personal value and purposeful autonomy. Yet for most female protagonists in Victorian fiction, such journeys toward independence and individuality are foreclosed by social custom and narrative convention. Even in the witty, sharp-eyed comedies of Jane Austen, the heroine achieves her moral and social education through her intimate attachments to her own family (especially her sisters) and in courtship and marriage attains greater self-understanding within the circle of landed gentry families that constitutes the dominant arena of middle-class women's work and leisure.[23]

Some devotees of Alcott's *Little Women* might be disturbed by Armstrong's and Swicord's willingness to radically revise the novel's lessons in nineteenth-century social conduct and morality for young women. Yet I find the film especially interesting because it in fact accommodates far more contemporary cultural expectations about the roles of women in society. For Alcott, the happy ending of marriage is also the end of the narrative and storytelling, since, as Nina Auerbach notes, the novel's "perfunctory concluding marriages give a twilight flavor to the enforced passage into womanhood proper." But Armstrong's adaptation realigns the constricted narrative destinies of the novel's Victorian female characters with the ideals of mainstream feminism in the 1990s: it shows that emotionally intimate relationships between women should not have to end with marriage, nor should women's careers preclude the joys of heterosexual romance.[24]

Armstrong's film also softens the important and edifying conflicts between the sisters that occur in the novel. Unlike the novel, the film does not show Jo March's complex relationships with Amy, her rival artist-sister, and Beth, the angel in the house, as important way-stations in her moral education but as stages in the female artist's emotional growth into an adult woman. The distinction between Alcott's moralizing and the film's presentation of sisterly love and forgiveness is subtle and especially apparent in Jo's relationship with Amy.

As the other ambitious artist in the family, Amy, the youngest and the most vain and self-preoccupied of the sisters, sometimes becomes the catalyst for competition and jealousy. She envies her older sisters' happiness and Jo's talents, and in a fit of rage she burns Jo's manuscript. When shortly thereafter Amy breaks through thin ice in a lake and nearly drowns before Jo's eyes, Jo becomes aware of her feelings of revenge, hesitating for a moment before rushing to her sister's aid. Working through her "sins" of bad temper and anger, which put one of her sisters in real danger, is an important element in Alcott's education of the sentimental heroine. In the film, the story is divested of its serious moral lesson: Jo immediately saves Amy from drowning in the icy water, and the sequence ends with the sisters gathered closely around Amy, in bed, as Jo pronounces that she could never love anyone better than her sisters. In order to highlight sisterly accord and harmony, the film here deemphasizes the sibling rivalry and anger that occasionally surface in the novel. As Marchalonis suggests, "In the recent films, the underlying message is that love solves everything, a message that the late twentieth century finds acceptable . . . and perhaps the film-maker's belief that love solves everything is its own kind of naive sentimentality."[25]

While the novel puts her relationship with Beth at the center of Jo's sentimental education, the film folds it into her coming of age as an artist. Jo is independent, head-strong, and ambitious; Beth is self-effacing, shy, and eternally childlike in her dependence on her family. Yet they are the most invested of the four sisters in keeping the childhood sister bond intact, and both are selflessly devoted to their art, Beth to her music and Jo to her writing. The film suggests this intimacy through recurrent two-shots, as when Beth expresses her faith in Jo's literary talents or comforts her after Jo has rejected Laurie's marriage proposal and finds out that Amy will accompany their Aunt March to Europe.

Jo cannot ultimately prevent her favorite sister's slow fading from the family circle after she contracts scarlet fever. Critics of the novel have pointed out that Jo is tamed by the more compliant, selfless sister and that gentle Beth's impending demise "marks the penultimate stage in the heroine's moral transformation" from "wild girl" to "strong, helpful, tender-hearted woman."[26] On her deathbed, Beth asks Jo to take her place and to renounce her ambitions as a writer to become a comfort to her family. But in Armstrong's *Little Women*, the well-known death scene, played affectingly by Claire Danes and Winona Ryder, emphasizes the breakup of the sisters' childhood foursome rather than Jo's moral development. An overhead shot of Beth's empty bed covered with flower petals and a close-up frame of her doll collection symbolically suggest the loss of sisterhood and childhood. In the novel Jo renounces her grand ambitions as a writer and internalizes to some degree Beth's character and values; in the film, Beth's death triggers Jo's desire to recreate the all-female family in her own writing and to become a respected author.

More serious objections to Armstrong's and Swicord's revisions to the novel, however, can be raised about their highly selective use of Louisa May Alcott's life as a basis for their adaptation. Just as Alcott romanticized her own life and family relationships in *Little Women*, it is telling that Armstrong's and Swicord's merger of fact with fiction also avoided Alcott's brilliant but impractical father, a prominent proponent and idealistic practitioner of Transcendentalist philosophy. Bronson Alcott's progressive educational philosophies, which stressed self-reliance and learning through experience, encouraged Louisa May's writerly ambitions, yet his paternal exhortations to continually improve herself and curb her "wild spirits" created within her a life-long struggle between self-expression and self-censorship. Bronson Alcott's relentless supervision of his four daughters' moral and spiritual perfection during their childhood and adolescence left Louisa May competing with her sisters for her parents' attention and affirmation. In some respects, the contradictory messages about femininity and creativity in *Little Women* are the products of Bronson Alcott's deep influence.[27]

The failure of Bronson's utopian community at Fruitlands in Harvard, Massachusetts, forced Louisa May into the difficult role of the family breadwinner. Her literary success with *Little Women* in 1868 at the age of thirty-six placed the burden of the Alcott family's economic survival solely on her shoulders. It was a position in the family she filled with some reluctance, for she had to tailor her writing for the literary marketplace to maintain her commercial success as a popular author. Eventually, after some years of turning out profitable books, Louisa May admitted her dissatisfaction with her publisher's charge to write a "girl's book," confessing that she had grown "tired of providing moral pap for the young."[28]

The 1990s film, not surprisingly, appreciates *Little Women* as Jo's highest artistic achievement, a cathartic memorialization of her sisters. Professor Bhaer, after all, advises Jo to write "from life, from the depths of her soul." At the end of the film, when Bhaer delivers to Jo the galley proofs of *Little Women*, he declares, "Reading your novel was like opening a window onto your heart." The creative transformation of loss into family memory and literary achievement is here linked to romantic love, and the film ends with Jo March and Professor Bhaer kissing under an umbrella. This ending markedly contrasts with Bhaer's awkward courtship in the novel: the oedipal overtones of Jo's relationship to an older man have been excised; the guardian of the heroine's morals in the sentimental tradition has metamorphosed into an attractive hero who will enter into a coequal relationship with Jo to work on educational reform. And just as Bhaer falls in love with Jo through her novel, a new generation of female viewers is invited through Armstrong's adaptation to enter and find inspiration in Alcott's story.

It perhaps is no accident that in our era of ideological conflicts within feminism, recent film adaptations of nineteenth-century domestic novels should articulate the vision of a powerful unifying sisterhood—Armstrong's *Little Women*, and to a lesser extent Ang Lee's *Sense and Sensibility*. Remarking on how "Alcott's novel transforms the middle-class home into a force for redeeming the world," Elizabeth Francis points out that "the film does the contemporary work of making the feminist home a hospitable place for women." By encouraging female spectators' consumption of an idyllic screen fantasy of harmonious sisterhood, the film implicitly acknowledges both the enduring influence of the women's movement of the 1960s and 1970s and its cross-generational complications and divisions during the 1980s and 1990s, as modern feminist ideas have moved into the cultural mainstream. As Francis suggests, Armstrong's interpretation of Alcott's novel is necessarily retroactive; in contrast to edgier, ironic, and more unorthodox films that probe present-day complexities in women's interrelationships, *Little Women* takes women's cinema back in time to Alcott's Victorian reverie of childhood in the attempt to recover the elusive ideals of devoted sisterhood for a postfeminist age. And it links this nostalgic return to a fantasy of preoedipal bliss, the all-perfect mother who presides over the development of her daughters into self-confident and productive women. "We are asked to recognize Jo's faith that sisters are made in the home, by feeling not only a nostalgia for a lost sisterhood but also the sentimental feminist desire to create it anew," Francis suggests. Indeed, reviewer Terrence Rafferty remarks that "Armstrong gives the March girls' idyll such a rich glow that when the sisters scatter, the movie evokes a freezing sense of loss. This *Little Women* makes Alcott's seductive fantasy, of a protected place that is both a schoolhouse and a wonderful playhouse, look real; you believe in it strongly enough to feel, as Jo does, the ache of being cast out."[29]

Little Women contrasts with Armstrong's more problematic, tougher vision of sisterhood and family relationships in *The Last Days of Chez Nous*, as I noted earlier, and indeed with many other films about adolescent sisters that I discuss in this book. In a review of the relationship between Armstrong's "edgy" Australian contemporary films and her Hollywood "costume dramas," Lizzie Francke writes:

> One hopes that she [Armstrong] can carry the March sisters beyond the "coming of age" through the more complicated entanglements characterized by her Australian films. *High Tide* and *The Last Days of Chez Nous* both centered on the shifting and perplexing nexus of female relationships in fragmented families—families only the potentially feckless Amy March could ever have imagined. These are films about the hollowing out of aspirations, the cutting down of dreams into pragmatic reality. And both end speculatively, pointing a way forward but without making promises for the true great-grand-daughters of Sybylla [in *My Brilliant Career*] and Jo [in *Little Women*].³⁰

The Last Days of Chez Nous probes the fragility of the modern bourgeois family by examining the conflicted bonds between sisters, husbands and wives, adult daughters and fathers. Scripted by the Australian novelist Helen Garner, the eldest of four sisters herself, *Chez Nous* portrays a middle-aged female writer, Beth, who lives in a bohemian Sydney household with her French husband, JP, and her teenage daughter, Annie.³¹ When Beth's younger sister, Vicki, a reckless free spirit, returns from traveling abroad and an unhappy affair that has left her pregnant, the hard-won but fragile footing of Beth's life is exposed. Opening shots of Vicki's legs, blue miniskirt, and flame-red hair announce her awkward yet aggressive sexuality. She roams the empty house and greedily devours a chunk of the pink-frosted, heart-shaped cake prepared for her homecoming, a scene that foreshadows her careless and rash involvement with her sister's husband.

Domestic spaces are here employed quite differently than in *Little Women;* no longer protective, comforting havens, they become much more ambiguous, both inviting and menacing, symbolic of the shifting alliances between the family members. Multiple scenes of eating, drawing, face painting, piano playing suggest an easy and open camaraderie between the family members, yet Vicki's secret plundering of her sister's wardrobe to play dress-up with Annie portends more sinister emotional "raids" between the sisters: Vicki's intrusion into her sister's marriage; Beth's urgent demand that Vicki get an abortion; and Beth's plagiarism of Vicki's writing for her own novels. The viewer understands that Vicki is challenging her elder sister in a destructive way, and that Beth cannot resist treating Vicki like a wayward child. Yet there is also an underlying search for love and affirmation between the sisters, although one fraught with sisterly rivalry and insecurities.

The Last Days of Chez Nous offers a vision of sisterhood that remains open, unresolved, conflictual. The particular modernity of this film is visible in its focus on the mundane and brittle aspects of human relationships. As John Orr writes, "[Modern pictures] seek revelation through images of the ordinary and like the modern novel from Joyce onwards, develop their own matrix of epiphanies not out of great events or melodramatic spectacle but out of the textures of everyday experiences."[32] Although the affair between JP and Vicki is the stuff of melodrama, Armstrong handles the sexual betrayal quite matter-of-factly, and her final shot of JP and Vicki in their new empty home shows a relationship already marred by discord. The complicated bond of affection and competition between Beth and Vicki is at the center of the film—JP even refers to Vicki as Beth's little echo. Unlike other films that feature sisters divided by their love for a man, in *Chez Nous* JP becomes, in effect, an incidental conduit through which the sisters work out or fail to work out their differences.

The "shifting and perplexing nexus of female relationships" that Lizzie Francke writes about in her review of Gillian Armstrong's Australian films is also visible in the subject of the next chapter, Jane Campion's *An Angel at My Table*. The film contains many textual similarities to *Little Women* with its focus on a female artist and her relationship with her three sisters, the dramatic impact of a sister's death in adolescence, and the social constraints placed upon a woman's growth toward creative self-expression. However, Campion's film probes more critically than do either Alcott in the novel or Armstrong in the film version of *Little Women* the ways in which sisters negotiate the particular contradictions and conflicts for young women growing up in a patriarchal culture.

An Angel at My Table

Sisters, Trauma, and the Making of an Artist as a Young Woman

The adolescent time now became a whirlpool, and so the memories do not arrange themselves to be observed and written about, they whirl, propelled by a force beneath, with different memories rising to the surface at different times and thus denying the existence of a "pure" autobiography and confirming, for each moment, a separate story accumulating to a million stories, all different and with some memories forever staying beneath the surface.

Janet Frame, *An Autobiography*

n evoking the close bonds that develop between sisters in their youth, the modern cinema can return us nostalgically to the childhood family romance, as does Gillian Armstrong's film *Little Women*, as I discussed in chapter 1, and as Jane Campion's 1990 film adaptation of Janet Frame's autobiography *An Angel at My Table* emphatically does not. Campion refracts Frame's life through moments of acute emotional experience that are almost always connected to her ambivalent identification with her sisters. *An Angel at My Table* is representative of how modernist filmmakers are concerned with the provisionality of both memory itself and the representational modes through which the past can be reconstructed in the cinematic orchestration of sounds and images.

In recalling her life as an adolescent in New Zealand, writer and poet Janet Frame attempts to distill in language the process of remembering. For Frame, as the epigraph suggests, there can be no "pure" autobiography, for the very act of recollection is elusive, fragmentary, kaleidoscopic. Her disavowal of a unitary sense of personal history, her suspicion of a grand narrative that holds all perceptions as if in the palm of one encompassing truth, is a particularly modernist insight. It recalls Virginia Woolf's repudiation of the artifices of generic story conventions in favor of literary characterization drawn from the stream of subjective perceptions, thoughts, and feelings:

> Examine for a moment an ordinary day. The mind receives a myriad impressions—trivial, fantastic, evanescent, or engraved with the sharpness of steel. From all sides they come, an incessant shower of innumerable atoms; and as they fall, as they shape themselves into the life of Monday and Tuesday, the accent falls differently from of old; the moment of importance came not here but there; so that, if a writer were a free man and not a slave, if he could base his work upon his own feeling and not upon convention, there would be no plot, no comedy, no tragedy, no love interest or catastrophe in the accepted sense. . . . Life is not a series of gig-lamps symmetrically arranged; life is a luminous halo, a semi-transparent envelope surrounding us from the beginning of consciousness to the end.[1]

Jane Campion's adaptation of Janet Frame's autobiography is clearly based upon "feeling and not upon convention." In exploring this well-known New Zealand author's relationships with her three sisters, Campion scrupulously avoids melodrama and instead employs the imagistic and impressionistic powers of cinema to convey the psychological terrain of a young woman writer's interior world. Although hardly an experiment in stream-of-consciousness narration, the film attempts to translate to the screen the elliptical, episodic, and self-explorative quality of Frame's modernist memoir, drawing from the whirlpool of Frame's remembrances those eventful moments of perception that form the "envelope" containing the woman artist's story of growing up.

The film incorporates a distinctly modern conception of time and memory, departing from the narrative conventions of the traditional Hollywood cinema and from the linear construction of a film such as Armstrong's *Little Women*. Campion, like Frame herself, refuses to mythologize the past and instead exposes the fundamentally subjective nature of remembering and comprehending it.

One of the film's most impressive features is its sensitive and involved depiction of personal trauma in Frame's life, if we take trauma to mean the repeated suffering of a catastrophic event or wounding experience, beyond the shock of the first moment. Frame never fully assimilates the experience of her brother's illness and the death of two sisters at an early age. These events tear apart not only her family but also her sense of security in the world. The late critic of modernity Walter Benjamin observed that the modern subject is deprived of opportunities to assimilate events directly into a larger and collective tradition of consciousness and memory. The modern subject often adopts a defensive posture, protecting itself against the myriad stimuli and "shocks" that assail it.[2] While in Louisa May Alcott's nineteenth-century world the death of a sister could be mourned in recognition of the religious virtues of suffering and sacrifice, the sibling deaths in *An Angel at My Table* seemed to the young Janet Frame arbitrary and unexpected, changing her life forever and making impossible an uncomplicated story of her coming of age.

Though never deviating from the chronology of Frame's experiences, Campion and her screenwriter, Laura Jones, skillfully evoke the unconscious psychic processes, the repressions, displacements, and associative proliferations of personal memories, that always destabilize a reconstruction of family history. As the epigraph to this chapter attests, Frame herself questions a linear and organic coming-of-age narrative, underscoring the fragmentary and overdetermined nature of memory. Her autobiography clearly belongs to a twentieth-century literary mode of modernism and psychological self-reflexivity, and her perspective gave Campion the perfect lens to problematize the affectional bonds between female siblings in the context of family, class, and gender relations.

An Angel at My Table examines a woman artist's struggle to define herself amidst the most difficult obstacles. The daughter of a very poor, working-class family in provincial New Zealand during the 1940s and 1950s, Janet Frame lived through a series of traumas that began in early puberty with the accidental drownings of two of her three sisters. She wrote in her autobiography that these deaths were defining moments in her life, and her journey as an artist was inextricably linked to the process of mourning their loss and, perhaps more importantly, of comprehending how their lives and deaths shaped her consciousness of her identity. The losses seemed to magnify the young Janet's long battle with feelings of social inferiority and intense shyness. A poor, gawky, and sensitive teenager in the rural provinces of New Zealand, where cultural norms of gender and class were rigidly conservative, Frame's only feelings of self-worth came from her family and in particular from her idolized older sisters. Their deaths precipitated her misdiagnosis as schizophrenic in her late teens, and she was forcibly confined to a mental asylum for eight years of electric shock treatments. In truth, unlike her more conventionally "feminine" older sisters, she had simply not adapted satisfactorily to the prevailing cultural standards of adult womanhood. Campion presents Frame's eventual escape from her incarceration as intricately intertwined with her need to come to grips with her sisters' impact on her personal identity. Ultimately, her odyssey in search of the past is brilliantly realized through the act of writing.

A New Zealander herself who grew up with an artistic sister, Anna (now also a film director), Jane Campion was attuned to the vagaries of sisterhood and placed special emphasis on this relationship in her adaptation of Frame's autobiography. Before directing *An Angel at My Table*, Campion had made the 1989 film *Sweetie*, a dark comedy about two adult sisters, one of whom, the mentally unstable and grotesquely excessive Sweetie, dominates her family's existence through her compulsive desire for attention. Sweetie invades the life of her more introverted and shy sister, Kay, throwing it into complete turmoil. Through her surreal, decentered cinematic style, Campion captures the emotional chaos engendered by the annoying Sweetie, and in doing so she also probes the emotional ambiguities that lie below the surface of modern family life. Hinting that one or perhaps both sisters were victims of some unnamed and unacknowledged traumatic experience, Campion makes the ungovernable Sweetie the most obvious expression of the family's dysfunction and a mirror image of her sister's repressions.[3] Even though Kay seems to be liberated in the end by her reckless sister's death (Sweetie falls out of a treehouse), the film comes to rest with a poignant image of a younger and more innocent Sweetie as she dances for her father, a sorrowful vision from memory of Sweetie's unfulfilled potential and terrible need. This coda to Campion's debut film conveys the director's strong empathy for the grotesque, pathetic Sweetie and her quest for love. The image speaks to Campion's talent as a filmmaker for balancing a complex range of emotions, also on display in her exploration of the psychological connections between sisters in Janet Frame's modern memoir.

Campion's film of *An Angel at My Table* preserves the three-part structure of the autobiography. The first segment, "To the Is-Land" presents

Frame's unstable Depression-era childhood as the second oldest daughter of a poor railway family in southern New Zealand—their frequent moves, the multiple family tragedies, but also the importance of poetry and imagination in their everyday life. The second part, "An Angel at My Table," focuses on Frame's troubled college years, when her excessive shyness, nervous breakdown, and attempted suicide were misdiagnosed as schizophrenia. During eight years in a mental institution, Frame suffered more than two hundred electroshock applications, which, as her character in the film declares, were "each equivalent in degree of fear to an execution." Frame escaped a lobotomy only because her first published book of short stories, *The Lagoon*, written during her confinement in the mental asylum, received the prestigious Hubert Church Memorial Award. After her release from the asylum, while living under the protection and tutelage of Frank Sargeson, an older New Zealand writer, she wrote and published her first autobiographically inspired novel, *Owls Do Cry* (1957). The final segment, "The Envoy from Mirror City," traces her travels to Europe on a literary grant after she was released from the hospital, her growing confidence in her mental health, and her gradual evolution to internationally recognized writer and poet.

Although Campion follows Frame's story from childhood to adulthood and underscores the character's continuity by casting strikingly look-alike actresses in the roles of Janet as a child, adolescent, and young adult, her film is very much concerned with the discontinuities in Janet's life, the interruptions in her story, and the haunting ghosts that surface from her past. Campion's off-beat visual style, eccentric framings, and expressive mise-en-scène capture Frame's unstable life from the opening shots of the film—an infant's point-of-view shot of its mother's breasts looming over her and a close-up of a toddler's legs moving through sharp blades of grass—signaling the film's concern with the subjective experience of a precarious external world rooted in childhood images. As Freda Freiberg has noted, "[Campion's] films invest the everyday, domestic and trivial scenes and situations with an edge of menace."[4] The unsettling opening frames are the perfect prelude to the portrayal of a female artist for whom a sense of wonder and nightmarish visions, imagination and reality, are closely aligned. Unlike the linear story of the March sisters' development in *Little Women*, announced by images of the changing New England seasons, *An Angel at My Table* follows an episodic yet tightly constructed narrative of memory fragments, recurring shards of painful experiences, and deferred desire. Its opening shots establish the child Janet's deep insecurity, introducing visual motifs and strategies that in the course of the film will repeatedly highlight her continuing anxiety and sense of estrangement from adult society.

The first scene in the childhood segment of the film shows a young, plump, frizzy-haired Janet walking alone down a straight dirt road toward the camera, as a voice-over by the adult Janet mentions the infant death of her unnamed twin in the context of announcing, "This is the story of my childhood." The early death of an alternate double-self foreshadows the many disappointments and losses of Frame's family life—her brother Bruddie's epilepsy, the untimely deaths of her vivacious and outgoing sisters, Myrtle and Isabel, and economic instability. The film's dramatization of the sisters' deaths—and the reactions of Janet and her surviving siblings—reveals the importance of sisters as attachment figures and objects of fantasy and desire. Furthermore, the losses deepen Janet's personal struggle to define her femininity and creativity outside the restrictive gender stereotypes of her era and culture.

Janet Frame grew up in a close-knit family that was all the more isolated for its poverty. Ostracized because of her frizzy red hair, bad teeth, and plain looks by the middle-class girls who exemplified standards of femininity in her school and community, Janet suffers numerous humiliations that lay the foundations for her progressive retreat from the outside world. Shame comes to dominate her early emotional experience. Early scenes in the film show a young Janet during the Depression being shamed and branded as a thief by a teacher after she had taken some change from her father's pocket to buy candy for her classmates, and then being singled out by a school doctor along with the other visibly "poor and dirty" children for a special examination.

In the face of such humiliations, Janet relies on her three sisters, Myrtle, Isabel, and June, as her closest childhood friends. The emotional intimacy between them (reminiscent of that in *Little Women*) is often displayed in terms of physical closeness. In the early segments devoted to Janet's childhood, Campion typically frames the sisters as a tight-knit group. In one poignant and humorous scene she employs an overhead shot to disclose the four sisters sleeping together in a single bed far too small to comfortably accommodate them, their young bodies so tightly crowded beside one another that the normal tossing and turning of slumbering children becomes a night-long drill of coordinated movements, with older sister Myrtle commanding her sisters to turn from side to side in unison.

Lying awake with her sisters in bed, Janet reads to them "The Twelve Dancing Princesses," a story that Patricia Mellencamp regards as a metaphor for the film as a whole.[5] In this Grimm's fairy tale a king's twelve beautiful daughters escape their locked room every night and dance until their shoes are in shreds. Eventually, when a prince marries his favorite of the sisters, the princesses' sororal bonds abruptly part. In the film the Frame sisters later recreate this powerful fantasy through play. Campion, in a lyrical scene, shows the four sisters dancing in a moonlit forest dressed as fairy tale princesses in homemade costumes. The magical episode perfectly conveys how the young Frame siblings temporarily escape the misery of their daily lives—in fantasy, make-believe, and symbolization, which psychoanalysts from D. W. Winnicott to Daniel Stern and Jessica Benjamin have designated as vital for mutuality and intersubjectivity.[6]

As so often in her films, Campion employs fairy tales and their magic objects to evoke a complex nexus of psychological and social references. Indeed, in an astute coda to this forest scene of children's fantasy she establishes the emotionally rich, if socially ironic, parallels between the twelve dancing princesses and these working-class sisters by panning across the tattered pairs of shoes lined up at the foot of the communal Frame bed. In fairy tales, shoes and boots confer special powers on their wearers (typically, male heroes), or, in the case of females, identify the "good" sister destined to marry the prince. (In *Cinderella*, the glass slipper becomes a sign for femininity, enveloping Cinderella's foot perfectly while her evil stepsisters hack off their toes and heels to fit into the dainty shoe.) Screenwriter Laura Jones draws on this potent gendered image for Janet's precarious search for her own identity. As a recurrent motif, shoes become complex and polyvalent visual markers of Frame's social identity as well as symbols of her psychological states. After Myrtle's sudden death, a close-up shot of her red pumps with Janet in the background signifies not only the loss of the vibrant sister but also her sexuality and femininity, from which Janet feels excluded. Later in her life, on the verge of mental breakdown and suicide, Janet removes her own pumps as she runs from the teaching position she despises. And in the third segment of the film, Janet the award-winning author must wear high pumps and a black cocktail dress to her first social soiree with her British publisher, where her awkward and uncertain gait not only exposes her discomfort in assuming the constrictive accoutrements of femininity typical of the 1950s but also reveals her inability as a serious woman writer from the colonies to fit into the fashionable world of London book publishing.

In one of the last and most affecting scenes of *An Angel at My Table*, Janet, by now a celebrated writer, has returned to New Zealand after her father's death to stay in the abandoned family homestead. There she discovers her father's large boots, and in a secretive, childlike tribute to him, she literally steps into his shoes. Imitating his forceful walk and authoritative voice, Janet simulates the bodily strength and rough bravura she had always admired and envied in him, a brilliantly conceived moment of psychological revelation: it connects the grown-up daughter's tentative steps toward a more assured sense of selfhood with socially venerated traits of masculine power and authority.[7] For Janet, the province of the writer represents the power and self-confidence in her time typically reserved for men. Stepping into her father's boots, she symbolically assumes the iconic shoes typically worn by male heroes in the kingdom of fairy tales, preferring the magical powers of the writerly imagination to the passive femininity of Cinderella's fragile slippers.

By walking in her father's shoes, Janet also enacts an unconscious gesture of private mourning. Her playacting both exhibits her need for consolation for her immediate personal loss and recalls her psychological reaction to her sisters' deaths. The scene is both hopeful and elegiac, suggesting the inextricable connections between her imaginative life as a writer and her personal tragedies and disappointments. Here, at the end of the film, the death of the father represents the last of the many losses that shaped Janet Frame's painful journey from childhood into maturity.

Perhaps the most psychologically devastating event in this dramatization of Frame's story is the first family tragedy she experiences as a fully aware adolescent—the death of her older sister, Myrtle, who drowns while swimming in a local pool after her heart fails. Campion and Jones stress the disturbing emotional impact of sibling loss on young Janet's impressionable female sexual identity, revising the conventions of popular female romance, with its emphasis upon male-female relationships, to highlight the psychological importance of sisters' friendships in adolescence. As Patricia Mellencamp has observed in this regard, the screenplay takes interesting poetic license with its fairy tale allusions, for the intimate bonds between the Frame sisters, unlike those of the twelve dancing princesses, are broken not by marriage but by Myrtle's sudden demise."[8]

For Janet, Myrtle's romantic sensibility and sexual charisma represented an ideal, if socially traditional, model of female sexuality. Many
of the films about adolescent sisters discussed in this book depict older
sisters as role models for their younger siblings. As Elizabeth Fishel
writes: "Because sisters are peers, not unequals, because they share the
daily intimacies and proximities of eating, playing and sleeping, and
because their relationship is not traditionally fraught with shoulds and
shouldn'ts (the soldiers of parental command), the channels between sister and sister are more easily viable, less guarded and defended against
than the byways between mother and daughter."⁹ Female sexuality is
potentially one of the most important and sensitive areas of sororal influence. Upon leaving puberty, younger sisters may closely observe an older
sibling in order to learn how to cope with the stirrings of their own genital sexuality and to reconcile their emotional desires with the social conventions of the adult world. Conversely, before puberty children can
hardly appreciate the meanings of the moral taboos enforced by adult
society over sexual activity, but they can nonetheless witness how their
older siblings are rewarded or punished for their sexual conduct.

Even as a young child, Janet literally becomes a spectator as she and
her friend Poppy, eating sweets as if in a movie theater, watch as Myrtle
has sex behind a fallen tree in the woods. (Candy and sweets are, as we
shall see, consistently metonymically linked to illicit pleasure and sublimated female sexuality, and their consumption is repeatedly followed by
punishment from some authority figure.) When Janet reports Myrtle's
sexual adventure at the family dinner table, naively expecting it to be
cause for celebration, their father brutally batters Myrtle and forbids
Janet to ever again see her friend Poppy. This severe punishment of
Myrtle creates for Janet feelings of sexual guilt and shame that will last
into her adulthood. The scene truly recreates a classic "double bind" (or
what psychoanalyst R. D. Laing called an insoluble "knot"): women are
supposed to fulfill sexual roles, a basis for their sense of positive self-
worth in adolescence, and yet are punished for their sexual feelings and
actions. This double bind is later reenacted when Janet develops a college "crush" on her psychology professor—his response is to recom-
mend her confinement to a psychiatric ward and later a mental asylum.
Significantly, after the scene of Myrtle's punishment, Campion cuts to
an image of Janet and her sisters walking through a cemetery, a grim symbolic foreshadowing of Myrtle's untimely death. Indeed, throughout the

film Campion conjoins imagistic and narrative allusions to the deaths of Janet's sisters and the social repression of female sexuality.

Beyond the enabling and affirming significance of sisters in childhood play, Frame, the sister-artist, also defines herself in opposition to her more conventional siblings. In childhood she largely idealizes Myrtle and defers to her authority as the elder sister, but Campion includes a pivotal scene in which Janet disagrees with and resists Myrtle's influence and conventional aesthetics. One evening, when Janet is writing her first poem for school, Myrtle looms over her, insisting that she change her innovative phrase "stars touch the sky" to "tint the sky," arguing that certain words and phrases must be used together. Janet balks at the literary cliché but reluctantly changes the line in her poem. Yet, in the following scene, we see that she has stubbornly held fast to her writerly tastes after all, when she reads her original phrase to her classmates, who applaud her creative use of language. The poem is a personal triumph, yet even here Campion's inclusion in the scene of the teacher's son, born with Down's syndrome, is a subtly disturbing reminder of how Janet's creativity will later be seen as "odd" or "mad." Janet's refusal to accept Myrtle's advice characterizes the artist's life-long struggle against normative ways of seeing and being. In the process, she will be forced to assert her unique creative vision and extricate herself from her romantic identification with the cultural stereotype of the "mad artist," which will also entail coming to terms with the haunting presence of her idealized sisters.

When the four Frame sisters reach midadolescence, they pair off, with Janet becoming closest to Myrtle, revering her exuberance and natural curiosity. Myrtle openly defies her father's authority, smoking, wearing pants, and sporting a red sweater as a sign of her romantic passions and modern independence. In contrast, Janet wears muted colors and refitted school uniforms, the image of the younger, obedient, studious sister. But she vicariously enjoys her older sister's fantasized world of romantic love and adventure. Janet is pleased to brush her hair and help her dress, and she watches admiringly as Myrtle dons the red lipstick of a grown-up woman. On the day she drowns, Myrtle embodies the glamorous image of the feminine sophisticate, attired in a daring scarlet dress with a bathing towel wrapped around her head à la the turbaned movie stars of the 1930s. Janet, with a mixture of longing and envy, gazes after Myrtle as her fashionable sister leaves for the swimming pool, sashaying across the street to a jazz tune on the sound track. The next day, a grieving Janet tenderly spreads out her dead sister's scarlet dress on the bed they had shared through most of their childhood.

Myrtle's death signifies a serious injury to what psychoanalyst Louise Kaplan has termed healthy teenaged narcissism, bodily love, and self-esteem, whereby the adolescent remodels the self-centered ways of infancy and accommodates them to the future definition of self. Losing her sister is particularly traumatic for Janet because it occurs during her vulnerable early adolescence. For solace and escape, Janet increasingly turns to literature and poetry, a world of imagination that gradually becomes what Kaplan calls a "resting place at which the broken world can be made whole again."[10]

George Pollock, who has written extensively about the impact of childhood sibling loss on families, claims that a number of factors can influence the sibling bond "beyond the grave" and "exert a powerful shaping influence on the as yet unformed personalities of the sibling-survivors."[11] Among these factors he mentions the risks involved in psychological replacement and resurrection of the dead sibling in the eyes of the parents. Indeed, as a result of her parents' troubled relationship with the rebellious Myrtle, Janet begins to conceal her thoughts and feelings, confining her adolescent sexual emotions and romantic imagination to the realm of books while maintaining the persona of a compliant daughter, a "lovely girl, no trouble at all." Indeed, with Myrtle gone, Janet enters a psychological state that she describes in her autobiography as "an adolescent homelessness of self."[12]

In the film Campion reveals how Janet reacts to these tragedies: deprived of her mirroring and recognizing older sister, she often gazes into mirrors, trying to emulate other people's ideals—the romantic sweet girl, the talented writer, and other feminine personae. Campion emphasizes Janet's social isolation, her intense shyness and fear of personal rejection, by repeatedly framing her alone in close-ups and medium shots, while she gazes with loneliness and longing at groups of girls in school. Without the support of her sisters, Janet feels socially and sexually undesirable among her peers, lacking the narcissistic confidence to adopt the kinds of popular feminine behaviors and poses at which Myrtle excelled.

In the second part of the film, when Janet and her younger sister Isabel go to college, Isabel has developed into a version of the sociable and spontaneous Myrtle. She and Janet share a tiny room in their aunt's house, where a bedridden uncle reminds the sisters of ever-present death ("It's like a morgue in here," Isabel complains). Isabel dominates their conversations; her furtive but excited confession that her boyfriend "wanted me to go all the way" provides Janet with a vicarious glimpse into the conundrums of romance, with all its titillating private temptations and emotional satisfactions—and with all its social penalties.

Janet refuses Isabel's invitations to participate in social activities at the college, avoiding the dating rituals expected of marriageable young women during the 1950s. Paradoxically, her debilitating shyness is an unconscious defense against deeper fears of failing to comply with social and sexual mores. For Janet, Myrtle's punishment by their father and her death are bound up with unconscious apprehensions about the price women pay for their sexuality, pleasure, and identity.

In dramatizing the ways in which Janet's repressed desires find an object, Laura Jones's screenplay recreates a scene from the autobiography in which Janet and Isabel secretly gorge themselves on their aunt's sacred collection of boxed chocolates while fantasizing about their aunt's and bedridden uncle's perversely sublimated sex life. Naturally, they are caught by their aunt and explosively expelled from the house. This comically bizarre episode underscores the sisters' deprivation and also their experiences with death, illness, and sexuality—all shameful if not taboo subjects in middle-class New Zealand society. It also echoes earlier moments in the film, such as when Janet secretly devours candy bars in her college bedroom to assuage pent-up appetites and fend off loneliness. Later, as a young woman struggling with depression on her own in Dunedin, she repeatedly visits a cemetery plot on her way to work in order to hide bundles of leftover candy wrappers and soiled menstrual pads. The visual motifs in this last scene especially point to Janet's shame-based body image and insecure feminine identity. The cemetery is, of course, a poignant reminder of her dead sister, Myrtle, whose sexual self-confidence and curiosity Janet lacks so completely. And in Janet's mind Myrtle's death is linked to the social prohibitions and embarrassments she has encountered during her childhood and adolescence over both "sweets" and female sexuality.

After their expulsion from their aunt's house, Isabel and Janet return home to their parents along the rolling hills of the New Zealand coast. Isabel wears Myrtle's red dress, a foreshadowing of her own impending death almost ten years after Myrtle's. In an uncanny repetition, Isabel also drowns while swimming, and Janet relives the agony of losing a sister. Not long afterward Janet suffers a nervous breakdown and attempts suicide. Then comes the mental hospital.

Campion effectively depicts Janet's social experiences in the mental ward as frightful, exaggerated versions of the ones she had experienced outside its walls. The asylum is not only a space of incarceration but one that delimits and circumscribes femininity. In obedience to the paternalistic ideology of the male doctors and administrators, the female inmates are kept compliant by the latest technologies of electroshock and lobotomy for their failure to live up to the era's social ideals of femininity. Indeed, Janet's bizarre "treatment" in the mental ward seems to confirm Michel Foucault's definition of the "madhouse" and the prison as institutions dedicated to social control rather than to healing.[13] In a particularly grotesque reflection on social norms and rituals, the female mental patients are prepared by the asylum staff to meet their male counterparts for a "party." Janet is brutally made up by the attendants with garish red lipstick and a wild hairbow—a reminder of Myrtle's adolescent experiments with cosmetics and provocative dress—and then forced to dance with her partner, a disturbing parody of the middle-class parties from which Janet felt alienated in her youth.

To escape from the asylum, Janet Frame learns that she must rely on the very thing that she has always turned to under acute stress—her writing. Too shy, too self-conscious, she had always expressed herself through writing rather than through speech, shaping and adapting her memories and feelings into communicable form. Her storytelling magically revealed her inner self and thoughts to others. In the asylum Janet literally writes her self into being: Campion frames her in an overhead shot in her isolation cell, feverishly scrawling on the walls to escape the terrors of electroshock therapy and the looming lobotomy, from which only the award of a prestigious literary prize rescues her.

The third segment of the film depicts Frame's gradual emergence from fear and shame. Campion, however, offers recurrent reminders of Janet's dead sisters and their persistent hold on her imagination, beginning with the opening memory scene of the four sisters sitting by the sea, singing "To France." The initial long shot of the sisters against the wild New Zealand coastline in the sparkling sunshine and the subsequent four-shot of Myrtle, Isabel, June, and Janet in profile transport us momentarily to the happy sisters' collective world where they once longed for a brighter future on the other side of the sea.

Janet fulfills their fantasy and goes to Europe on a literary grant, singing the sisters' childhood song in a low voice by the window of her Paris hotel room; in Spain she has her first sexual experience—with an American history professor and would-be poet, Bernard. In Ibiza, Janet sadly watches three girls playing in the street below her window, and later she looks on in shock at a funeral procession of men carrying several caskets of dead infants down the narrow streets—a reminder of the dreaded morgue, the shadow of death, and the return of Isabel's body in a metal casket on the train. Still in Europe, she miscarries after her affair with the callous Bernard ends—a cruel visitation of earlier losses. These sequences are accompanied on the soundtrack by variations of the musical theme "To France," augmenting the psychic connections between Janet's childhood attachments and losses and her adult experiences.

In this final section of the film, Janet makes tentative forays into Myrtle's world, opening herself up to Bernard instead of "blocking all entrances and exits to her body." In spite of the misery she feels later from his rejection, her affair seems to give her greater self-confidence, removing the stigma attached to sexuality and the body. Shortly afterward, Janet unpacks a pair of men's pants, shocking the traditional Spanish women who are her hosts: these pants resemble the ones that Myrtle wore in the first segment, rebelling against her father's strictures on sex. Here Campion again pays close attention to costume and dress as markers of identity and symbolic representations of psychic states, not only linking the adult to the child, but also indicating Janet's new, if provisional, triumph over adversity.

With its multiple levels of symbolic detail, Campion's film succeeds in both cinematic and narrative terms in capturing Frame's sense of the constant presence of the past as an accretion of experiences and internalized objects. Janet Frame writes in her autobiography: "Time past is not time gone, it is time accumulated, with the host resembling the character in the fairy tale who was joined along the route by more and more characters, none of whom could be separated from one another or from the host, with some stuck so fast that their presence caused physical pain."[14] In many ways, Frame's life task became one of peeling away the accumulated layers of experience that shaped her identity, unleashing her creativity but ironically also revealing an absence at the center. In London, Frame discovers that she never suffered from schizophrenia, a stunning revelation. All her life she had accepted her diagnosis as the mark of the "mad" artist, a romantic if fatally flawed idea that at times had allowed her to rationalize coping with loss through social withdrawal. Campion's film suggests Janet must work through her painful attachment to her dead sisters and reconnect with the childhood sense of community and intimate sharing of the sisters' relationship—poems and novels read together, songs sung, and fairy tales staged[15]—in order to finally go her own way. Campion visualizes Janet's return to her family in the final scene: she is living in a trailer home parked at her surviving sister's house, writing her poetry. Living close to, yet not in her sister's home, Janet continues to move between the external social world, dancing a few tentative steps to the twist, and the realm of the imagination where she must venture alone.

PART

Negotiating Sameness and Difference: Sisters in Adolescence

The desire to be and have a sister is a primitive and profound one that may have everything and nothing to do with the family a woman is born to. It is a desire to know and be known by someone who shares blood and body, history and dreams, common ground and the unknown adventures of the future, darkest secrets and the glassiest beads of truth.

Elizabeth Fishel, *Sisters: Shared Histories, Lifelong Ties*

A woman's desire for a sister, for the shared intimacies of the sister bond, is often strongest during the adolescent years. The reasons are not hard to fathom: girls, upon reaching puberty, leave behind their comforting dependency on the parent and the freedoms of childhood make-believe for the increasingly complex roles and realities of adult existence, undertaking journeys of self-transformation and discovery that are not only enriching and exhilarating but often bewildering and painful. Girls entering adolescence embark upon quests for a sense of personal selfhood, for autonomy and moral integrity, for a worthwhile existence in the face of a potentially destructive world.

Some of the most acute portraits of sisters in the modern cinema are renderings of female adolescence. This is hardly surprising, since in modern times the adolescent years have come to be perceived as a crucial period for self-definition, for learning what it means to be human and alive, for understanding what binds the self to the larger society and to the natural world. "More than birth, marriage, or death, adolescence entails the most highly elaborated drama of the passage from one realm of existence to another," remarks psychologist Louise Kaplan. "It is that critical point in human life when the sexual and moral passions come to fruition and attain maturity. And it is then that the individual passes from family life into cultural existence."[1]

Sisters, who are usually developmental peers, are often the most privileged witnesses to their sibling's adolescent experiences, close enough in age to encounter in tandem the consequent bodily, emotional, and social transformations, playing the roles of competitors and adversaries as well as of friends and confidantes. Throughout the developmental changes and challenges, sisters become actors in each other's consciousness. Engaging in a kind of intersubjective shadow-play, sisters may serve each other as psychic mirrors or alternate selves, as they lead and follow one another through adolescence, that dynamic if uncertain boundary-realm where they come to embody for each other both past and future identities.

The modern feature films that I examine in this part of this book represent the sister relationship as a significant psychological component in the adolescent conflicts of their central protagonists. Dramatizing some of the myriad ways in which sisters come to share, as Elizabeth Fishel puts it, "blood and body, history and dreams, common ground and the unknown adventures of the future," each film depicts female siblings as key players in identity and personality development during the teen years. Revealing how sisters' interactions are often shaped by the developmental exigencies of adolescence, the films also disclose how the sibling bond can itself influence the nature and even the outcome of a young woman's progress toward adulthood.

Virtually all these films belong to a much larger narrative family in late-twentieth-century cinema, usually referred to as "coming-of-age films" or "rites-of-passage films." Such films organize their action around young male or female protagonists, dramatizing situations and relationships that are meant to capture some of the experiential characteristics of childhood, adolescence, or early adulthood. Far too diverse to be defined as a traditional genre, the films in this broad class exhibit a wide range of aesthetic approaches, social and psychological interests, cultural themes, and source materials, and more often than not are indebted to narrative traditions associated with their particular national cinema. Yet, despite these disparities, the contemplation of childhood and adolescence is what unifies these films, among them some of the most memorable works in the modern canon of world cinema.[2]

Although almost all of the films I treat in the following three chapters fall into the category of the coming-of-age film (the 1995 British chamber drama, *Sister My Sister*, is the one exception), they also share an unusual sensitivity to the psychological complexities of women's interrelationships and identifications, which sets them apart from many other films about female adolescence. This difference is especially apparent if one compares them to the large number of contemporary Hollywood-produced, commercially oriented films about female teenagers and young adult women.[3] All are the products of the contemporary wave of revisionist films that since the 1970s have attempted to represent female subjectivities through cinematic lenses unclouded by either the excessive sentimentality or the polarized morality so characteristic of traditional film melodramas about women.

Indeed, beginning in the 1970s a host of women filmmakers have created works that, to borrow Inez Hedges's characterization of the modernist cinema of the 1960s, have sought to "break the frames of our normal perception and ultimately have a positive influence on reality itself." Their emergence largely reflects the influence of the women's movement on world cinema, especially in the West, and the ascension of women directors into the international ranks of modern filmmakers. As critic Barbara Quart has noted, many narrative films about female adolescence by women directors have refused to adhere to traditional narrative conventions based upon male fantasies of female fulfillment, longstanding cultural stereotypes of women's social destiny and desires, or both. Instead they have critically explored the gendered differences of female development in light of contemporary transformations in women's identities.[4]

The revisionist spirit of these female coming-of-age films cannot be understated. As recently as the decades following World War II, when postclassical Hollywood directors and New Wave European filmmakers began to challenge paternalistic screen images of the male adolescent in such landmark postwar films as Nicholas Ray's *Rebel Without a Cause* (1955) or Truffaut's *The 400 Blows*, focusing on juvenile deviance from conformist social norms and the male youth's conflicts with adult authority, they continued to depict the female adolescent solely in relation to the desire for love and marriage.

In contrast, many female coming-of-age films since the 1970s have resisted or undermined the narrative imperatives of courtship and marriage common to classical women's melodrama, romantic film comedy, or male-centered realism. Women directors, most notably, have instead emphasized the adolescent heroine's emotional attachments to mothers, sisters, and female friends, refusing to treat women's adolescent life stories as merely a conventionalized rite-of-passage from the familial bonds of childhood into the adult pleasures of heterosexual love or the duties of motherhood—although few neglect the influences of fathers, brothers, lovers, and other male figures in the developmental dramas of their adolescent heroines. Whether writing autobiographically inspired scripts or drawing upon literary works about growing up, women directors such as France's Vera Belmont (*Red Kiss*, 1986), Hungary's Marta Meszaros (*Diary for My Children*, 1982), China's Lu Xiaoya (*The Girl in Red*, 1984), Hong Kong's Ann Hui (*Song of the Exile*, 1989), Holland's Marleen Gorris (*Antonia's Line*, 1995), and U.S. independent Alex Sichel (*All Over Me*, 1997) have offered original and sometimes startling perspectives on the female quest for identity.[5] In addition, a number of iconoclastic male directors have attempted to articulate the fundamental importance of female interrelationships during adolescence and postadolescence. Besides Todd Solondz (*Welcome to the Dollhouse*, 1996, treated in chapter 3), they range from Victor Nunez (*Ruby in Paradise*, 1996) in the United States to Great Britain's Mike Leigh (*Life is Sweet*, 1991; *Career Girls*, 1997), and from Taiwan's Ang Lee (*Eat Drink Man Woman*, 1994) to Russia's Vyacheslav Kristofovich (*Adam's Rib*, 1992).

Several recent works by American independent directors illustrate through their storylines and psychological perspectives the expanding range of female coming-of-age films in the 1990s. In both Lisa Krueger's *Manny and Lo* (1996) and Mo Ogrodnik's *Ripe* (1997), sisters negotiate their identities and sexualities in an uncertain and hostile social world. Krueger's film focuses on two orphaned sisters, Amanda (Manny) and Laurel (Lo), who escape their respective foster families and live on the run, driving from town to town in their late mother's station wagon, shoplifting from convenience stores, and spending the night in unoccupied model homes. Their precarious lifestyle reaches a crisis when Lo can no longer deny her advanced pregnancy and convinces her younger sister to help her kidnap and hold hostage a woman shop clerk in a maternity store whom the sisters mistakenly believe to be an expert on motherhood. Hiding out in a vacation cabin in the woods, the unlikely trio builds a reluctant improvised family, with the shop clerk assuming a motherly role. Much of the off-kilter humor in this film derives from the visual perception of eleven-year-old Manny, who has both a firm grasp of reality and a child's eye for wonder. Loyal and protective of her hardened but self-deluded older sister, she nevertheless longs for a maternal figure and family.

Director Mo Ogrodnik's edgy and much harsher film, *Ripe*, concerns fraternal twin sisters, who, after the death of their mother and abusive father in a car crash, run away as "outlaws" and hide out on a run-down army base, a hyper-masculine world that forces the sisters to confront their emerging sexuality. Conceived by Ogrodnik as opposites, the two represent polar extremes of female pubescent attitudes towards sexuality: Violet is curious about exploring her sensuality, while Rosie, who cannot let go of childhood and her close bond with her sister, reacts with violence and anger toward sexuality.

Despite their differences in tone and style, both *Manny and Lo* and *Ripe* draw upon fairy tale tropes made surreal: the motif of the journey through the forest; the focus on female siblings who have lost their parents and must, on their way to adulthood, rely on each other to survive. Manny's and Lo's yearning for and final discovery of a substitute mother provides an ironic meditation on family and female bonding.[6] *Ripe* takes a tough feminist perspective on the confusions of female adolescent sexuality, which ultimately shatter the sisters' symbiotic childhood bond. Ogrodnik has commented on her use of the fraternal twins as a metaphor for adolescent women's conflicted attitudes toward sexuality and, in that sense, the film is less concerned with the relationship *between* the sisters than in their symbolic value as exaggerated representations of a split female self.[7] Nevertheless, the film's depiction of sisters bonded together against an abusive parent and its psychological reflections on female sexuality strongly echo issues and themes that appear in the two films I discuss in chapter 5, *Heavenly Creatures* and *Sister My Sister.*

It is worth taking a moment here to explore the intersubjective dynamics between sisters in adolescence; in this crucial stage of identity formation, it is hardly surprising that the negotiation between self and other, sameness and difference, should occupy the main arena of their search for selfhood. What is significant here is that the sisters' process of self-definition necessarily occurs within the relational matrix of the sister bond itself. The search for identity among adolescent sisters is a mutual, dialogic quest. As Jackie Stacey comments, "Recognizing oneself as different from, yet also as similar to, a feminine ideal other produces the pleasures between femininities which has been referred to as the 'intimacy which is knowledge.'"[8]

The search for recognition is particularly active and significant in adolescence. As recent studies of female development have argued, young adolescent women face a major psychological crisis around issues of body image, sexual object choice, identity formation, and cultural values and prohibitions on female sexuality and behavior.[9] Unlike boys, whose internal and external worlds seem to expand during adolescence, girls tend to focus inward, often undergoing intense conflicts over separation from the primary family and its values, accompanied by self-doubt and a loss of their prepubescent confidence. Sisters become major players in this process both as figures of identification and as intimate antagonists, participating in what Marian Sandmaier has termed the "rivalry over attributes that society still promotes as essential to feminine adequacy—physical beauty, thinness and the ability to attract men."[10]

The films I discuss in the next three chapters concern themselves with this rivalry to varying degrees, critiquing social norms of "feminine adequacy" through the ways siblings collude with or resist the attributes sanctioned by male desire. In *Eve's Bayou* (1997) and several others, the relationship between sisters is mediated by the oedipal scenario between daughters and fathers. The father, who also represents paternal authority and law in a larger cultural sense, is an important if ambivalently experienced figure for the sisters—an object of fascination and dread.[11]

Sisters also engage in the preoedipal struggle over maternal love. Films that portray sisters in adolescence often stage the process of self-definition through the protagonist's keen observation of her sister and her sister's relationship with the mother, a dynamic that complicates fantasies of pre-oedipal merging with the mother—which, according to many feminist psychoanalytic critics, shapes and influences female identity from childhood through adulthood. As Terry Apter points out, "However strongly one sister influences another, the influence is not simply from sister to sister but from mother/sister to mother/sister/sister. The girl is not simply influenced by what the sister is or does, but also [by] how the mother responds to her sister's behavior, and how she contrasts this response to her mother's responses to her."[12] As we shall see in *Peppermint Soda, Gas Food Lodging, Welcome to the Dollhouse*, and others, the triangulated bond between sisters and mother calls into question any simple identification between mother and daughter or sister and sister.

Female siblings play a unique role in the female adolescent's search for identity between family and the larger society, sharing each other's worlds and also observing each other from afar. A case in point is Diane Kurys's *nouvelle vague*-inspired *Peppermint Soda (Diabolo menthe*, 1977), which anticipated subsequent films about female adolescence and sisterhood. Its rueful, unsentimental look at the complex relationship between two adolescent sisters growing up with a single mother is distinctively modernist in perspective and tone, combining irony and humor with a bittersweet sense of loss. Set in the epochal year of 1963, as France stood poised on the brink of major sociohistorical change, *Peppermint Soda*'s autobiographical portrait of youthful sisterhood is a remembrance of the coming of age of a new generation of young women who, in searching for self-definition as they prepared for adulthood, were to redefine the values and ideals of femininity in French society through their own experience and their relationships with other women. The film captures the important role of the sibling relationship for each of its female protagonists as they carve out their female identities not only in relationship to their mother but also to their most intimate peer—the sister—during an era of social transformation.

In chapter 3, I discuss Kurys's film as well as Allison Anders's independent American feature, *Gas Food Lodging* (1992), and Todd Solondz's seriocomic film about adolescent alienation, *Welcome to the Dollhouse* (1995). In all three works the sister relationship serves as a medium for the quest for self-knowledge. However, compared to those in *Little Women* or *An Angel at My Table*, the sister relationships they dramatize are far more contentious and ambivalent, highlighting the sisters' vexed parental identifications with the mother, who in each film becomes a central figure or object in the constellation of the sisters' desires. In all three films the power struggles between the sisters over dominance and recognition in the family are connected to the ways in which the mother treats and values them differently, to her conscious or unconscious regulation of the sisters' competition for her attention and love; each film portrays these power struggles from the perspective of the sibling who is the outsider in the family. Cinematically, the films also force a critical distance from the dramatic action, presenting a "dual narrative" that allows the viewer to enter the sister-narrator's thoughts, perceptions, or feelings, while at the same time maintaining ironic distance from her.[13]

The two films I consider in chapter 4, *Double Happiness* (1995) and *Eve's Bayou* (1997), explore the role of the father in sisters' relationships and female development. *Double Happiness*, the first feature film by Canadian-Chinese director Mina Shum, visualizes two sisters' problematic relationship with their autocratic father. Although Shum treats important identity issues for young women, her inventive blending of documentary realism, expressionistic point-of-view shots, and fantastical montage sequences reflects the buoyant imagination and emotional complexity of the film's protagonist. The younger sister in the film is the only character who not only comprehends the double bind of identity imposed on Chinese-Canadian women of their generation, a central theme, but also sees and understands her sister as an individual with her own thoughts, feelings, and creative ambitions.

Eve's Bayou, written and directed by African American filmmaker Kasi Lemmons, is also a highly original debut film by a woman. A contemporary gothic melodrama set in the Louisiana bayou during the 1960s, the film tells the story of ten-year-old Eve Batiste, whose position in her African American family's complex relationships ensnares her in a narrative of loyalty and deceit when her fourteen-year-old sister Cisely's adoration of her father threatens to cross the taboo barrier of incest. In contrast to the recent black family "feel-good" melodrama featuring three sisters, *Soul Food* (1997), *Eve's Bayou* poses more challenging and disturbing questions about unconscious and incestuous desire in family relationships, the close ties and hidden jealousies between sisters that influence their respective interpretation of truth.

Both *Eve's Bayou* and *Double Happiness* follow in a line of breakthrough films in North American ethnic cinema that began in the 1960s and 1970s and was accelerated by the emergence of the New Black Cinema in the 1980s. The two films present two ethnically or racially specific family contexts—African American and Chinese Canadian—that expand the vision of the cultural influences on deeply rooted bonds between sisters. The relationships between the sisters and their response to paternal authority are played out in the context not merely of the nuclear family but of the larger problematics of racial and ethnic history: *Eve's Bayou* reaches back into the history of African American enslavement, while *Double Happiness* calls into question Chinese women's longstanding subjugation to the Confucian law of filial piety.

In the two works that I examine in chapter 5, Peter Jackson's 1994 New Zealand film *Heavenly Creatures* and Nancy Meckler's 1995 British production *Sister My Sister,* the tensions and conflicts between mothers and their daughters produce far more disturbing outcomes than in the works discussed in chapter 3. Family murder is again a central theme, as it was in *Eve's Bayou,* but in these films the outcome is matricide.

Heavenly Creatures and *Sister My Sister* each feature extreme cases of sibling mirroring and psychological enmeshment, and this twinning effect between sisters is played out in two historical cases of matricide or murder of a symbolic mother substitute. Despite their potentially sensationalistic subject matter, each film is concerned less with the crime itself than with the complex subterranean relationships between the female characters, the powerful fantasies of seduction and attachment that lead up to the two matricides. *Heavenly Creatures* is the only film in this book that deals with female friends rather than blood siblings, but the relationship between Pauline and Juliet is remarkable for its ardently desired and fantasized sisterhood—Fishel's "primitive and profound desire to be and have a sister."

Both films highlight the psychological dynamics in troubled sibling relations where identity boundaries have been erased and sisters become symbiotic mirror images of each other. Significantly, they treat the murderous sisters not as monsters or freaks but as complex victims of parental neglect, social prejudice, and class differences. Once again, a dual narrative prevails in each film: the spectator is positioned to empathically enter the protagonists' internal worlds but permitted critical distance from the dramatic action through the deployment of both realist and expressionist mise-en-scène and montage.

Jackie Stacey's assertion that women on- and offscreen define themselves actively rather than passively through a female other is borne out in all these films.[14] In each, the female protagonist's search for psychological truth and identity occurs in the matrix of sororal relatedness. Like *Little Women* and *An Angel at My Table,* these films explore in other historical periods the "differences between femininities" that, as Stacey points out, have been insufficiently understood in a cinematic context as important forms of identification and differentiation for female spectators.

Sororal Rites of Passage

Peppermint Soda, Gas Food Lodging,
and Welcome to the Dollhouse

he power of adolescent sisters to shape each other's psyche, which first became a subject of women's cinema in the 1970s, has since appeared more frequently as a thematic focus in rites-of-passage films, including the three I consider in this chapter: *Peppermint Soda* (1977), *Gas Food Lodging* (1992), and *Welcome to the Dollhouse* (1995). Psychologically, the character of one sister's progress through adolescence can exert a powerful influence on a second sibling, who may assimilate and translate her sister's experiences into a desirable ideal or cautionary tale for her own life. This internalization by one sibling of her adolescent sister's experiences and perceptions, dreams and illusions, and her recognition of her sister as a real other, testify to the strength of the intersubjective sororal bond that is forged in the childhood years. Originating in the recesses of childhood consciousness and fantasy, the sister bond furnishes for each sibling a crucial link between past and present, the family and the outside world. Conversely, siblings' different memories and renderings of the past—what Paula Gallant Eckard has called "the prismatic past"—call into question a single, linear family history and suggest a more dialogic reconstruction of childhood worlds.[1]

The often autobiographical nature of women filmmakers' representations of family relationships means that memory and the reconstruction of family history play an important role in films about sisters in childhood and adolescence.[2] Two of the earliest films to explore the "hidden" memory of female family bonds between sisters and among mothers and daughters were Michelle Citron's feminist avant-garde piece *Daughter-Rite* (1978) and Diane Kurys's feature *Peppermint Soda*. *Daughter-Rite* is noteworthy for its experimental mixing of documentary, narrative, and avant-garde modes, its blending of cinema verité and melodrama. Citron describes *Daughter-Rite* as "the story of two pairs of sisters and their relationship to their respective mothers. The themes of betrayal, anger, love and manipulation between mother and daughters and between sisters are presented through an interweaving of cinematic techniques: scripted and acted scenes shot in the visual language of *cinéma vérité* and optically printed home movie images accompanied as voice-over by a narrator reading entries from her journal."[3]

The layering of narratives in this film suggests the fragmentary nature of memory shot through with resistance and desire and articulates the multiple viewpoints in the triangulated relationship between a mother and two sisters. While the home movie footage shows the three acting out the stereotypes of femininity associated with the ideal middle-class family for the husband's paternal camera eye, the cinema verité sequences portray an ostensibly more complex and authentic picture: we witness the adult daughters sharing painful and conflicted memories of growing up, feelings of sibling rivalry, and then anger toward their mother's controlling and invasive surveillance. When the viewer realizes that these cinema verité scenes were consciously constructed, enacted performances, the sisters' conflicted memories of their mother and relationship to the past are exposed as artifice as well. The true relationship between the sisters and their ambivalent identification with and rejection of the mother is not so easily captured in a coherent narrative; through the collision of different cinematic modes of representation, *Daughter-Rite* emphasizes the conflicted search for an interrelational definition of self.

E. Ann Kaplan has rightly argued that in *Daughter-Rite* the narrator-daughter's and sisters' dominant point of view, their unconscious anger and resentment, relegates the mother to silence, absence, and marginality, ironically underscoring the negation of the mother by patriarchial structures. However, the film is an instructive early example of how women have used the medium to explore the ways in which images and memories of self and relationships to parents are refracted through siblings' different perspectives.[4] *Peppermint Soda* is much less formally adventurous than *Daughter-Rite*, but it too self-consciously announces its personal, testimonial retrospective of the past and family history from the very first frame and explores the triangulated bond between a mother and two adolescent sisters.

Peppermint Soda's primary focus is the younger sister—the director's thirteen-year-old alter ego—and her subjective response to her family and the world around her. In two later films about her family life, Kurys expanded her internal, even narcissistic, point of view to include the intersubjective others—her mother and older sister—articulating her mother's history and experience in *Entre Nous* (1983) and her older sister's perspective in *C'est la Vie* (1990); she perhaps also wished to acknowledge the distortions, repressions, and transformations at work in *Peppermint Soda*.[5] I focus here on that film because it offers the most developed and nuanced reflection on Kurys's relationship with her sister in adolescence, and one of the first narrative examples in modern international cinema of the interrelational world of adolescent girls.

Along with *Peppermint Soda* I consider in this chapter two American independent features, *Gas Food Lodging* by Allison Anders and *Welcome to the Dollhouse* by Todd Solondz. They all represent very different cultural milieux but nevertheless continue the theme addressed in *An Angel at My Table* (see chapter 2): a non-nostalgic return to childhood and adolescence and the female adolescent's struggle with autonomy and intimacy in relation to the sister and mother. Like many films on female adolescence and sisterhood, these three incorporate some of the directors' life experiences. In addition to Kurys's purely autobiographical *Peppermint Soda*, Allison Anders based her film on her experience of working her way through film school as a single mother with two rebellious teenage daughters.[6] Todd Solondz has denied any overt autobiographical references in *Welcome to the Dollhouse* but admitted that the film captured his feelings about what it meant to be a high school kid feeling alienated in the New Jersey suburbs.[7]

What marks these films as modern is their subtle self-reflexivity, their keen awareness of point of view, and their positioning of the adolescent protagonist as spectator, observer, and narrator of her relationship to her sister and mother. It is the "invisible" sister, the daughter who perceives herself to be neglected or not favored by the mother, who tells the tale in each. The relationship between mothers and daughters and between sisters is particularly conflicted and volatile during adolescence—the sisters' struggle to separate from the mother and from each other to establish their own identities rivals their desire to remain attached. Feminist psychoanalytic critics have described the difficult psychosexual journey that the girl is socialized to undertake in adolescence: the imperative to identify with her mother because of their shared gender and to separate and individuate from her, and finally to turn her attachment from the mother (her first love object) to the father and the social world of adult sexual love. In these films, as in life, the sister relationship is intertwined with the mother-daughter matrix. A sister may serve, as Marian Sandmaier has written, as "accomplice, as support, as validator, as co-explorer of one's most intimate history" with one's mother, and she simultaneously represents a rival for the mother's fantasies about the preferred, perfect daughter.[8]

Peppermint Soda and *Gas Food Lodging* are particularly moving and insightful in their representation of the female adolescent's search for self-knowledge, a quest that requires her to mourn the loss of her "infantile love dialogues" before she can transfer her maternal attachment to other objects.[9] In each film, the older daughter's emerging active sexuality coincides with her mother's regrets and disappointments in love and her ambivalent feelings about aging. This mother-daughter conflict serves as an object lesson for the younger sister's rite of passage. By contrast, *Welcome to the Dollhouse* dramatizes the failure of an intersubjective relationship between mother and daughter and between the sisters, largely because of the mother's extreme preferential treatment of her youngest daughter. The potential intimacy between the sisters is aborted and so is the coming of age of the protagonist—the invisible daughter—whose experience of the family is never validated by her siblings.

Peppermint Soda

Peppermint Soda (1977) begins with a shot of its sister protagonists, Anne (Eleonore Klarwein) and Frederique Weber (Odile Michel), posing with their father and Frederique's boyfriend on the beach for an off-screen photographer at the end of their annual summer vacation. The self-reflexivity of this scene, its acknowledgment of the presence of the camera, its frame within a frame, is distinctly modernist in its visual articulation of the film as an artistic construction, violating the illusionist conventions of realist cinema. As spectators, we are immediately aware of filmmaking as an act of seeing and remembering, and the potential of the camera for scrutinizing the human image and family relationships.

One soon learns that Frederique's and Anne's parents are divorced—still a rare occurrence in the early 1960s—and thus the family, like those in many modern films, is not taken for granted but comes under scrutiny, as does the sisters' relationship to each other and their parents. Kurys's dedication of this autobiographical film to her older sister, "who still hasn't returned [her] orange sweater," playfully asserts the importance of the sibling relationship in the film and its lasting significance in Kurys's life.

Made some fifteen years after the works of the French New Wave with their predominantly male adolescent protagonists, *Peppermint Soda* was one of the first films to introduce a *female* adolescent perspective, focusing on the search for identity and the importance of female bonding in adolescence. The most innovative scenes in the film incorporate cinema verité–style observations of girls in school and the all-female world of a divorced mother and her two daughters at home. The "photomontage" structure of the film—short elliptic scenes—replicates the perspective of the adult filmmaker recollecting her experiences as a thirteen year old in 1963. Kurys also sketches out the landscape of the generation coming of age in the 1960s: "In *Diabolo menthe*, I tried to show how we were raised and educated, which explained why we exploded in May '68."[10] Set in the year of Kennedy's assassination, the film reveals how Anne and Frederique must submit to the strict discipline and conformity of high school as the world outside is undergoing dramatic social changes. Frederique engages with these changes through her first experiences of love and social activism, while Anne finds it difficult to leave behind her childhood. The beginning of worldwide political turmoil and unrest among the younger generation reflects Anne's intrapsychic transformation and her insecurities as a child of divorced parents. Torn between her desire for her mother's love and her identification with her father, oppressed by the authoritarian atmosphere of the lycée, and ambivalently attached to her older sister, Anne often feels like an outsider.

Ultimately, Anne negotiates her entry into adolescence and female sexuality through her sister rather than through her tie to her mother. From the very beginning, she seeks to emulate and vicariously participate in her sister's life. Indeed, Frederique becomes a role model and "mirror" for Anne—as older sisters often do—suggesting alternative selves and embodying the pleasures and pains of late adolescence. Kurys repeatedly frames the sisters' interactions in mirrors, underscoring Anne's desire to play a part in Frederique's world. Fascinated by her sister's experiences of

first love, she steams open Frederique's letters from her summer boyfriend
to steal his picture, which she then takes to school to show to classmates.
Much of the humor in the film derives from Anne and her friends spec-
ulating about the mysteries of sexual intercourse. Anne craves the trap-
pings of adult femininity, wearing a bright red hat, begging her mother
for permission to wear pantyhose, and taking her sister's tampons even
though she has not yet begun menstruating. Yet she is also afraid of men,
as we detect from the intermittent scene of her spontaneous bolts from a
male stranger on the street. She tags along with her sister to a dance and
has her first encounter—shy and awkward—with a boy. For her part,
Frederique experiences a passionate teenage romance but grows bored
with her boyfriend during a camping trip (significantly, this trip is conveyed through a montage of still shots like the sequence in which the sisters take a winter vacation with their father—a visual cue that these experiences are not part of the everyday homosocial world of mothers and
sisters). When Frederique nonchalantly tells Anne during a shared bath
that the relationship with her boyfriend is over, Anne bursts into tears, for
she had invested her sister's relationship with the alluring mysteries of an
ideal adult love affair. Her emotional response also conveys her painful discovery of the fragility of relationships, aggravated by her sense of loss as
the daughter of divorced parents.

Kurys never idealizes the sisters' relationship but instead presents the
complex range of emotional colorations that inform it. Frederique
asserts her position of authority, refusing to include Anne in "grown-
up" activities. In an episode that inspires the title of the film, Anne and
her friends go to a cafe to drink diabolo menthe (peppermint soda, a
French brand of popular beverage associated with growing up as a
teenager), but Frederique appears with her own clique and humiliates
Anne by ordering her to go home. Kurys claims that in the film she took
her revenge on her sister for abusing the authority with which their
mother had entrusted her.[11] When Anne tries to participate in conversations about boyfriends, sex, politics, or the latest movies, Frederique
and her friends repeatedly rebuff her. At one point, Frederique and a
friend discuss a schoolmate who has run away from home. Excluded,
Anne takes her revenge by making a prank phone call to her sister.
When Frederique discovers Anne's trick, she beats her up, realizing
only later that Anne's actions stem from her desire for Frederique to
notice her, to recognize her. But at other times Frederique pays close
attention to her sister in ways that underline their solidarity. For

instance, when she, Anne, and their mother visit a wholesale garment retailer, Frederique observes the salesman's voyeuristic look at Anne, who is trying on clothes between racks, and as an act of protest refuses to purchase anything. Here the male objectifying gaze, which eludes the mother who is exchanging pleasantries with the salesman, is exposed through the sisters' protective bond. In another scene, Anne steals something from a shop, and while the mother walks away in anger and humiliation, Frederique puts her arms around her sister, assuring her that "she [the mother] will get over it."

The central conflict between Frederique and Anne concerns their rivalry for their mother. Director Diane Kurys has described her feelings as an adolescent who felt excluded from her mother's attention:

> I grew up without a father. As I show in *Diabolo menthe*, there were no men in my world, at home or at school. It was an exclusively feminine milieu. I lived with my mother and older sister and I not only idealized my absent father but I felt I must have resembled him and therefore, at times, I felt I was rejected the way he was. It was a difficult time for me—today children have more of a dialogue with adults—but I didn't want to sentimentalize. It was entirely autobiographical.[12]

Less confident than Frederique of her mother's love and affection, Anne feels shut out from the close relationship that exists between her mother and older sister. Recurrent scenes shot from Anne's point of view reveal her mother and sister lying together in the maternal bed, whispering and talking to each other, followed by a shot of Anne observing them through the half-open bedroom door. The mother has chosen the older sister as her confidante. In one scene, the camera pans around the sisters' dark room as we hear the mother's and Frederique's muted voices. Disturbed by her older daughter's boyfriend's passionate love letters, the mother warns Frederique about the difference between youthful passion and "true love," sharing her own experiences of heartache. The scene is constructed to suggest both intimacy and distance, as the viewer, like Anne herself, is both privy to the conversation and kept out of the mother's room. Anne responds to her feelings of rejection by lying to her mother about her schoolwork and by stealing, two acts that psychoanalyst D. W. Winnicott has claimed are often the child's way of symbolically reclaiming the mother's love of which she feels deprived.[13]

Frederique experiences her own share of traumas and challenges typical of middle adolescence: a fickle romance, betrayal by a close female friend, and a displaced oedipal attraction to the father of her friend

Muriel. In addition, Frederique's consciousness raising in a politically turbulent era, and her assertive self-identification as a Jew in a nation haunted by its World War II anti-Semitism, express her need to become her own person as she moves into young adulthood. She rebels against her mother first by staying out late after a dance and later by becoming involved with an antinuclear group at a time when political activities were banned from all-girls schools. All these events are portrayed in the framework of Frederique's struggle to grow up in the all-female family—her resistance and her need to separate from the symbiotic relationship with her mother. Toward the end of the film, Frederique has left the preoedipal space of her mother's bedroom, and, as if to substitute for this loss, she experiences a fleeting, erotically charged moment of connection and "sisterhood" with a female friend whose political commitment she shares—an acknowledgment of the homoerotic bonds between women that Kurys later explores in *Entre Nous*.[14]

Anne's position as an observer-outsider forever peering into her mother's and sister's lives embodies Kurys's complex perspective on her own attempt to reclaim her childhood and adolescence and her relationships with her mother and sister. After completing *C'est la Vie*, she claimed in an interview that her parents' divorce made her into a writer.[15] There are numerous self-reflexive references to her own development in *Peppermint Soda*. For instance, Anne's defiant refusal to pose for her mother's lover's camera during a family picnic suggests Kurys's adult decision to change her career from actress to director behind the camera. A school production of a Molière play in which Frederique acts hints at Kurys's own career as an actress. Many of Kurys's subsequent films—*Molotov Cocktail* (1981), *Entre Nous*, and *C'est la Vie*—rework the autobiographical material of her parents' divorce and its effect on herself and her sister.

Peppermint Soda concludes with scenes from the sisters' annual beach vacation with their absent father. A year has gone by since the similar beach scene that opened the film. This time, however, Anne wanders along the shore by herself, apart from her sister and her sister's new boyfriend. Having entered puberty, Anne has left behind her childhood self and seems skeptical of the future that lies ahead. The final medium close-up of Anne against the seashore looking directly at the spectator— one of several citations from Truffaut's autobiographical film, *The 400 Blows*—articulates the space she occupies between childhood's maternal attachments and the search for independence in adolescence—an independence won by her sister. However, unlike *The 400 Blows*—in which Truffaut's antiheroic protagonist escapes from juvenile reform school and permanently severs his ties to his family and childhood self— the cyclical structure of *Peppermint Soda* suggests the future importance of female relationships for young Anne. For Kurys's autobiographical heroine, the process of growing up will entail not only coping with new freedoms and responsibilities but also eventually discovering new meanings in her bonds with longtime friends, parents, and sister.

Diane Kurys's cinematic recollection of the crucial role her older sister played during her adolescence recognizes the significance of siblings as "bridging or connecting objects" between familial and social worlds.[16] The sister bond can aid in the primary task of adolescence, which psychoanalyst Louise Kaplan has described as the reconciliation between genital sexuality (instinctual drives) and the moral authority of the social order. For Kaplan, the adolescence of each new generation provides a "potential space" for the redefinition of the cultural and moral aspirations of a society, based on youth's belief in and urge toward ethical perfectability.[17] This redefinition of self and society is often negotiated between siblings in opposition or relation to parental figures, and entering the wider social world is often fraught with conflicts, especially for young women who do not easily comply with the sometimes absurd social ideals for femininity— as will be particularly evident in the sister relationships depicted in *Gas Food Lodging* and *Welcome to the Dollhouse*. Both achieve distinction as modernist texts by self-consciously critiquing or parodying conventional identifications with social constructions of femininity.

Gas Food Lodging

Made thirteen years after *Peppermint Soda*, American independent director Allison Anders's debut film, *Gas Food Lodging*, also presents a woman filmmaker's perspective on the triangular relationship between a single, divorced mother and her two daughters; again a younger sister, Shade, comes of age under the influence of an older sibling. While the film is based on Richard Peck's novel for young adults, *Don't Look and It Won't Hurt* (1972), Anders's screenplay also draws upon her experiences and observations as a mother raising two teenage daughters. Her film, like Kurys's, rejects the melodramatic framework that characterizes American films about the domestic world of mothers, daughters, and sisters for a nonsentimental look at female maturation in the 1990s.[18] However, *Gas*

Food Lodging is more explicitly concerned than *Peppermint Soda* with the emotional consequences that arise from the adolescent's self-destructive compliance with conventional female gender roles. One of the key reasons for the film's emphasis on the emotional hardships of growing up female is its social context: the "trailer park" culture of New Mexico in the early 1990s, where female gender roles are influenced by both the absence of men in the daily lives of working-class women and the threat of male sexual violence—in those fleeting moments when lonely women and transient men drift into each other's paths in roadside cafes, highway convenience stores, and the other temporary gathering spots of a place marked by a history of impermanence. In comparison to *Peppermint Soda*, in which the adolescent negotiation of sexual identity is treated rather matter-of-factly, *Gas Food Lodging* looks at its insecurities and cruelties. The gang rape and teenage pregnancy of Trudi, the older sister in the film, are symptomatic of an Anglo American culture in which sexual behaviors are conditioned by a frontier history of vagabond men "who leave" and women who are left behind to set down "roots" in the desert landscape. In evoking sexual difference as a central topos of American frontier mythology, the film presents a revisionist picture of the modern West, focusing on the psychosocial challenges confronting adolescent sisters in a world traditionally identified with the individualistic prerogatives of male "freedom" and sovereignty over women and nature. In examining the ways in which women carve out domestic spaces in the Southwestern landscape, it invokes the social connections between the marginalized Anglo women and Mexican Americans.[19]

In *Gas Food Lodging*, Nora (Brooke Adams), a hard-working waitress at a roadside diner, is trying to bring up her adolescent daughters, the restless, rebellious Trudi (Ione Skye) and the younger, introverted Shade (Fairuza Balk). They live in a trailer park in the dead-end town of Laramie, New Mexico. The title of the film emphasizes the material world that Nora and her daughters must contend with, but as a road sign it also symbolizes the transience of a white Anglo culture moving through a more rooted Mexican American culture, and of men—fathers and lovers—who flee to escape domesticity. During the credit sequence, a traveling tracking shot of the desert highway from a moving car and subsequent shots of abandoned swimming pools, telephone poles, and industrial parks suggest a modern wasteland disfigured by the destruction that accompanied the westward movement and increasing commercialization. A single mother, Nora struggles to make ends meet, while Trudi tries to escape from a life of poverty and cramped living circumstances by seducing local middle-class high school boys. First used and then rejected by one boy, Trudi later has a brief relationship with a visiting British geologist, Dank; when his accidental death during a cave exploration goes unreported, Trudi assumes he has abandoned her. Her romantic and sexual traumas seem to recreate her mother's disappointing encounters with local married cowboys. In fact, Nora jokingly laments that loneliness is the latest trend for women in the 1990s.

Shade dreams of finding her father, who left the family long ago. She treasures a grainy home movie that shows him playing with her as an infant and with two-year-old Trudi. In her other free moments she avidly watches old Mexican movies starring the fictional actress Elvia Rivero at the local Spanish-language theater, and arranges dates for her mother with potential suitors who remind her of the masculine heroes in the Rivero films. Nostalgically longing for a romantic father figure, she stages her dreams of "doing all the dumb things normal families do." Eventually, however, Shade is destined to confront the transferential web of hopes and dreams that have kept her ensnared in a fantasy relationship with her idealized, absent father. When she finally meets him, he is gray and middle aged, living with another woman and working menial jobs. In time, Shade falls in love with Javier, a Chicano man whom her sister, Trudi, dismisses at the beginning of the film as a "wetback," but whose family has lived in the area for five generations (far longer than the Anglos who have colonized the desert with their trailer parks); Shade sees in him a counterpart to her own misunderstood self.

Like Anne in *Peppermint Soda*, Shade is the focal point of the film, the first-person narrator in the voice-overs and a close observer of her sister and mother in their intense battles over sexuality and independence. And like Anne, she feels excluded and invisible within the family; at one point, as daughter and mother face each other across a quiet breakfast table, Shade realizes that they never talk except when Trudi is around.

We are first introduced to Shade as she sits in a dark movie theater by herself, a spectator of Spanish melodramas, subconsciously associating her own mother with the characters played by Elvia Rivero. Always cast in the part of a long-suffering female heroine who is exploited, abandoned, or oppressed by father, husband, or Church, Elvia Rivero is predictably and happily reunited with the repenting male hero at the end of each movie. Shade marvels in a voice-over: "Elvia Rivero made

everything come alive. She put into words what I couldn't say. It was
Elvia who first gave me the idea." Shade's idea, we soon discover, is to
search for her own father, her lost "hero." This scene is significant for
a number of reasons: it self-reflexively comments on Shade's fantasy of
the "family romance," a fantasy facilitated by the narrative of cinematic
melodramas. This opening scene also foreshadows Shade's eventual
embrace of the Chicano/Mexican culture that provides her with a genuine alternative to the transient Anglo culture that she grew up in. Here
screen romance becomes a potential space of play for Shade, allowing
her to imagine her future by reconnecting to her childhood—a trajectory that in the course of the film we find has been obstructed for her
older sister, Trudi.

Winnicott places the child's experience of transitional objects during
separation from the mother in an "intermediate area," a "potential space"
between fantasy and reality, inner objects and external subjects, subjectivity and objectivity. The child both invents and discovers the object in this
early stage of the use of illusion, which is retained throughout life as a
capacity for creativity and creative looking. This definition of "potential
space" can be extended to the female spectator's relationship to on-screen
illusion, with the advantage of allowing the spectator an active rather than
passive relation to the screen image. Not only is Shade's view of femininity constructed by the Mexican film industry, but like all spectators she
imaginatively appropriates from the films she sees the meanings that make
sense to her own life and experience. Shade's association of Elvia Rivero
with her mother—an identification that for all its disparities is in fact later
affirmed by the arrival of her mother's new lover, Hamlet Humphrey—suggests the unconscious power of cinema as an imaginative space of creative
identification.[20] Shade's identification with Spanish melodramas is, of
course, that of a very young and naive adolescent, whose enthusiasms will
be tempered by real experience, but they nonetheless serve an important
psychological purpose, allowing her to emotionally move past her sense of
familial loss toward a more adult understanding of human relationships.

Gas Food Lodging contrasts Trudi and Shade, who define themselves
differently in the face of love, rejection, and abandonment as well as in
relation to each other and their mother. The sisters share a small bedroom in their mobile home, but their separate spaces and fantasies are
clearly demarcated: Anders's camera pans the walls, revealing images of
rock stars, male models, and cowboys on Trudi's side and posters of an
androgynous David Bowie and the fictional Mexican film star Elvia

Rivero on Shade's. From the very beginning, Trudi constructs her identity in opposition to her mother around images of women as sex objects
promoted in the mass media. In an early scene at the diner where her
mother works, we see Trudi dressed in a provocative skimpy dress and
leather jacket, refusing to eat anything but a salad to keep her figure
slim. Whereas Shade searches for a connection with her father, Trudi's
flamboyant sexuality and her promiscuity are linked to her struggle with
her mother over the desire for emotional and physical contact. Louise
Kaplan describes the preoedipal dilemmas that resurface for a girl in
adolescence: "A woman's aggressive, rivalrous feelings toward her
mother will always have an admixture of erotic, libidinal yearnings—
sometimes to be the passive, cared-for baby, sometimes to be the active
lover who can satisfy all her mother's desires."[21] Indeed, Allison Anders's
use of a "feminized" desert landscape in the film's mise-en-scène situ-
ates Trudi's sexual rebellion in the context of an unconscious return to
a maternal space. When Trudi becomes involved with the British geologist Dank, she accompanies him to a desert cave where he is excavat-
ing rock formations that reveal their exquisite colors under a special
light. The cave is clearly a metaphoric space for the female body, the
wonder of its desert flora and secret colors illuminated as the backdrop
to Trudi's and Dank's lovemaking. It is in the "womb" of the earth that
Trudi enjoys, for the first time, a fulfilling and transformative sexual experience, later conceiving a child by Dank. Yet this maternal space also
becomes an occasion for a feminist critique of the male explorer/scien-
tist penetrating the female landscape. A brief close-up of a black scorpion
caught under glass foreshadows Dank's eventual death in the cave accident and also represents a visual correlative to Trudi's secret of having
been gang raped as a young teenager by local cowboys (a story she in fact
confesses to Dank in the cave).

The maternal symbolism of the cave as a space of wonder, awe, and mystery and as a locus of danger and dread—a commingling of preoedipal fantasy and adult sexuality—captures visually the overdetermination of Trudi's
sexuality and her ambivalent attachment to her mother. Trudi's resistance
to what she perceives as her mother's omnipotence and control is, to take
Jessica Benjamin's suggestion, at the same time an intense search for recognition that has broken down.[22] This desire for recognition, which also
fuels her promiscuous sexual relationships with men, is complicated by the
early experience of gang rape—the ultimate degradation and negation of
her subjectivity. Trudi's sexual rebellion represents her attempt to assert

control, yet it makes her vulnerable to objectification by men. Her inability to recognize her mother and herself as independent but interrelated subjects entraps her in a domination-submission matrix, oscillating between aggressive defensiveness and a passive longing for a man to take her away. Ironically, in trying to separate from and resist her mother, Trudi follows in her footsteps: after quitting school she works as a waitress at the same diner as her mother, and like Nora she becomes pregnant as a teenager.[23]

Trudi's pregnancy represents a return to the mother and precipitates a crisis that further separates her from the family. One of the most violent exchanges between mother and daughter occurs when Nora wants her to have an abortion and Trudi defends her right to keep the baby. As they scream at each other across a picnic table, the mother sees her own life repeated in her daughter's actions, and Trudi accuses her mother of wishing she had aborted her. Trudi's decision to carry the baby to term is an active attempt to resist her mother's control and to affirm herself in the face of her perception of being an unwanted child. For Trudi, the mother only functions as an omnipotent, destructive other, a projection of her own fears against which she must constantly defend herself. Trudi's decision to give the baby up for adoption and to leave for Dallas and an uncertain future as a model are among the many losses Shade must overcome. And Trudi's choice of modeling as a career continues her identification with the kinds of conventional male fantasies of femininity that have ensnared her from the beginning.

In contrast to Trudi, who defines herself primarily in terms of others' desires, Shade undergoes her initiation into the world of adult sexuality in scenes that implicitly comment on prefabricated images of femininity and the female masquerade. Like many younger siblings, she seeks advice from her sister on techniques to sexually attract a boyfriend, in this instance their neighbor Darius (Donovan Leitch), an androgynous young window dresser at a retro clothing store. A misfit in the masculine cowboy culture, he fantasizes to Shade about his "dream girl," pop star Olivia Newton-John, in his eyes an icon of daring female sexuality. Mistaking for a sexual proposal to her his desire to *be* Olivia Newton-John, Shade follows Trudi's advice to make the first move and dresses up as Olivia in a 1970s disco-style costume—sequined hot pants, platform shoes, and blond wig. Her attempted seduction fails miserably as Darius becomes confused and frightened by Shade's masquerade of his fantasy persona.

The episode becomes an important step in Shade's internal development. She ultimately rejects playing the role of "dream girl" in an adolescent male's narcissistic fantasy, a role her sister Trudi has urged her to accept. Instead, she identifies with the older Mexican culture in the Southwest. Unlike Trudi, she works through her intersubjective bonds with her sister, mother, father, and lover; her identification with Mexican Americans functions as a kind of transitional space for her. Through Javier she develops a sense of another person's needs and desires that obviates the kind of narcissistic self-centered involvement characteristic of Trudi's obsession with popular images of femininity.

After her unsuccessful attempt to seduce Darius, Shade meets Javier on a dusty road filled with tumbleweeds, where he gently teases her about her identification with movie stars and her outlandish disco costume.[24] Initially influenced by Trudi's prejudices against Chicanos, Shade eventually overcomes her biases and develops a genuine friendship with Javier. When she visits his home in the desert, his deaf-mute mother invites Shade and her son to dance to some contemporary Latin music, sensing the vibrations of the music with her feet. One of the less developed, perhaps somewhat idealized, characters in the film, the mother becomes an important alternative figure for Shade's identifications across cultural difference. Velvet paintings of John F. Kennedy and other American icons mix with Spanish religious and folk art on the walls of her traditional adobe house, symbolizing the historical fusion of Anglo and Mexican cultures in the Southwest and signifying the cross-ethnic identification between Shade and Javier without collapsing their differences. After Javier professes his love for Shade, they share their appreciation of the subtle beauty of the desert landscape that is home to each of them. Shade describes their relationship in voice-over: "It's like we finally met our twin and together we made up a whole. It was enough to just be myself, Shade." She develops a sense of identity that partakes of feelings of genuine belonging to a cultural and natural environment, more meaningful than Trudi's pop culture fantasies. Shade discovers the enchantment of the desert through her relationship with Javier, and the camera celebrates in low-angle shots the barren landscape transformed into a flowering, multicolored garden, recalling Georgia O'Keeffe's erotic paintings.[25] Instead of a dead, empty environment, the desert becomes for Shade a space of discovery and liberation that promises the possibility of renewal.

Even though Shade defines herself quite differently from Trudi, she remains connected to her sister till the end. She searches for family resemblances as she views Trudi's baby behind the glass divider in the hospital, mourning the child's loss of origins: "She will never know where she came from, the desert where she was conceived." This loss is, of course, connected to the larger sense of transience and loss of cultural and familial roots that has been critiqued in the film. Shade visits Trudi in her hospital room, begging her sister to return to Laramie, but Trudi refuses. Shade retrieves from her purse the rock Dank gave Trudi as a token of their love, but its plain surface only reminds Trudi of her aborted relationship and the disillusionment she has come to expect in romance. For Shade, the rock that only reveals its colors under special light becomes a metaphor for ways of seeing, for discovering a world beyond the surface of social convention. It is, in fact, the social convention of men leaving and women staying behind that shapes Trudi's image of herself. Significantly, it is Shade who finally discovers that Dank died in a collapsed mine and that Trudi had merely imagined his desertion. This new knowledge leads Shade to redefine her sister's disappointment and sorrow as signs of hope—for herself, her sister, and "the path of daughters not yet born." Indeed, if for Shade her sister's life serves as a doubled image of her female identity, it is an image she learns to resist, one that reflects the most crippling emotional losses and instabilities generated by the caprices of male desire (symbolized perhaps by the Western's trademark tumbleweeds blowing loose across the desert landscape). For Trudi, Dank's desertion is a reality—a confirmation of her mother's past in her own, and the catalyst for her own desire to fall further into male conventions of femininity by becoming a model. Her breathtaking physical beauty, inherited from her mother, is, like the shimmering rocks of the cave, something to be sold to tourists. But for Shade the knowledge of Dank's death renders Trudi's abandonment as illusory as the belief that one's femininity must always be defined in a marketplace defined by male idealization.

In *Gas Food Lodging*'s closing long shot, Shade walks home across the blooming desert landscape, which has become a symbol of her burgeoning self on the threshold of adulthood. Unlike Trudi, she has found a way to assert her individuality and remain connected to her family and her community. Abandoning her fantasy of the perfect family, she establishes a relationship with her father, accepts her mother's need for a life of her own and a new relationship with Hamlet Humphrey, who is "in it for the long haul." Most of all, Shade grounds herself in the multiethnic culture of the Southwest, among people who have managed to find in the desert country a home and identity.

Welcome to the Dollhouse

One of the most incisive contemporary films about rivalry between sisters, Todd Solondz's independent *Welcome to the Dollhouse*, about the trials and humiliations of eleven-year-old Dawn Wiener (Heather Matarazzo), avoids the nostalgia or sentimentality typical of more mainstream films about childhood and adolescence. A black comedy, satiric and edgy, the film is a lineal descendant of the modern Jewish-American social satires that during the 1960s and 1970s were exemplified by the works of Woody Allen and Paul Mazursky. Although the Wiener family are thoroughly secularized, assimilated Jews who lead a middle-class American life in the New Jersey suburbs, the middle daughter, Dawn, struggles to overcome her outsider status and alienation in a version of the seriocomic "Jewish-American bildungsroman," in which the adolescent hero faces the cruelty and prejudice of the wider world.[26] Bernard Sherman has described this genre in the Jewish-American novel as "the initiation into experience of a boy or youth, tracing his passage from innocence to awareness, his realization of the particular meaning of the life of a Jew in the American city."[27] In *Welcome to the Dollhouse* the city has been replaced with a slightly surreal suburbia with monotone ranch houses, manicured lawns, and backyard barbecues. Dawn, moving from innocence to experience, does not transcend her feelings of alienation and uncertainty by the end of the film. To director Todd Solondz,

> it is a comedy, a sad comedy, sometimes a harsh, even brutal comedy. But it is a comedy nonetheless. . . . But I think this brutality, this cruelty—there's something about this particular time of life, this farewell to childhood, the onset of adolescence, that brings into relief this quality. And contending with these forces of cruelty I think is part of the process of growing up. . . . But if it were just cruelty, it wouldn't interest me as much as the fact that there's a struggle to transcend it.[28]

While some critics have faulted Solondz for building his film around a young girl's perspective rather than a boy's experience of early adolescence—which might have resulted in a more autobiographically authentic film—the director deliberately chose to explore female adolescence.[29] Solondz is aware of undermining some stereotypical representations of girls in American cinema in the process:

> I think that girls do mature more quickly than boys in certain key ways. Since it was cuteness I wanted to avoid at all costs, I felt that a girl's romantic yearnings and longings would be taken more seriously and that there would be a

little more room for emotional complexity. In hindsight, I am particularly pleased that I have a little girl at the heart of this movie because there is a certain myth that girls are more sensitive than boys, that girls must only be in these cute, sensitive little movies. As if girls were more sensitive than boys, as if girls cannot handle the things that a boy can handle emotionally. To have a movie that's as acid as this one and have a little girl at the center of it, I think, is a novelty.[30]

From the first slow zoom-in on Dawn in an artificially posed family photograph during the credit sequence, Solondz represents all of her complexity and ambivalence. She is both persecuted victim and persecutor, awkwardly navigating humiliations by her schoolteachers and peers, venting her frustration on her only friend and on her younger sister, Missy, the prime target of her adolescent rage.

Dawn first appears in a medium shot in the school cafeteria, looking desperately for a place to sit. Her hunched shoulders, thick glasses, unbecoming flowered dress, and permanently furrowed brow immediately render her an outsider to the self-appointed hip clique at Benjamin Franklin Junior High (the name a sly nod at the U.S. ethos of self-improvement). Dawn's younger sister, Missy, is ballerina-pretty with long blond hair and blue eyes, dancing and pirouetting through the film in a pink tutu, the perfect favorite daughter. In a hyperreal scene Solondz satirizes Missy's prettiness and cleverness as a display of childish grandiosity, the camera following her self-absorbed prancing across the family's suburban front lawn.

A narcissistic extension of the doting mother who continually hugs her, Missy sits next to her mother at the dinner table and takes her side against Dawn's accusations and defenses. Early on Missy tells Dawn she is not allowed to drink in the family television room, and Dawn calls her a "lesbo" in retaliation—an epithet that her classmates have taunted her with, projecting their own fears of not "fitting in" on the most obvious misfit. It is, according to critic Stan Schwartz, "one of the film's major notions that children appropriate adult language of violence, use it without fully understanding the true import of what they're saying, and occasionally even transform it (unintentionally and hence very poignantly) into meaning something very near the opposite."[31] Spontaneous expressions of aggression and affection contrast with the dinner-table scene: Mrs. Wiener forces Dawn to apologize to her sister and tell her that she loves her. A close-up of Dawn's face registers her disgust at Missy's contrived expression of love. She saws off the head of Missy's Barbie doll in retaliation for her sister's humiliation of her—clearly a displaced gesture of her wish to destroy her sister. In a psychoanalytic context, Winnicott has argued that the fantasized destruction of the "object" and its survival precedes a healthy "use" and love of the object outside of the individual's narcissistic projection of the other.[32] However, in a family where the parents routinely ignore Dawn and lavish praise and admiration on Missy, Dawn cannot relate to her sister as another subject—instead, Missy becomes a projection of all Dawn hates and cannot be.

Like many of the films about sisters in adolescence, *Welcome to the Dollhouse* articulates the preoedipal rivalry between sisters for their mother's love and attention. As the middle child and a daughter, Dawn is virtually invisible to her family (an older, computer-obsessed brother is bound for college); it is her desire to be considered "special" (particularly by her mother) that fuels her actions and her attempts to connect with other people. Beneath Dawn's sullen and stubborn demeanor, Solondz captures her grief over her mother's evident greater affection for and approval of Missy, the "good daughter." In the words of Marian Sandmaier, Dawn is the "unchosen" daughter who often feels that "her mother identifies with her sister in some deep, unspoken way that she is powerless to dilute, and which relegates her to the status of perpetual outsider."[33]

Dawn's relationship with a school bully, Brandon, who threatens to "rape" her because she called him a "retard," must be seen in the context of her search for recognition. In a pivotal scene, filmed in a long tracking shot, Dawn follows Brandon quietly to a remote spot, ready to acquiesce to his attack. However, the threat of violence quickly and unexpectedly turns into a moment of tenderness and mutual vulnerability as Brandon talks about his retarded brother; his aggressive posture is revealed as a defensive mask for a sense of isolation and hurt. Not coincidentally, this scene is immediately followed by another family dinner humiliation sequence in the Wiener household, which exposes the cruelty of the impatient and uncomprehending mother, who punishes Dawn by denying her dessert for not tearing down the backyard clubhouse—Dawn's only private space in the family household—for the parents' anniversary party. Missy asks her mother for Dawn's uneaten piece of cake. In juxtaposing Dawn's encounters with Brandon with this humiliating confrontation, Solondz is clearly contrasting a cruelty that derives from deprivation with a psychological brutality that arises out of selfishness and middle-class banality.

Like the sisters in the films discussed earlier, Dawn and Missy share a bedroom, but the cramped single space only emphasizes the gulf between them. The room is decorated in feminine pastels and filled with Missy's toys and dolls; Dawn looks out of place—her frilly clothes and pajama suit, rather than making her look endearing, accentuate her gawkiness.

Dawn's sense of rejection reaches a climax with her parents' twentieth anniversary party. Looking down on the party in the backyard, she observes how Steve, whom she has awkwardly and unsuccessfully pursued, swings Missy in the air. Later she must endure her family watching a videotape of the party and laughing at a scene in which Missy pushes Dawn into a wading pool. During the night, Dawn destroys the tape with a hammer and, in the following powerful scene, returns to her room wielding the tool over her peacefully sleeping sister. The fantasy of killing her sister is absolutely believable after the string of humiliations Dawn has endured at school and at home, with Missy taking center stage all the while. The camera pulls back from a low-angle shot of Dawn holding the hammer over Missy's head to a high-angle shot of her sitting dejectedly on her bed, as she says to her sleeping sister, "You're so lucky."

Dawn's fantasy of murdering her sister is psychologically linked to the last part of the film when Dawn is indirectly responsible for Missy's kidnapping, having failed to tell her to catch a ride home from ballet class with a friend. Solondz comments on how this kidnapping scene plays out Dawn's (and the audience's) secret aggression toward Missy:

> Part of the process of growing up is beginning to understand the reality underlying the fantasies we might have or the language that we use.... You might fantasize that you want your little sister to be kidnapped or killed or something horrible; once the reality of that happens, however, it jolts you in a way that forces you to grow up.
>
> Of course, Dawn is ravaged by guilt, although you can't say that it is her fault. She didn't mean for her sister to be kidnapped and she does feel terrible about what has happened. Yet there is a certain ambivalence there. Therein lies the irony that this is the little girl that you—that probably everyone in the audience—had wished something terrible might happen to. It's that kind of irony I'm playing to.[34]

Solondz confronts viewers with their own secret desires and guilt elicited through an identification and empathy with Dawn, destabilizing the spectator's position of mastery and knowledge. As Elizabeth Cowie has argued in *Representing the Woman*, to tell a story (on film) is to narrate a scenario of relationships to others, not a singular identity or desire, hence the fluidity of narrative identifications.[35] The kidnapping scene places the viewer in relation to both Dawn and Missy: we are shocked at the latter's abduction but perhaps we have also secretly desired it—hence, the viewer's own fantasy of "goodness" is called into question.

Solondz further complicates the ironies of identification by having Dawn fantasize about rescuing her sister and being embraced by her mother. She leaves during the night for New York City after the police have heard that Missy's tutu was found in Times Square; there she hands out missing-person flyers to misfits on the city's streets. A quick montage of slightly distorted close-ups reveals Dawn's fantasy of people expressing their love to her—her mother, father, brother, and vain Steve, whom she has idolized and who so unkindly dismissed her a few scenes earlier. This sequence is psychologically overdetermined: her rescue fantasy represents Dawn's desire both to repair the damage of her hostile act toward her sister and to upstage her, to be a heroine whom everyone admires. In a final ironic twist, Dawn learns that Missy has been found and that in the excitement over her rescue, her parents had hardly missed Dawn at all—she has, once again, remained invisible, and Missy has become a local celebrity.

While some of the characters are intentionally overdrawn for satiric purposes (critics have commented on the unsympathetic portrayal of the mother), the film consistently stays with the perspective of an eleven year old struggling to make sense of her place in the world. This is no doubt the reason that *Welcome to the Dollhouse* has resonated so with audiences: its uncompromisingly ironic and yet sympathetic view of adolescent alienation and ambivalence toward family. The familiar splitting of roles between "good" sister and "bad" sister is ironically undercut as Solondz elicits the viewer's ambivalence. And Missy's favored position in the family is by no means enviable; as Solondz has said, "I'm sure that ultimately Missy will be just as damaged as Dawn from the excessiveness [of the mother]."[36]

Having straddled psychological realism and modern social satire throughout, the film ends with the conflicts between Dawn and her family, siblings, teachers, and schoolmates unresolved. As her brother Mark says to Dawn in response to her question of whether things improve in high school, "They still call you names but not to your face." Todd Solondz has said that he was interested in documenting an adolescent girl's *struggle* (not necessarily its successful resolution) to overcome rejection and an almost primal sense of cruelty at a pivotal phase of development before "we become much more adept at camouflaging as we get older."[37] It is in Dawn's survival of this struggle and her understanding of her own capacity for cruelty and carelessness that a small measure of hope can be glimpsed.

4

Sisters, Fathers, and the Modern Ethnic Family
Double Happiness *and* Eve's Bayou

The family is your first love, and thus ultimately they must be your first heartbreak.

Mina Shum

The story of antagonism and competition among sisters for the love of a father or a husband within the patriarchal family abounds in classical myth and literature. The many versions of "Cinderella" and Shakespeare's *King Lear*, for instance, are among the numerous Western variants of this age-old tale, pitting sisters (or stepsisters) against each other in pursuit of male approval and affection, property and social rank.[1] Films often reproduce this oedipal scenario as well, particularly in the female-twin melodramas that critic Lucy Fischer has analyzed in relation to sisters' competition for the "rewards"—in exchange for exhibiting "acceptable" feminine traits—of their father's favors or betrothal to a desired romantic object. In these scripts the rivalry between sisters always moves toward a narrative solution celebrating filial love or matrimony at the expense of sororal friendship.

This familiar pattern in literature and film coincides with Freud's bleak model of women's psychosocial development, which stresses the daughter's lifelong struggle to turn away from her mother and libidinally attach herself to her father—

or later, a father substitute; the struggle begins with the girl's realization that she lacks a phallus and continues through her passive desire to achieve fulfillment as daughter, marriage partner, and mother. As Lynda Boose writes, "Daughterhood is, in fact, inseparable from absence in the psychoanalytic definition of social development, for it is the daughter's recognition of 'castration,' her renunciation of the active, phallic state, and her acquiescence to passivity that, in Freud's assessment, constitutes the prerequisite step backward that sets her on the pathway to 'normal femininity'."[2]

Feminist psychoanalytic critics have challenged Freud's view as a problematic fiction that disguises the father's incestuous desires toward the daughter beneath a mask of paternal protection, perpetuating patriarchal authority and legitimizing the nuclear family.[3] Furthermore, the nature of the daughter's psychological conflict with her father, according to Freud, is quite different than the son's oedipal rebellion, which emphasizes his desire to displace the father in order to individuate himself and ultimately assume the mantle of adult authority in the larger social order. But as Boose argues, Freud's model of female development fails to consider how the daughter's struggle to psychologically separate from the father is complicated by women's lack of power in traditional patriarchal cultures. Boose takes note of Lévi-Strauss's observation that daughters are frequently treated as objects of exchange between their fathers and future husbands.

Psychologically, then, the father plays a contradictory role in the daughter's development. On the one hand, he is the daughter's first male love object and a figure of protection and security. Hence, daughters' rebellions in most father-daughter narratives are muted or channeled through other characters as a result of "the daughter's need for paternal approval and her residual awe of the godlike father," an emotional bond that seems "to override the violent impulses of revenge and competition." On the other hand, the father is an authority figure who monitors a daughter's desires and social conduct. Indeed, in some instances the father's possession of a daughter is so uncompromising that he assumes total control of her destiny. As Boose points out, "Father-daughter stories are full of literal houses, castles, or gardens in which fathers . . . lock up their daughters in futile attempts to prevent some rival male from stealing them."[4]

Few feature films, even by women directors, focus on the relationship between adolescent sisters and the problematic affiliations between fathers and daughters. However, Chinese Canadian writer-director

Mina Shum's *Double Happiness* (1995) and African American writer-director Kasi Lemmon's *Eve's Bayou* (1997) challenge traditional iconic images of sisterly rivalry for the father. Although both draw on the sisters' oedipal bond to the father, they explore how sisters, though bonded to their fathers in love, nonetheless resist or rebel against paternal authority. Interestingly, both directors examine the conflicts between sisters and their fathers through ethnic-specific lenses, and in each film the father symbolizes a past that is both personal and collective; rebellion against his paternal authority allows the protagonist to become aware of her place within both the family and the larger historical world that has shaped it. To borrow Rocio G. Davis's description of similar ethnic narratives in literature: "This type of fiction explores the ethnic character and history of a community as a reflection of a personal odyssey of displacement and as a search for self and community."[5]

Double Happiness dramatizes the familial and social conundrums that beset Jade, the older of two adolescent sisters born to Chinese immigrant parents in present-day Vancouver, Canada, caught between Western values of individualism and traditional Chinese Confucian ideals of filial duty. Jade's father, Mr. Li, plays a pivotal role in her life and that of her sister, Pearl, representing a patriarchal legacy against and through which they must define their identities.[6]

With this focus on the conflict between old-world fathers and new-world daughters, Mina Shum joins the company of Asian Americans such as Maxine Hong Kingston, Amy Tan, and Fae Myenne Ng, women who have written about the ambivalent position of Asian American daughters. Like them, Shum resists the lure of assimilationist myths: *Double Happiness* is highly critical of the racism toward and marginalization and silencing of Asians in Canada, yet it does not advocate an unproblematic return to ethnic traditions and heritage. The supreme self-reflexive theatricality of the film emphasizes the performance of identity inside and outside the Chinese Canadian household. Working in a mode of sharp-eyed social comedy, Shum uses the dramatic vignette as the central building block of scene construction and a stylized blend of expressionistic and cinema verité shooting methods to capture the disjunctures within the family home as well as the cultural disparities Jade feels in modern Vancouver.

Kasi Lemmon's acclaimed first film, *Eve's Bayou*, also emphasizes the subjective point of view of its central female character, Eve Batiste, whose voice-over narration as an adult frames the film, recalling the history of her family and her turbulent childhood. Set in the early 1960s in an African American community on a Louisiana bayou, the film unfolds in a retrospective, almost novelistic, fashion the story of Eve's fall from childhood innocence and the disintegration of her middle-class family. Weaving symbolic allusions to the biblical story of the Fall with legends and rituals from African American folklife—dream visions, supernatural manifestations, magic, and conjuring—*Eve's Bayou* reveals how the past can metaphorically haunt the present.

In the two films, Kasi Lemmons is far more concerned than Mina Shum with the unconscious psychological dynamics of family relationships, addressing the taboo of father-daughter incest and its ramifications for Eve, her older sister, Cisely, and the entire family. However, Lemmons sets the sisters' troubled relationship with their father in the context of cultural forces that have historically menaced the social identities of African American men and women and sometimes problematized the emotional affiliation of the child to the parent.[7] Hortense Spillers's provocative work on the uncertain status of the father in the African American family because of the history of slavery is instructive here: "The original captive status of African females and males in the context of American enslavement permitted none of the traditional rights of consanguinity." The disruption of the black family complicated the notions of fatherhood, as the father's African name was erased in cultural memory, since children—whether or not they were the products of miscegenation—bore the name of the white slaveholder. "In this fatal play of literally misplaced/displaced names," writes Spiller, "the African father is figuratively banished; fatherhood, at best a cultural courtesy, since only the mother knows for sure, is not a social fiction into which he enters."[8]

Eve's Bayou also explores a strong matrilineal connection handed down through folklore and magic. The ancestor slave woman Eve emerges as a powerful influence in the lives of Eve and Cisely, leaving matrilineal legacies of her name, her property, her magic gifts of healing, and voodoo. Combined with the dilemma of African American fatherhood, these legacies provide a historical framework for the Batiste sisters' harrowing rites of passage into the perplexities of human perception and truth.

Double Happiness

Mina Shum's *Double Happiness*, a modern comedy-drama about growing up and moving out, is a wry and often satirical depiction of the ways in which two adolescent sisters attempt to navigate the contradictions and conflicts that arise from coming of age in a Chinese Canadian immigrant family. Like *Peppermint Soda* (see chapter 3), *Double Happiness* begins with a self-reflexive acknowledgment of the process of filmmaking and the presence of the director: the central character, twenty-two-year-old Jade Li (played by Sandra Oh), addresses the camera in a frontal medium shot: "I wanted to tell you about my family; they're very Chinese, if you know what I mean." After Jade rhetorically asks why her Hong Kong immigrant family could never be the Brady bunch, she says that the Bradys never needed subtitles, hinting at her double consciousness as both an insider and outsider to Canadian or American popular culture.

The camera cuts to a gossipy dinner scene to introduce the family— Jade, her mother (Alannah Ong), father (Stephen Chang), and younger sister, Pearl (Frances You)—as they discuss the need to find a "nice Chinese husband" for Jade. As in many Asian films, such as Ang Lee's *Eat Drink Man Woman* (another film about sisters and their negotiation of traditional Chinese culture and the patriarchal family), food becomes an important cultural metaphor. The Chinese sign of the film's title, "Double Happiness," means marriage and also refers to a traditional dish that perfectly balances opposites in texture, color, and flavor, capturing the thin line Jade struggles to walk between the traditional expectations of her Chinese family and her desire to live in the Western world and make her own decisions. Jade's difficulties with her bicultural identity place this film in the tradition of Asian American immigrant narratives, which, as playwright David Henry Hwang has pointed out, typically explore the question of constructing and maintaining one's cultural identity and heritage while making a new life in a new land.[9]

Jade's and Pearl's traditional Chinese parents emigrated to Vancouver, British Columbia, to provide their children with better opportunities in life, but they still expect their daughters to enter into financially stable marriages to Chinese men or embark on lucrative careers in broadcasting, like Connie Chung (a running joke in the film that refers to the stereotype of the Asian immigrant as model minority). As the parents dutifully perform their daily rituals or anxiously monitor Jade's encounters with the dates they have arranged for her, Shum satirizes them yet avoids caricature by giving each their moment of speaking to the camera: The father reflects on his confusion over no longer holding the position of patriarchal authority wielded so effortlessly by his own father in prerevolutionary China; the mother compares her sense of loss over her daughters' modern behavior to that of a young broken-hearted woman in China whose daughter was killed in infancy by her husband.[10]

Meanwhile, Jade's attempt to define her identity independently of her family is reflected in her ambitions to become an actress—ambitions tolerated by her parents as long as she agrees to fulfill her filial duties and comply with their matchmaking efforts. She effectively lives a double life as a respectful, selfless, and nearly invisible Asian daughter and a bold, playful, and ambitious Canadian "twenty-something." It is one of the central ironies of the film that while all its characters must act out roles assigned to them by traditional cultural values, they also participate in a masquerade: traditionally, Chinese women would not be educated to become self-sufficient; the parents themselves are "modern" in relation to traditional Chinese culture. The mother asks her daughters to play the roles of traditionally submissive *and* academically successful children in front of their uncle Ah Hung, visiting from China, and to pretend that their disinherited brother, Winston, is a successful businessman and that their father has managed to preserve Chinese customs in Canada. Ah Hung himself, Jade finds out, leads a double life, as he is secretly involved with his former maid with whom he has had a child. He advises Jade to "choose her path carefully" in life, contradicting her father's insistence that she follow his dictates.

The sister relationship plays a central role in Jade's negotiation between the two worlds of tradition and freedom from ancestral obligations, serving as a positive space of mutual recognition and affirmation for each sister. Pearl is still young enough to be bound within the tight orbit of her parents' activities and supervision; in family shots she is often framed with her mother and father while Jade is isolated by the camera from the family circle. However, if Pearl generally complies with her parents' wishes and fears her father's disapproval, she also shows signs of an independent spirit. Jade offers her an alternative role model to that of their mother, who does not challenge the father's authority. Like Shade in *Gas Food Lodging* and Anne in *Peppermint Soda*, Pearl becomes a kind of spectator within the diegesis of the film; she understands and identifies with her sister's dilemma—how to be true to one's desires and not offend the family—a dilemma she will almost certainly face in a few years. Jade's final decision to make a life of her own paves the way for Pearl's future choices, even as Jade's leave-taking remains a painful reminder of their beloved brother, Winston, disowned by their father because of an undisclosed transgression of filial duty. Tellingly, Jade hides a photograph of the three siblings under her bed, a visual sign of a secret family shame but also of the siblings' solidarity and distance from their traditional parents.

Much like Anne and Frederique in *Peppermint Soda*, Jade and Pearl often exchange knowing glances, laughing together at the follies and pretenses of the adult world and the contradictions of immigrant life. Bridging the worlds represented by her parents on the one hand, and her older sister on the other, Pearl is frequently framed with her parents and in two-shots with Jade. For example, early in the film during a family gathering, when Jade's parents are matchmaking and charting her future with the uncomfortable Andrew, a Chinese lawyer later revealed to be gay, Pearl and Jade face each other in a doorframe, discussing Andrew's looks while Pearl teases her sister good-naturedly about the long line of potential suitors their extended family has assembled for her. In another scene, Jade conspiratorially tells her sister about getting a major audition for an acting part, and Pearl takes great pleasure in her success, giving her a "high five," as their mother and uncle prepare a meal in the background. Through a private ritual of gestures and language established since childhood, Pearl and Jade affirm each other's sense of agency and self.

The empathy between the sisters is associated with their mutual position as young Chinese women caught between the value system of their parents and the prejudices and misconceptions of white society toward Asians. In a sequence where Pearl and her mother are watching Jade's humiliating debut on television as a Chinese waitress in a soap opera, not only is Jade reduced to a stereotypical, marginalized role, she is literally pushed to the edge of the television screen so that only her voice marks her presence. Jade's mother is confused: "I don't understand. Where are you?" she asks, searching the screen for her daughter's face. While she sees Jade's absence as evidence of her failure as an actress rather than as a sign of television's marginalization of ethnic minorities, Pearl is supportive of her sister and in the next shot strokes her hand affectionately.

A recurrent scenario in *Double Happiness* reveals the sisters' common subordination to their father's authority in the household: Jade repeatedly plays the obedient daughter by bringing her father his favorite red-bean buns as an offer of appeasement after her "transgressions." As she waits patiently, holding out the pastries and tea, the camera focuses on the father and relegates Jade to the edge of the screen; she is as marginalized in her own family as she is in the world of television and film, where she is stereotyped as an Asian (later in the film, she is ironically also rejected by a Hong Kong casting agent for not being able to read Cantonese dialogue).

Mina Shum's interest in exploring the convergence of problematic roleplaying in family, relationships, and work for Asian immigrants and particularly their children is also foregrounded when Jade responds to the clumsy attempts at conversation with Mark, a Caucasian university student, outside a club that has discriminated against her, by assuming the stereotyped role of the submissive "Oriental woman."[11] Only by working through their mutual pre- and misconceptions and expectations can Jade and Mark meet as individuals. As a spectator of her sister's negotiation of a bicultural life, Pearl closely observes Jade's roleplaying, in particular the ritual of submission and reconciliation between Jade and their father, until Jade realizes that her father will never recognize her individual needs and that she must leave her family in order to find some measure of personal happiness.

Jade reciprocates Pearl's admiration and support, initiating Pearl into the ethical compromises and dissimulations required to survive in the family. For instance, Jade changes Pearl's one "C" on her otherwise straight-A report card so that her younger sister will not have to face her father's stern lectures about family honor and filial obligations. Pearl asks Jade rather than their mother for advice about dating a Chinese boy. As with Trudi's relationship to Shade in *Gas Food Lodging*, Jade becomes an important sounding board for the younger Pearl in discussions about love, relationships, and female identity. As Marian Sandmaier suggests, "Sisters also show sisters how to be women." Sandmaier has found in her research that many women feel "that a sister had an enormous, enduring impact on their female self-concept, their expectations for relationships with men, and their acceptance or rejection of traditional norms of femininity." She contends that particularly during adolescence, "women with older sisters talked of closely watching this process of growing up female, copying this, editing out that, seeking information through questions or snooping or both, in the process of piecing together a personal vision of womanhood."[12]

Jade's involvement with a Caucasian man, which contradicts her parents' strict and vigilant supervision of their daughters' dating within their own ethnic group, leads to a scene in which Pearl asks her sister, "So what's wrong with Chinese guys?" Jade supports Pearl's first forays into dating and affirms, "Chinese guys are great." She shows Pearl how to dance the twist, and the high-angle shot of their coordinated moves emphasizes a casual intimacy and easy camaraderie that can withstand the conflicts between parents and children.

At the farewell dinner for uncle Ah Hung, Jade announces her departure—after she asks her father whether he really needs her, and he responds with rejection and embarrassment. One by one the family members leave the dinner table in anger or shame, until only the sisters are left sitting opposite each other, Jade mourning the inevitable loss of her childhood closeness to her parents and Pearl witnessing the breakup of familial and cultural harmony that had been so precariously preserved throughout the film.

In the final scene, Jade calls her lover, Mark, about painting her new basement apartment, repeating a joke that Pearl told her in their first scene together. This auditory cue suggests the enduring bond between the sisters despite Jade's painful and permanent departure from the family. Furthermore, Jade's first gesture in the apartment is to set up the group portrait of herself, her sister, and their brother, a visual affirmation of the importance of sibling ties that survive the frequent tensions between traditional immigrant parents and their culturally more ambivalent second-generation children. Unlike the two stage characters with whom Jade had identified earlier—Blanche duBois, who "depends on the kindness of strangers," and Joan of Arc, who "is alone on earth but not in heaven"—she has asserted her independence while remaining connected to and recognized by her sister.

Eve's Bayou

Kasi Lemmons's 1997 first feature, *Eve's Bayou*, places the intense rivalries and love between two adolescent sisters at the core of its portrayal of African American Creole life in the early 1960s.[13] The film draws liberally on the narrative and symbolic traditions of southern Gothic melodrama, with its focus on slavery, family secrets, the transgression of sexual and racial boundaries, and the house as a site of family trauma and dissolution. These motifs reflect Lemmons's self-acknowledged debt as a screenwriter and director to Tennessee Williams's plays and Harper Lee's *To Kill a Mockingbird* (the novel and film), but one can also detect echoes of William Faulkner's novels and Toni Morrison's "gothic fables" of growing up black and female in America.[14] Indeed, Lemmons weaves African American folk legends, ghostly apparitions, and other magical and fantastical elements into her film, recalling the way in which Morrison's novels recast Gothic forms through the narrative techniques of magical realism in order to probe the psychological impact of slavery and oppression on the cultural history and family life of African Americans.

The Gothic and magical realist elements in *Eve's Bayou* are closely associated with the film's thematic exploration of the psychological complexities of perception, subjectivity, and memory, with Lemmons's concern for the ways in which human passion shapes the telling of personal and collective history. As I commented in my discussion of Janet Frame's *An Angel at My Table* in chapter 2, the problematic nature of reconstructing the past is a preoccupation characteristic of modernist narratives. In *Eve's Bayou* this theme is revealed in the very first frames, a montage of brutal, if blurry, black-and-white images of a copulating couple, which are soon reflected in the eye of a woman, Eve Batiste. "Memory is a selection of images," says Eve. "Some elusive, others printed indelibly on the brain. . . . The summer I killed my father, I was ten years old. My brother, Poe, was nine, and my sister, Cisely, had just turned fourteen." As we come to realize later, this opening montage evokes the primal scene (the child's primordial fantasy of her parents' lovemaking, her initiation into sexual knowledge), hinting at the powerful and irrational sexual passions that will become associated in Eve's mind with acts of emotional trespass, betrayal, and violence.

Next a series of black-and-white images of the bayou suggests mysteries as elusive as the passions hidden below the threshold of the waking mind. Through voice-over narration Eve returns us to the mythic origin of the Batiste family, when her ancestor and namesake, the African slave Eve, received her freedom and a homestead after saving her white master from death with her powerful folk medicine. Still the site of the family home, it is also the seat of a tangled history so powerful it continues to shape the family's self-perceptions and emotional lives. Eve speculates that her ancestor bore her master sixteen children out of gratitude for her freedom, but as spectators we sense that the illicit relationship was forged also out of coercion, passion, and violence. The tale of the slave ancestor and the slaveholder alludes to the intersecting history of black-white relations, miscegenation, and cultural creolization that has existed since slavery times, a blurring of racial, sexual, and cultural boundaries that still affects the lives of the Batistes. In her essay "Rootedness: The Ancestor as Foundation," Toni Morrison has written about the significant presence of an ancestor in much of African American writing as representative of a "timeless people whose relationships to the characters are benevolent, instructive, and protective, and [who] provide a certain kind of wisdom." Indeed, the slave woman Eve's secret knowledge of African healing rituals ensured her survival in slavery times and, as Kasi Lemmons points out, "folklore is the legacy of power handed down from woman to woman."[15] However, Lemmons also dramatizes how this ancestral knowledge complicates and disturbs the middle-class world of the contemporary Batiste family, for Eve Batiste will have to learn how suffering and loss are the consequences that accompany her exercise of that power for destructive ends.

Heading the affluent Batiste household is the father, Louis Batiste (Samuel L. Jackson), a well-liked and respected but philandering physician; the family includes his long-suffering, elegant wife, Roz (Lynn Whitfield), and their three children, Cisely (Meagan Good), Eve (Jurnee Smollett), and their younger brother, Poe (Jake Smollett). The story chronicles the disintegration of the family the summer that Eve discovers her father in a tryst with a married woman, Mattie Mereaux. She witnesses her parents' violent quarrels and later believes her sister's claim to have been molested by their father.

Eve is particularly attached to her father's sister Mozelle (Debbi Morgan), a psychic healer gifted with second sight who is ironically unable to foresee her own future, for she has already lost three husbands to death. A conjuring woman and Mozelle's competitor, Elzora (Diahann Carroll), brands Mozelle as cursed and warns the unhappy Roz and her family of an ominous but ambiguous future. Influenced by Elzora's advice to "look to [her] children" and by Mozelle's fragmented premonitions of a child's death, Roz virtually imprisons—in true Gothic fashion—her three children in the house for the summer, hoping to protect them. But the danger to the family lies within, when her own repressed anger and Louis's long history of adultery are finally revealed to their children.

Cisely, who adores her father and blames her mother for alienating him from the family, is also grappling with her own budding sexuality. And in an attempt to keep her father bonded to the family, she waits up every evening for him to come home. One night after a particularly violent quarrel between her parents, Cisely goes to comfort her drunken father, and their kiss is tinged with erotic desire. When the confused Cisely confides in her sister that Louis molested and hit her, Eve's love and adoration for her father turns to hate; she vows to kill him. She not only hints to Mr. Mereaux that his wife is having an affair with Louis Batiste, thus unleashing the cuckolded husband's jealous rage; she also enlists Elzora's help in casting a deadly voodoo spell on her father. The conflict culminates in a violent confrontation between Louis Batiste and Mr. Mereaux in a bar by the railroad tracks, during which Eve witnesses her father's murder: after Louis defies Mereaux one more time and says goodnight to his mistress, the enraged Mereaux shoots him.

Perhaps fulfilling Elzora's prophesy that "sometimes a soldier fall on his own sword," Louis Batiste's death also becomes the source of Eve's intense guilt; she believes she has orchestrated his demise to avenge her sister. Eve is the "child with the blues, never too young to pay her dues," as the credit song suggests at the end of the film. However, *Eve's Bayou* ends on a note of redemption and forgiveness. Eve discovers among her father's papers a letter he wrote to his sister Mozelle that presents a different version of the events: Louis reflects on his failings as a husband and father; he denies kissing his daughter in a sexual way but assumes responsibility for not reestablishing boundaries in a confusing situation, for indulging his need to be adored as a hero by other women and his own daughter. In the final scene, Eve confronts Cisely at the edge of the bayou about the truth of the fateful night's events. In a familiar gesture of psychic connection she has inherited from her aunt Mozelle, Eve touches Cisely's hands and finds that the memories are confused— Cisely's and Louis's versions of the past event seem to mingle, and boundaries of desire are blurred in memory. Eve forgives Cisely, and Cisely seems to absolve her father, as both submerge Louis's letter in the muddy waters of the bayou. As they look out upon the river, holding hands, the adult Eve resumes her narration from the beginning of the film: "Memory is a selection of images . . . some elusive, others printed indelibly on the brain. . . . Each image is like a thread . . . each thread woven together to make a tapestry of intricate structure . . . and the tapestry tells a story. . . . And the story tells our past."

The film's modern open-endedness emphasizes ambiguity, employing the metaphor of the web or tapestry to suggest the complexity of history not as given fact but as an act of storytelling, endlessly susceptible to interpretation by the participants. At the center of this struggle over the meaning of the past and family relationships are Cisely and Eve, rivals for their father's attention; yet Eve loves her sister to such a degree that she is willing to murder her father for hurting her. Lemmons has claimed that *"Eve's Bayou* is about loving so deep that it hurts, that you make mistakes. The sisters love each other, they live for each other, and they can't live without each other."[16] It is their complicated intersubjective bond, firmly situated within the matrilineal tradition of the Batiste family, that leads to the sisters' self-knowledge, to Eve's realization of her own power, and to Cisely's recognition of her own desires, all of which signify a fall from innocence and illusion.

The sisters' oedipal competition for their father as well as their strong attachment to each other are introduced in the first scene of the film to occur in the present, when Eve is ten years old. At a party the Batistes host for friends and neighbors, we are ushered into the adult society of the bayou community from Eve's perspective; she clearly adores her elegant parents but at the same time is acutely aware of her exclusion from their grown-up universe. Close-up shots of adult couples dancing seductively in the Batiste's living room refer back to the sexual imagery of the opening montage, and overheard conversations between gossiping guests hint at Louis Batiste's illicit affairs and sexual narcissism. Meanwhile, Eve tries to catch her mother's and aunt Mozelle's eye by offering them chocolates. When her younger brother Poe comes running into the room, the film turns to slow motion as Eve observes her mother embracing and kissing her favorite child. Feeling slighted and ignored as the middle child and as a daughter, Eve takes her revenge, offering Poe sweets that are really chocolate-covered bees. This is the first hint of Eve's impish streak and her role as a conjuring or trickster figure who, like her aunt Mozelle and her female ancestors, will use her power in subversive ways.[17]

Cisely enters the party scene in a white, luminous dress, admonishing her younger siblings to behave themselves, yet shortly thereafter they form a tight-knit group, toasting each other with champagne glasses. When their father asks Cisely to dance, Eve jealously observes them become the center of attention as they dance a complicated Zydeco step. Feeling rejected by her father as well as her mother, she runs away from the party to the carriage house, falls asleep, and awakens to her father and Mattie Mereaux having intercourse against the wine racks. That Eve observes this scene in the liminal state between waking and dreaming foreshadows the loosening of other boundaries, such as those between father and daughter, Louis and Cisely. When the couple notices Eve, Louis tries to comfort and reassure her and strikes an implicit bargain with her by promising to dance with her at every party in the future. Yet the facade of the picture-perfect family has cracked, and Eve later comes to suspect that Louis has many casual affairs with his female patients.

When she tells Cisely what she saw in the carriage house, Cisely refuses to believe her. Gazing into the bedroom mirror at their own images, she "revises" Eve's narrative of the event: the camera cuts to Cisely sitting in the carriage house with her arm around Eve, as she replays the scene and tries to convince her sister that Louis and Mattie Mereaux were merely laughing together. Throughout the film, Lemmons strategically employs the mirror shot to introduce the deliberate crafting of past events through storytelling, conveying the coexistence of different realities and perceptions, the ambiguity of memory shaped by desire, and the doubling of reality and fiction.[18]

In the transitional stage between the seemingly safe childhood world of her siblings and her desire to be treated as an adult woman, Cisely desperately tries to uphold the fiction of the perfect family even as she unconsciously attempts to replace her mother in her father's affections. Her revision of Eve's story is the first instance of how her own desires and fears cloud her judgment and perspective, intersecting fatefully with her father's sexual indiscretions and arrogance. Like her mother, who at one point confesses to her sister-in-law Mozelle that before her marriage she saw Louis as a kind of god, a healer who could fix anything, until she discovered that he was only a man, Cisely must come to terms with the fallibility of her father.

Out of a sense of failure that he may be just another country doctor who "is pushing aspirin to the elderly," Louis Batiste is particularly susceptible to sexual temptation. Although Lemmons never makes explicit the parallel between his constant competition with other men for possession of women and the history of black men's disempowerment and exclusion during slavery (their double break from the African family and disenfranchisement from white power), the film seems to suggest such an unconscious motivation for Louis's philandering through the legend of the slave woman Eve's relationship to her white master.[19] Roz's seemingly irrational fear of losing her children can also be seen in historical terms, as slave mothers were often threatened with being separated from their children.

In a moment of defiance, Cisely leaves the house against her mother's wishes and returns with the same hairstyle as her mother—a demonstration of sexual competition that leads Roz to forbid her daughter to wait up for her father and unleashes a violent confrontation between husband and wife. Eve observes Cisely's increasing alienation from their parents, and in the process the sisters become more tightly bonded to each other, visually conveyed by a shot, from the back, of the sisters' close embrace. The volatile family situation reaches a climax when Cisely has her first period, a sign of her adult femininity and distance from her sister's childhood world. Eve taunts her sister about menstruating, and Cisely becomes hysterical, attacking Eve and wrestling her to the ground. Cisely refuses to be examined by her physician father, who has, in her mind, become a sexually threatening ogre. When she decides to leave home to live with her grandmère, Eve is heartbroken, believing herself to be the cause for the family's breakup.

It is at this point that Eve and the viewer hear Cisely's version of the events that occurred on the stormy night when she tried to comfort her father. In Cisely's account, the kiss between father and daughter turned sexual before Louis, in shock and then sudden anger, slapped Cisely. The memory of the incestuous kiss is reflected in a large mirror, creating a doubled image and an unstable vision of reality. Nevertheless, the viewer becomes sutured into the drama of the event, empathizing with Cisely's trauma as well as Eve's fierce loyalty toward her sister when she promises to kill their father for hurting her. At the same time, Cisely is revealed as an unreliable narrator when she admits to knowing all along that her father has been unfaithful with Mattie Mereaux. A medium shot of Eve and Cisely sleeping in the same bed in a close embrace confirms their bond of solidarity and love, and on the morning of Cisely's departure, the sisters silently communicate their understanding to each other—a secret bond that only their aunt Mozelle witnesses.

Mozelle represents in many ways the central connecting figure in the film: she is her sister-in-law Roz's confidante and, as Kasi Lemmons calls her, the "mirror image" of her brother Louis. Lemmons juxtaposes sister and brother to comment on the cultural scripts for gendered sexuality: "There's a stigma against women like Mozelle. Her brother, Louis, gets away with being extremely sexual because it's a man's world. Mozelle, who has the same sexual weakness as Louis, gets labeled as crazy. Her sexuality is perceived as dangerous because it is the 1960s and the South."[20] The film repeatedly associates Mozelle with extradiegetic images of a spider, "the black widow," and indeed she believes she is responsible for the death of her three men, that her barrenness is a sign and a curse. The film makes clear, however, that these are patriarchal images and perceptions that have imprisoned Mozelle in a particular role. While the traditional visual symbols for dangerous female sexuality and power—the spider woman, femme fatale, the snake and apple—

are evoked in *Eve's Bayou*, the film significantly rewrites the patriarchal Christian story of Adam and Eve. In the corrupted Eden of the New World, where Africans were enslaved and brutally mistreated, black women's power, which Mozelle has inherited, became a survival strategy, albeit one that coexists with guilt for the loss and disempowerment of African American men. Mozelle embodies African American women's history of suffering and survival, an experience of loss that has made her compassionate toward the loss of others. She is a healer like her brother, but whereas Louis tends to the body, Mozelle nurtures the soul. She has inherited the legacy of folk medicine and spirituality, and, combining them with Christian faith, she represents a bridge between Old and New Worlds, a synchretic form of African American folklore and culture.

Mozelle also functions as an alternative role model for Eve to that of her passively suffering mother—a Cinderella figure waiting for her prince—and embodies the matrilineal tradition inherited by Eve and her sister. Yet even she, despite her insight into people's pasts and futures, has been enslaved by her passions and her past. After Louis's death, Mozelle tells Eve of her dream of flying and watching her other self drown, a dream she interprets as a sign of a new beginning. Flying is, of course, a recurrent trope in African American slave narratives, folklore, and contemporary black literature for escaping slavery for freedom. Mozelle's dream of flying in the end becomes a metaphor for escaping various forms of enslavement, a sign of her ability to let go of the past to begin anew. Thus she embodies the ambivalence of a simultaneous return to and flight from history.

The film does not ultimately answer the question of whether Louis was killed by voodoo, that is, by Eve's hatred, or died of self-destructive arrogance and hubris. Cisely's painful confusion as she tells her sister, "I can't [tell you the truth].... I don't know what happened.... I don't know," ends *Eve's Bayou* on a note of ambiguity, the essential unknowability of the truth in light of the psychological propensity to fictionalize history. Throughout, the adolescent sisters have served as unreliable narrators of family history, whose different points of view on the same events yield completely different meanings.[21] In the final scene of the film the camera pulls out of a close-up shot of the two sisters, revealing them as tiny dots in the landscape. As they hold hands gazing out over the bayou, we see them framed between two tall trees reflected in the opaque water—a metaphoric doubling of their own images. This concluding image of the sisters as they overlook the seemingly placid but shifting undercurrents of the bayou is one that evokes disparate and heterogeneous visions of the past, the fluctuating ebb and flow of memory. As the voice-over of the adult Eve reflects on the elusive nature of remembering, we realize that the question of what really happened that night when Louis and his daughter Cisely kissed will remain a mystery as impossible to unravel as why the African slave woman Eve saved the life of the white man who enslaved her and in her newfound freedom bore him sixteen children.

Despite its popularity and critical acclaim, *Eve's Bayou* lost in that year's NAACP awards to *Soul Food*, an African American film about three sisters whose competitive and contentious relationship is resolved sentimentally through the mediating influence of the matriarch and her grandson. *Eve's Bayou* ends on a more precarious note, affirming the close affiliation between sisters and the matrilineal bond, yet refusing to resolve the emotional confusion that exists between them and their father as it examines the historical gender conflicts in the African American family. The film as a whole—particularly the final scene—emphasizes the ambiguity of perception and the powerfully subjective nature of memory, as well as the legacy of suffering and spiritual survival among contemporary African American women. As Lemmons points out, the prominence of the bayou in the film's mise-en-scène suggests the reflective "pools of memory," a visual metaphor for the impenetrable mystery of the past and its mirroring and doubling of the characters' desires or delusions.[22] The Louisiana bayou itself signifies a cultural space where slaves escaped to hide from their masters and worked as exploited labor to drain the swamps. Mozelle's many visions of her clients' contemporary experience of pain and suffering—drug addiction, sexual betrayal, death—are set against black-and-white wipes of the bayou swamps. The bayou also represents a metaphorical female space visualized by the opening black-and-white shots of the mythic female slave ancestor entangled in the vegetation. Eve's and Cisely's submersion of their father's letter in the murky waters signals a silent pact between the sisters to survive and reconnect, even as they share guilt and grief over their personal and communal history.

Sororophilia and Matricide

Shared Fantasies in Heavenly Creatures
and Sister My Sister

The two girls are bound to each other heart and mind. They depend on each other for emotional and intellectual sustenance. They dress alike, talk alike, eat the same foods, read the same poets, daydream about the same boys, idolize the same idols, despise the same enemies. . . . The shared fantasies are a blend of the stereotypes from television soaps, comic books, ladies' magazines. . . . But such passions can get out of control. The breakup of a special friendship can be as devastating as any other love affair. Between friendships the girl is bereft. And Mother, as usual, pays the price.

Louise Kaplan, *Adolescence: The Farewell to Childhood*

In describing the intimate bonds between adolescent female friends, Louise Kaplan highlights the importance of shared fantasies in the girls' creation of mutual self-definition and an exclusive relationship, and this is especially true of sisters. The intersubjective dimension of fantasy as a shared discourse between sisters has tremendous impact on the imaginative construction of their lives. Connected through memories and a common origin, sisters often reinforce their bonds through a kind of insider language and mutual play that grow out of their individual subjectivities; they also create a shared space of fantasy that draws upon and is shaped by the cultural discourses that surround them. Sisters' fantasy worlds are often the wellspring for broader artistic endeavors and life ambitions, as is apparent in, for example, *Little Women* and *An Angel at My Table*, discussed earlier.

Heavenly Creatures (New Zealand, 1994) and *Sister My Sister* (U.K., 1995) also observe the close bonding between two "sisters" through their intersecting fantasy lives, which decisively shape their relationship to each other and the world around them.[1] However, these films depict far darker aspects of sisterhood, dramatizing how young women's imaginative play can intersect with fantasies of revenge and death, a theme discussed in relation to *Eve's Bayou*, where sisters competed for their father. But *Heavenly Creatures* and *Sister My Sister* are concerned with sisters' ambivalent attachment to the mother, revealing how preoedipal conflicts between daughters and their mothers can resurface in adolescence and, in the heat of adolescent passion, descend into violence.

Both films are based on real crimes committed by pairs of young women. Peter Jackson's *Heavenly Creatures* treats the brutal 1954 murder of Honora Parker in Chistchurch, New Zealand, committed by her daughter Pauline Parker and Pauline's best friend and "sister," Juliet Hulme. Nancy Meckler's *Sister My Sister* is adapted from Wendy Kesselman's play *My Sister in This House*, which recreates from a feminist perspective the case of the Papin sisters, a pair of housemaids who savagely murdered their middle-class female employer and her daughter in LeMans, France, in 1933.

The French case triggered numerous sensationalized and politicized treatments at the time. Jacques Lacan published an early analysis, "Motives of Paranoiac Crime: The Crimes of the Papin Sisters," in the surrealist journal *Le Minotaure* in February 1933, alongside work by Dali, Leiris, Masson, and Breton. Existentialists Jean-Paul Sartre and Simone de Beauvoir and others debated the Papins' crime in terms of class politics, regarding the sisters as victims of domestic servitude and exploitation, as well as of the criminal justice system.[2] Jean Genet's play *The Maids* (1948) was based on the Papins' story. In later years, Christopher Miles's 1974 film adaptation of Genet's play and Nico Papatakis's *Les Abysses* (1963) brought the Papins' controversial tale to the screen. The matricide in *Heavenly Creatures*, however, which was known in New Zealand only as the Parker-Hulme affair, received muted public discussion. A source of national shame, it was erased from public memory for decades. Its female-on-female violence shook to the core the seemingly bucolic, respectable, and arch-conservative community of Christchurch in the

1950s—a place and era rather archly rendered in the montage of tourist bureau newsreel footage that opens the film.

By addressing these films, I run the risk of rekindling a debate over what some critics term negative or stereotypical cultural images of women's desires for each other.[3] Historically, female criminal behavior often has been constructed as sexual deviance and madness. Women's sexuality, particularly its expression outside heterosexual and familial norms, has been "specularized" as perverted or even murderous within a patriarchal framework.[4] One thinks of Charcot's eroticized staging of female hysterics in the Salpêtrière or the surrealists' celebration of nineteenth-century women hysterics as fellow artists. Only recently popular cinema has represented women as homicidal home breakers in *Fatal Attraction* (1987) and *The Hand That Rocks the Cradle* (1992) and as lesbian/bisexual killers in *Basic Instinct* (1992). However, *Heavenly Creatures* and *Sister My Sister* distinguish themselves from other representations of female crimes by refusing to dwell on the sensationalist aspects of the murders or the abnormality of their perpetrators. Instead, both focus entirely on the events that lead up to the murders, sympathetically examining how the shared fantasy lives of two pairs of young women were in each case misinterpreted by a narrow and conformist society, leading to tragedy.

Particularly rich and suggestive modernist films in the context of the problematic representation of female violence, *Heavenly Creatures* and *Sister My Sister* situate their crimes in a psychological context—the familial matrix of women's relationships—and in social and temporal milieux informed by conventional definitions of femininity. Both focus on a pair of adolescent girls—biological sisters in the case of *Sister My Sister* and close friends/would-be-sisters in *Heavenly Creatures*—who murder a mother or symbolic mother substitute; both thus place the acts of violence within the preoedipal drama between mothers and daughters. In paying particular attention to female psychosexual relations, Jackson and Meckler link actual and symbolic matricide to the intense, homoerotically charged bonds between sisters or close friends, what I call here "sororophilia."[5]

Rather than dwell on the extraordinary nature of the murders, both films dramatize, I believe, an unusually violent resolution to the very common conflicted relationship between mothers and daughters during adolescence, when a girl transforms her homoerotic passions of childhood for her first love object—the mother—into new libidinal desires that are directed outside of the family. Perhaps for this reason, director Peter Jackson has called *Heavenly Creatures* "a murder story about love. A murder story with no villains."[6] Implicit in the films are critiques of two societies—the conformist Anglican community of Christchurch in the 1950s and the repressive, middle-class world of provincial France in the 1930s—both of which turn ordinary preoedipal ties between women into something extraordinary, deviant, or "perverse."

A number of feminist psychoanalytic critics theorize that a daughter's particularly difficult maturation often entails both separation from and simultaneous identification with the maternal figure. Louise Kaplan writes in *Adolescence: The Farewell to Childhood:* "As with any deployment of passion from one realm to another, the event [of the separation from childhood attachments to the mother] begins with a variation of violence." While this violence is most visible in the adolescent male's turning away from the mother, "a woman's aggressive, rivalrous feelings towards her mother will always have an admixture of erotic, libidinal yearnings."[7] *Heavenly Creatures*'s coscreenwriter Frances Walsh and director Peter Jackson found that many female viewers closely identified with the world of the protagonists despite the brutality of the crime: "A lot of women have come up to us and said, 'I was Pauline. That was me. That was my childhood.' I don't think it's unusual. I think what is unusual about the whole thing is that these aspects of Pauline's character led to murder, and I don't think the sort of person she was was particularly unusual or freakish or weird."[8] Obviously, what viewers are responding to is not the crime but the familiar mother-daughter conflicts as well as the intensity of female bonds in adolescence, the ways in which girls find and respond to each other in an "us against the world" fantasy.[9]

Although both *Heavenly Creatures* and *Sister My Sister* draw self-consciously on the genre of women's melodrama, the films eschew its Manichean opposition of good versus evil and its emphasis on female suffering. Instead they offer a far more nuanced, psychological exploration of the murderers' perspectives and motivations. *Heavenly Creatures* in particular "denaturalizes" melodramatic form through its hyperkinetic style and self-conscious, even campy, use of opera, popular music, and cinema to portray the exuberant energy and creativity of the two central characters.[10] Pauline and Juliet are not shown as either passive melodramatic victims or visual spectacles; rather their experiential worlds and subjectivities become the foundation of the film. Their vivid, fantastical flights of imaginative play "break the frame" of melodramatic realism much as they rupture the rigid moral codes of adult authority. Jackson takes full advantage of such special effects as morphing and animation to create the hyperreal, kinetic fantasy world of the adolescent girls. On the complexity of the film's treatment of adolescent murderers, reviewer Luisa Ribeiro writes:

> The film's exuberant style and humor belie its equally serious and deeply disturbing tone that is weirdly empathic to the girls while paradoxically never undercutting the brutal nature of their crime. By turns comic, tragic, fantastic, and romantic, the film, much like its true-life source, defies simple interpretation, yet leads inescapably to an unsettling awareness of a guilt rarely untouched by innocence and an innocence not untainted by some degree of guilt.[11]

Ribeiro is here alluding to the "dual narrative mode" of the film, which allows the viewer to be both inside and outside the characters, to sympathetically identify with the girls' trials of adolescence and states of mind as well as to critically distance herself from their violent crime.[12]

Less daringly expressionistic than Jackson, Meckler painstakingly records with her camera minute behavioral details and silent gestures that convey the quiet but mounting tensions between the sisters and their employers within the claustrophobic domestic world of the chamber drama. However, this microscopic treatment produces a distancing effect on the viewer not dissimilar from that created by Jackson's more flamboyant expressionism. Indeed, Meckler seems to recognize that the closer she brings her camera lens to the quartet of women who occupy the drama, the more the spectator is forced to pull back to contextualize and reflect upon what is being seen at such close range.

Heavenly Creatures

Peter Jackson's *Heavenly Creatures* is primarily told through Pauline's point of view. Her voice-over narration in the film is drawn from Pauline Parker's actual diary entries from 1953 through 1954. However, the film ultimately stages what psychoanalyst Ethel Person has termed the enactment of "shared fantasies"—in this case, congruent fantasies—between two lonely adolescent girls from different socioeconomic and cultural backgrounds, whose common feelings of alienation from their families lead to elaborate fantasies involving sex, romance, revenge, and finally murder. Their intense emotional involvement with each other is not unusual for adolescent girls, and neither is Pauline's ambivalence toward her own mother and her fierce attachment to her best friend, Juliet

Hulme, and her family. The girls' mutual enchantment and teenage eupho-
ria are wonderfully captured in an early rapid montage sequence built
around the music of their idol, Mario Lanza's "The Donkey Serenade." The
camera captures Pauline and Juliet in a frenetic and ecstatic romp—they
read *Biggles* on the sidelines of the school court; play dogfighting planes;
shape Plasticine figures modeled on the fabulous creatures from their private fantasy world of Borovnia; rush deliriously out of the cinema and
cycle madly down a country road. The sequence climaxes as they run
through the woods dancing and singing, tearing off their clothes, shocking a bewildered farmer who sees them clad only in their underclothes.
Not missing a beat, they continue singing Lanza's song, falling into the
lush grass in a fit of laughter and kisses. This montage is a good example of Jackson's ability to evoke, through images, multiple facets of the
relationship: the erotically charged bond between the girls, their ebullient
defiance of social propriety and rigid gender roles, and Pauline's increasing identification with the Hulme family (she is shown in one shot playfully imitating the refined gestures of Mrs. Hulme). Moreover, this early
sequence serves as an emotional counterpoint to the scene of the later
murder, when after slaying Pauline's mother the girls run in horrified
delirium through the woods.

Pauline Parker's and Juliet Hulme's love for each other is intensified
and complicated by Pauline's "family romance." Freud observed this
recurrent fantasy in the dreams of his patients and in literary narratives:
a (typically) male child consciously or unconsciously imagines himself to
be a foundling of royal or upper-class origins. Freud associated this "family romance" with the child's necessary psychological separation from his
parents, the child's defense against the realization of his parents' imper-
fection and their failure to perfectly mirror his sense of omnipotence.[13]

Similarly, Pauline's fantasy of belonging to the Hulmes, which plays
such a central role in *Heavenly Creatures*, reflects the adolescent's narcissistic search for a new ideal that will replace the fallen idols of mother and
father. When Pauline visits the Hulmes' estate, Ilam, for the first time, her
awe and admiration are conveyed in a lingering point-of-view shot of the
large stately house set among beautiful gardens. Juliet appears as a magical figure, dressed in a chiffon gown, tinsel crown, and necklace, playing
the queen to her brother's evil prince. The Hulmes' aristocratic pretenses
to British cultural refinement are further reflected by the interiors: Pauline
delights in the ornate fireplace, paintings, and antique furniture, as well
as the "decorative" feminine elegance of Hilda Hulme, Juliet's mother, and

the scholarly aura of Juliet's father, who has recently taken up an academic rectorship at Canterbury College in Christchurch. The grounds of Ilam will later provide the setting for many of Pauline's and Juliet's fantasized medieval scenarios. Peter Jackson's depiction of Pauline's naive, wide-eyed response to the Hulmes' home, however, is a wonderful illustration of how the film manages to render Pauline's subjectivity while hinting that her appreciation of the Hulmes' upper-class life-style and rituals is misplaced. In a preceding scene Jackson has staged a bit of business—Mr Hulme's embarrassing discovery that he has forgotten to remove rotting salmon-and-egg sandwiches from his jacket pockets—that cues the audience to receive skeptically Pauline's idealization of the family and to understand that she is easily blinded by her fantasies. And it is one of a number of early hints that the glamorous facade Mr. and Mrs. Hulme present to the world hides some rather unsavory family secrets.

Apart from its focus on the girls, *Heavenly Creatures* also discloses the complex interrelationships between the families, vastly different in socioeconomic and cultural backgrounds. Pauline continually strives to escape her dull, working-class New Zealand origins and her too ordinary parents—her father, Herbert Rieper, who works in a supply store and her kindly but worn-out mother, Honora Parker (who though known as "Mrs. Rieper" to friends and neighbors, never legally married him), toils away in the kitchen and takes in boarders to make ends meet. Her older sister, Wendy, is utterly conventional, a dutiful, feminine daughter—hardly the sister Pauline's renegade spirit would wish for. When Pauline meets Juliet Hulme, Juliet's cool self-confidence, ethereal blond beauty, and cosmopolitan air immediately attract her. Juliet's interest in the arts embodies all of Pauline's own dreamy aspirations, which she feels are being stifled in her culturally undernourished family environment. Only much later in the film does Pauline become aware of Hilda Hulme's adulterous affair, which Mr. Hulme seems to tacitly condone as a ménage à trois arrangement. Yet neither she nor Juliet seem to hold the Hulmes responsible for the lengthy and repeated periods of parental abandonment that Juliet has endured in various sanatoria, recovering from bouts of tuberculosis.

Juliet's fear of abandonment and Pauline's desire to escape her family are powerful catalysts for their bonding. Pauline quickly becomes an adoring mirror and active collaborator in all of Juliet's imaginative endeavors. All forms of creativity and art—music, drawing, sculpting, and writing—play major roles in their self-definition as peerless "heavenly creatures" who together dwell far above the "plebeian" preoccupations of more homely and ordinary people. At first, their families look upon their exclusive friendship with amusement and incomprehension; later they become alarmed over the girls' intense fantasy lives and emotional attachment.

"Heavenly creatures" refers to Juliet's fantasy of entering the Fourth World, a place she describes as a "sort of heaven—only better, because there aren't any Christians." Filled with art and music and the girls' private array of "saints" drawn from popular film and opera, the Fourth World soon becomes a universe more vividly inviting and emotionally "real" to them than the lonely existences they experience when apart. Together they spin out the elaborate fantasy kingdom of Borovnia, which they fashion from films and fairy tales, their erotic yearnings for the romantic tenor Mario Lanza, and their sexual anxieties over the villainously libidinous persona of Orson Welles. Assuming various fictional identities in their letters and fantasies, Pauline and Juliet create an ever-thickening web of unconscious identifications, acting out in the Fourth World their innermost passions for each other as well as their hostilities against the outside world that threatens to separate them.[14]

Initially, a common history of childhood illnesses and sickbed confinements bring them together. Pauline's bone disease left her with a large scar on her leg, while Juliet's tuberculosis has isolated her from other girls. Illness becomes a badge of honor, a sign of their mutual aristocratic distinction. As Juliet herself asserts: "All the best people have bad chests and bone diseases! It's all frightfully romantic!"[15] Juliet's comparison of her own "romantic" disease to Pauline's more serious disfigurement is an early indicator of how their grandiose fantasies blur the social distinctions of their backgrounds.

The girls' powerful bonding and desire for a sisterly relationship are captured in a sequence toward the beginning of the film that shows Pauline spending a vacation with the Hulme family at Port Levy. Mrs. Hulme is combing Pauline's hair as if she were her own daughter, and she good-humoredly encourages Juliet's melodramatic fantasies. This happy family scene ends when a casual question by Mr. Hulme about passports once again threatens Juliet with abandonment, as her mother prepares to leave her behind to travel with her husband to England. It is in response to the specter of abandonment that Juliet and Pauline have their first shared delusional vision of the Fourth World. An airborne shot of Juliet's small figure running toward the edge of a hill and a close-up of her tear-stained, distraught face cradled in Pauline's arms gives way to Juliet's sudden vision of a paradisiacal fairy tale world filled with uni-corns, giant butterflies, and manicured gardens. As Juliet invites Pauline to join her, Port Levy dissolves and the chimerical Fourth World appears.

The term "heavenly creatures," from Pauline's poem "The Ones I Worship," explicitly alludes to her fantasy of the family romance and of being united with Juliet as "sisters." Pauline reads the poem in voice-over when she and Mr. Hulme collect Juliet at the sanatorium, where she has been recuperating from her recurring tuberculosis. The poem implies that Pauline imagines herself and Juliet as the daughters of Mr. Hulme:

> There are living among two dutiful daughters,
> Of a man who possesses two beautiful daughters,
> . . . .
> Compared to these two, every man is a fool,
> The world is most honoured that they should deign to rule,
> And I worship the power of these lovely two,
> With the adoring love known to so few . . .
> 'Tis indeed a miracle, one must feel,
> That two such heavenly creatures are real,
> . . . .
> And these wonderful people are you and I.

Throughout the film, Peter Jackson explicitly links, psychologically and visually, Pauline's overwhelming desire to be part of the Hulme family, as sister and daughter, to the murder of Pauline's mother. *Heavenly Creatures* begins with a disorienting tracking shot of a blood-splattered Pauline and Juliet running up a garden path, crying "Mummy, Mummy." The shot is intercut with a sepia-tinted dream or fantasy sequence of Pauline happily chasing Juliet across a cruise-liner deck toward Mr. and Mrs. Hulme, but never quite reaching them. The cross-cutting between reality and fantasy creates a spatial and psychological ambiguity as to whom "Mummy" refers—Honora Parker or Hilda Hulme. It suggests Peter Jackson is plac-ing deliberate emphasis on the girls' ambivalent relationship to their respective mothers, and on Pauline's desire to escape her own mother and run toward her fantasized ideal mother, Mrs. Hulme.

The fantasy is repeated shortly after Juliet and Pauline agree to kill Pauline's mother: this time Pauline and Juliet reach Hilda and Henry Hulme, who turn to embrace them. The fantasy clearly links the ful-fillment of a wish—Pauline's and Juliet's desire to be united as sisters, Pauline's dream of belonging to the Hulmes—to the death of Pauline's mother. In the closing moments of the film, after the murder, the cruise-liner fantasy appears for a third time, but now Pauline is left on the pier as Juliet calls out to her from the departing boat and Mr. and Mrs. Hulme pull her back from the railing. Ironically, the murder that was intended to bring Pauline together with Juliet's family makes such a reunion impossible, and the final fantasy scene suggests perhaps Pauline's intuitive understanding that the Hulmes have more to do than her own mother with her separation from Juliet.

Yet the lower-class mother is from the start designated the "main obstacle" to the girls' desire to stay together, the "bad object" that, in their delusional paranoia, needs to be eliminated. Mrs. Hulme, meanwhile, remains the idealized, unattainable love object, even though she is shown to be less loving and concerned about her children than Honora Parker, who is genuinely pained by Pauline's increasing withdrawal and hostility. As Pauline's and Juliet's inner worlds become increasingly enmeshed and the girls act out the family romance in fantasy scenarios involving Borovnia—a parallel world filled with royal couples and violent offspring, illegitimate affairs and the killing of patriarchal figures—we notice that maternal figures are conspicuously absent from these imaginary scenes. For, outside the girls' fantasies, Hilda Hulme and Honora Parker are split into respectively idealized and abject objects.

In *Powers of Horror* (1982), Julia Kristeva associated the phenomenon of the abject with the terrifying hold of the maternal body, against which the child constantly struggles. The result is a sometimes violent attempt to break away, "with the constant risk of falling back under the sway of a power as securing as it is stifling."[16] Point-of-view shots of Honora Parker present Pauline's distorted vision of her as grotesque and overwhelming, images that intersect powerfully with Juliet's uncertainty and tenuous hold on her own mother—hence the overdetermination of the murder of the maternal figure, perceived as both abandoning and persecutory. The girls' desire for the perfect mother who abandons them meshes with their fear of the mother as abject, an intrusive and oppressive presence who will not let them go. The intercutting of the murder scene and Pauline's fantasy of union with the Hulmes at crucial moments in the film, as well as her increasing dehumanization of Honora Parker, emphasizes this psychic splitting and ambivalence toward the maternal figure.

Ironically, the film shows that the Hulmes take the initiative in separating the girls. After observing them sleeping in a close embrace once Juliet has returned from the sanitarium, Henry Hulme works quietly behind the scenes to keep them apart. Suggesting to Honora Parker that Pauline needs to be "cured" of her "unhealthy" attachment to Juliet, he encourages her to take Pauline to a psychiatrist, Mr. Bennett. The psychiatrist, who shares Hulme's conservative prejudices, "diagnoses" Pauline a homosexual. Peter Jackson satirizes the doctor's ignorance and paranoia, and his homophobia masquerading as science precipitates the girls' increasingly violent responses to the hypocritical adult world. They discover Hilda's longtime adulterous affair and the final separation of Hilda and Henry Hulme, which leads to their decision to send Juliet to South Africa for schooling and recovery. As Luisa Ribeiro observes:

> Jackson and Walsh characterize the Hulmes' growing domestic misfortunes in a sensitive if sparse manner, focusing more harshly on Henry's trepidation over the fervor of Juliet and Pauline's friendship. Henry's anxiety easily mirrors that of the partriachal social milieu of the decade, scandalized at impermeable, uncontrollable feminine excess. Both the Riepers' and the Hulmes' inability to grasp the magnitude of their respective daughter's individual and combined alienation and emotional needs decidedly propels the situation toward catastrophe.[17]

As the Hulmes' family life unravels before Pauline's and Juliet's eyes, their illusions of an all-enveloping family romance are shattered and they react defensively, alternately contemplating suicide and sharing grandiose fantasies of escaping to Hollywood to become famous writers and actresses. Significantly, Henry Hulme overhears but does not see Pauline and Juliet acting out these unrealistic fantasies in the bathroom and once again projects his homophobic anxieties onto the girls' relationship. In a final tragic irony, the girls demonize the lower-class mother as "the greatest obstacle" to their future together and view Henry Hulme as "the noblest and most wonderful person." Just as Pauline and Juliet see themselves as victims of an uncomprehending, hostile social world, they see Henry Hulme as victimized by the impending breakup of his marriage. Later, in a manic delusion, Henry Hulme appears to Juliet and Pauline as a tragic figure in a world that has descended into madness, a king who has been turned into a fool. The fantasy reveals the girls' idealization of Mr. Hulme as a disgraced and fallen patriarch.

Sister My Sister

In Nancy Meckler's *Sister My Sister*, a similarly complex narrative of gender relations embeds the female world of the Papin sisters and their employers in the larger context of patriarchal authority and control. Male characters never enter the film's diegesis and only appear in voice-overs that frame and judge the relationship between the sisters. However, the males' authority and single-minded search for an explanation of the murder are called into question by the film's depiction of the very ambiguity and overdetermination of the women's relationships with each other. In her analysis of gendered use of sound and voice in cinema in *The Acoustic Mirror*, Kaja Silverman contends that in dominant (Hollywood) cinema the male narrative voice often appears as "disembodied, unlocalized, omniscient, and omnipotent," suggesting its aspiration to invisibility and anonymity.[18] Conversely, she argues, one rarely finds a female disembodied voice in classical, male-defined cinema, as this would grant women a narrative authority outside the diegesis of the film that they are generally denied.

In *Sister My Sister*, the men's pronouncements and questions are used ironically and self-reflexively to point to their ultimate *lack* of knowledge about the Papin sisters, and their failure to comprehend the complex emotional dynamics that exist between them and the Danzards, their female employers. For example, when the Papin sisters go to the same photographer as Mme Danzard and her daughter to have their portrait taken, the offscreen photographer literally frames the sisters in his camera as idealized twins, asking them whether their mother has always dressed them alike. Christine, the elder sister, resists the photographer's intrusive inquiries and fawning remarks, leaving him without answers. Similarly, at the end of the film, the disembodied voices of a medical examiner and judge describe the bizarre details of the murder and sentence Christine to death. As the camera entraps the frightened sisters huddled in bed in the film's final shot, the judge's voice commands them to speak: "What was the nature of your relationship? Was it simply sisterly love? Speak. You are here to defend yourself. You will be judged." The disembodied male authority figures thus represent the outside world's attempt to document and objectify the Papin sisters, and their physical absence from the intimate domestic sphere corresponds to their lack of understanding of the four women's internal world.

Screenwriter Wendy Kesselman and director Nancy Meckler probe the intertwining lives of the quartet bound by bourgeois social norms and religious conventions and the sisters' transgressions of both sexual and class boundaries. Despite inconclusive court records, Kesselman and Meckler show the sisters engaged in an incestuous relationship, yet they locate their sexual intimacy not within a pathological framework

but within the preoedipal mother-daughter bond and the sisters' longing for maternal affection.[19]

Sister My Sister takes place almost exclusively in the claustrophobic
bourgeois household of the Danzards, who employ Lea and Christine
Papin as maids. Unlike that of the protagonists of *Heavenly Creatures*,
these two sisters' flight from the oppressive social world is confined to a
small, womblike attic chamber they share in the house, where they replay
the rituals of childhood. Christine's repressed passions find a creative outlet only in the intricately embroidered linens that she makes for Lea—a
trousseau of bridal whites that later become the props for the sisters'
seduction. Within this domestic, "maternal" space, a closely observed
chamber drama unfolds between the rigidly exacting and conventional
Mme Danzard and her submissive yet perpetually resentful daughter,
Isabelle, on the one hand, and the servants on the other. Christine, emotionally scarred by her mother's abuse and bitter about her longtime preference for Lea, dominates her younger sister as Mme Danzard controls
her daughter. Through parallel editing, Meckler establishes Mme Danzard's and Christine's initial admiration for each other, their common
desire for control and perfection, and their domination of the younger
Lea and Isabelle, whose clumsiness and incipient rebellion threaten to
unbalance the carefully maintained power relationships between employers and maids. Julie Walters plays Mme Danzard with barely controlled
hysteria. Dependent upon her daughter's mirroring responses to her
emotional whims, she alternately solicits her daughter's opinion and love
and cruelly denies her affection or pleasure. Similarly, Joely Richardson's
performance reveals how much Christine relies on Lea for the affection
and affirmation she has sought in vain all her life—first from her mother
and then from a nun, Sister Veronica, in the convent the sisters grew up
in after their mother abandoned them. Richardson also subtly displays
Christine's resentment of her inferior social status and her fragile self-
control, which is easily unraveled by the less repressed and more impetuous Lea.

Although constantly emphasizing the class divisions through spatial
separation and costume, the film examines the subterranean psychological enmeshment between the two sets of women through a juxtaposition of parallel scenes. Not only are the power relations mirrored,
but parallels are drawn between Christine's and Lea's offscreen mother,
who has exploited and manipulated them financially and emotionally all
their lives, and Mme Danzard, who controls Isabelle's future and whose

miserliness and obsessive demands for cleanliness and obedience make the sisters' lives miserable as well.

As in *Heavenly Creatures*, the opening scenes of *Sister My Sister* situate the murder of Mme Danzard and her daughter in the context of a pre-oedipal drama. Black-and-white footage shows Christine and Lea as children locked in a small, dirty room, obviously suffering from maternal neglect. Christine takes care of her younger sister, feeding her and combing her hair. This scene ends with the mother suddenly entering the room and taking Lea away, and a close-up of Christine's face registers both her sense of loss and resentment of her mother's obvious preference for Lea. The film then turns to color, and a long tracking shot down some stairs displays the gruesome details of the murder scene itself, as Christine sings a lullaby to her sister in voice-over.[20] The final scene of the film reverses the trajectory of its opening: the camera moves upstairs to the sisters' attic room to culminate in a black-and-white close-up of Christine and Lea in a close embrace, frightened of being separated by the police, who are off-screen. The film thus articulates in spatial terms the psychological links between the sisters' early experience of deprivation and neglect, their simultaneous hunger for maternal love and fear of persecution, and the ultimate murder of their employers.

These psychological connections and the sisters' close ties are even inscribed in their bodies, much as Pauline and Juliet in *Heavenly Creatures* bonded through their bodily illnesses. Early in the film, Lea asks her sister to tell her a story about their childhood, when Christine rescued her from being run over by a carriage in the street. Christine remembers that she and her sister bled from the same wound, and a close-up shot of their arms reveals a continuous scar line, which a gypsy woman reads as a prophetic sign that the sisters "are bound for life, bound in blood." This scar and prophecy are overdetermined signs of the sisters' bond, their common wounding by a neglectful yet demanding mother, which symbolically foreshadows their bloody crime.

During the first part of the film, as the sisters struggle to extricate themselves from their mother's tyranny and financial exploitation, Christine manages to bring Lea into the Danzard household and gradually loosens her ties to their mother. In a psychologically resonant scene that occurs after the sisters have decided to no longer visit their mother or part with their wages, Christine and Lea gleefully unravel the baby blanket their mother knitted for Lea, a symbolic rending of the umbilical cord. Their social and economic entrapment in the small attic room of the Danzard household, however, leaves the sisters no room to breath or move, and Christine increasingly takes on the role of the controlling mother toward her sister.

The two spend all their time together, relying increasingly on each other for comfort and affection. When their tenderness turns into mutual seduction, this intimacy is tinged with preoedipal overtones, just as the erotically charged bonds between Pauline and Juliet in *Heavenly Creatures* signify both a flight from the overpowering mother and a return to the preoedipal maternal body. The incestuous twinning, Meckler suggests, must be understood in light of a preoedipal fixation that grows out of deprivation. This is underscored in the film by a particularly moving scene in which Lea performs a clever imitation of Sister Veronica. We see a flashback of the young Christine, standing in a starkly bare corridor of the convent as she gazes longingly after the nun, who has cruelly ignored her pleas for attention. The camera then cuts back to the present to show Christine sobbing in Lea's lap; Lea for the moment plays the mother-sister and provides the emotional warmth Christine has felt deprived of all her life.

Christine's and Lea's intimacies are thematically and situationally linked to Mme Danzard's unacknowledged yet powerful narcissistic seduction of her daughter, Isabelle. Crosscutting between the sisters' lovemaking and the Danzards' frenetic card playing, Meckler's parallel scene construction reaches simultaneous emotional climaxes in the sisters' bedroom and in the parlor as Mme Danzard is gripped by orgasmic delight after winning the game against her daughter. However, when the power relations shift in the Danzard household, the tenuous balance and separation between the pairs of women break down. Isabelle shows signs of rebellion, furtively eating chocolates that her mother has locked away and offering one to Lea. Christine jealously observes her sister combing Isabelle's hair—an intimate gesture associated with the sisters' private world since childhood—and she becomes increasingly paranoid that once Isabelle marries, Lea will leave her to work for Isabelle. Isabelle beholds the sisters in a tender moment, when Christine soothes her sister after Lea has clumsily knocked over a pitcher—a moment that brings home to Isabelle her mother's lack of affection. Mme Danzard is equally threatened by a loss of control over her household and her daughter, whom she sees only as an extension of herself. She takes out her anger on the maids, whose increasing independence and subtle transgression of class boundaries provide a perfect target.

In a deep focus shot, for example, Mme Danzard observes Lea dusting in the background, remarking with shock and incredulity that Lea is wearing a pink embroidered sweater over her maid's uniform, a sign of pleasure and extravagance that Mme Danzard immediately perceives as a transgression and a threat to her tight grasp on the household. Christine also chastises Lea for wearing this pretty garment in front of the Danzards, but in her eyes Lea's costume signifies a betrayal of their intimacy and Lea's growing independence. In this volatile atmosphere, intermittent shots of water slowly dripping from the kitchen faucet symbolically indicate the mounting resentment and anxiety among the quartet of women. It takes only the seemingly trivial trigger of a blown electrical fuse, a burned satin blouse, and Lea's fear of punishment to unleash Christine's feelings of oppression and emotional starvation in a brutal act of bloodshed.

In both *Heavenly Creatures* and *Sister My Sister,* we find images of class-bound societies where adolescent girls can find no socially acceptable outlet for their emotional desires; the combination of psychological and social pressures produces a volatile emotional milieu for the acting out of adolescent rage and paranoia against maternal figures, eventually resulting in their murders. In both films intimate and sisterly bonds are the products of a need for intense mutual mirroring and affirmation, symptomatic of maternal neglect and abandonment in early childhood. In both, the once all-good, adored preoedipal mother or symbolic maternal figure turns into a persecutory and oppressive object in the young women's fantasy lives, an intrusive presence perceived as abject.

Julia Kristeva has theorized the abject mother primarily as the product of male anxieties over the engulfing and unknown mother's body. However, these two films make a statement about young women's needs to differentiate their subjectivities from the mother's during a pivotal developmental stage of identity formation. Lynda Hart describes Christine's relationship with her mother as "matrophobic," because of her hatred for the mother and her fear of becoming the naughty daughter that her mother perceives her to be, a monster child who would be cruel to her own sister out of jealousy.[21] Kesselman and Meckler make a strong visual case in their film for Christine's murderous rage against Mme Danzard as a delayed reaction to her own tormented relationship with her mother. The murder not only represents Christine's efforts to prevent Mme Danzard from taking her sister Lea away from her (Lea is, after all, the only person who has ever shown Christine any affection); it is also an unconscious attempt to finally free herself from the double bind of maternal attachment.

Sister My Sister and *Heavenly Creatures* attempt to take us inside the emotional lives of the female criminals to better comprehend their intrapsychic and intersubjective worlds. In their own times the crimes were either declared incomprehensible or misinterpreted by male commentators who projected onto the events their ideological agendas and perhaps their unconscious fantasies. As in many cases of familial, female-on-female homicide, there was a reluctance to investigate the psychic motivations and fantasy structures underlying the relationships between perpetrator and victim. Indeed, by such an investigation one risks violating cherished illusions about the sanctity of mother-daughter and sister relationships as well as the popular myth of women as the gentle guardians of culture and morality. But the supreme challenge of interpreting the overdetermined causes of the crimes stands at the heart of the actual cases, and this challenge is carried over into Jackson's and Meckler's complex constructions of the protagonists' folie à deux. Both show that the motivations of their sisterly murderers—no matter how ghastly their crimes—are far more understandable and resonant than most of us are perhaps willing to acknowledge.

The films belong to a small oeuvre of serious narrative works that explore the nature of female violence. Bette Mandl has compared Kesselman's play, which inspired *Sister My Sister*, to Charlotte Perkins Gilman's 1892 novella "The Yellow Wallpaper" and Susan Glaspell's 1916 play *Trifles*; in both, subtle domestic oppressions and confinements drive women to madness or violence from motives incomprehensible and thus invisible to the male characters.[22] However, the chamber drama quality of *Sister My Sister* resembles in its basic form and central themes the sister films of Swedish director Ingmar Bergman—in particular, *Cries and Whispers*. As in his earlier film, *The Silence*, Bergman's portrayal of sisters' interrelationships in *Cries and Whispers* shows them to be profoundly complex, emotionally ambivalent, and the product of familial patterns of maternal seduction and abandonment and larger patriarchal structures for women's confinement. Much like Nancy Meckler in *Sister My Sister*, Bergman dramatizes how the psychological legacies of family life remain forever imprinted in sisters' memories of the past.

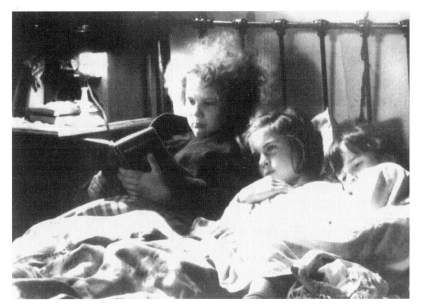

Photo 1. Scene from Jane Campion's *An Angel at My Table* (New Zealand, 1990). *From left to right:* Janet Frame (Karen Fergusson) reads to her sisters, Isabel (Samantha Townsley) and June (Sarah Llewellyn), in bed. Museum of Modern Art Film Stills Archive. Courtesy of the New Zealand Film Commission and Fine Line Features.

Photo 2. Scene from Diane Kurys's *Peppermint Soda* (France, 1977). Anne (Eleonore Klarwein, *center*) and a school friend look admiringly at Anne's sister, Frederique (Odile Michel, *right*). Museum of Modern Art Film Stills Archive. Courtesy of New Yorker Films.

Photo 3. Scene from Mina Shum's *Double Happiness* (Canada, 1995). *From left to right:* Mr. Li (Stephen Chang), Mrs. Li (Alannah Ong), Jade Li (Sandra Oh), and Pearl Li (Frances You). Courtesy of Stephen Hedyes, Quattro Productions. Photo credit: Kirk Tougas.

Photo 4. Still taken from the motion picture *Eve's Bayou* (Kasi Lemmons, USA, 1997). Roz Batiste (Lynn Whitfield) embraces her children *(from left to right)*, Cisely (Meagan Good), Poe (Jake Smollett), and Eve (Jurnee Smollett), after the death of their father. Museum of Modern Art Film Stills Archive. Provided through the courtesy of Trimark Pictures, Inc. © 1996 Trimark Pictures, Inc. All Rights Reserved. Photo credit: Chris Helcermanas-Benge.

Photo 5. Scene from Ingmar Bergman's *The Silence* (Sweden, 1963). The profile of Anna (Gunnel Lindblom) overlaps Ester's face (Ingrid Thulin) in the famous "cubist" shot of the two sisters. Museum of Modern Art Film Stills Archive. Courtesy of Svensk Filmindustri.

Photo 6. Scene from Ingmar Bergman's *Cries and Whispers* (Sweden, 1972). The two sisters, Karin (Ingrid Thulin, *left*) and Maria (Liv Ullmann, *right*), and their servant Anna (Kari Sylwan), dressed in white, wait in the red antechamber for their dying sister, Agnes, to wake up. Museum of Modern Art Film Stills Archive. Courtesy of Svensk Filmindustri.

Photo 7. Scene from Ingmar Bergman's *Cries and Whispers*. In this flashback scene, Karin (Ingrid Thulin), Agnes (Harriet Andersson), and Maria (Liv Ullmann), and their servant Anna (Kari Sylwan) stroll in the gardens. Museum of Modern Art Film Stills Archive. Courtesy of Svensk Filmindustri.

Photo 8. Scene from Margarethe von Trotta's *Sisters, or The Balance of Happiness* (Germany, 1979). *From left to right:* Anna (Gudrun Gabriel) and Maria (Jutta Lampe) visit their mother (Agnes Fink). Museum of Modern Art Film Stills Archive. Courtesy of Bioskop Film GmbH, Munich.

Photo 9. Scene from Margarethe von Trotta's *Marianne and Juliane* (Germany, 1982). Juliane (Jutta Lampe, *left*) and her sister Marianne (Barbara Sukowa) argue violently about their politics and personal past as prison wardens look on. Museum of Modern Art Film Stills Archive. Courtesy of New Yorker Films.

Photo 10. Scene from Margarethe von Trotta's *Paura e amore* (Italy/Germany/France, 1988). Framed by the arcades of the university, Maria (Greta Scacchi, *right*) confesses her ennui to her older sister, Velia (Fanny Ardant). Museum of Modern Art Film Stills Archive. Courtesy of Bioskop Film GmbH, Munich.

PART III

Loss, Memory, Recognition: Sisters in Adulthood

Long after they grow up and leave their childhood home, sisters continue to watch each other. Openly or covertly, each observes how the other navigates her intimate relationships, mothers her children, develops a career, confronts aging, copes with success and with loss. . . . Throughout this lifelong process of mutual awareness and influence, sisters continue to work through the fundamental issues of their relationship— issues of intimacy and separateness, of support and rivalry, of sameness and difference.

Marian Sandmaier, *Original Kin: The Search for Connection Among Adult Sisters and Brothers*

In her book about siblings, *Original Kin*, Marian Sandmaier recognizes adult sisters' life-long spectatorial relationship. Because siblings represent an irreplaceable connection to one another's earliest history, they maintain a central importance for each other well into adulthood, often acting as mutual figures of identification and comparison and finding in adulthood opportunities to renegotiate their childhood bonds. Sandmaier suggests how we retain our parents through sharing memories with our siblings, and as long as this connection remains intact "we are never entirely orphaned."[1] Not surprisingly, many contemporary films that feature adult sororal relationships are concerned with the theme of memory; sisters in these films undertake a literal or figurative journey home to revisit sororal and parental relations.

In her essay "Feminist Fiction and the Uses of Memory," Gayle Greene distinguishes between different uses of memory in women's writing, particularly feminist fiction, distinctions germane to the role that memory plays in many sister films.[2] Greene observes how modernist writers in the early part of the twentieth century foregrounded their concern with memory as a response to cultural crisis, a rupture in continuity with the past. In their effort to understand a world shattered by war and the social and cultural changes of modernity, some modernists adopted a nostalgic point of view, longing to retrieve a stable notion of reality. Others, including many women authors more critical and revisionist in their approaches, engaged history and the past more skeptically. According to Greene, novelists such as Virginia Woolf use narrative and memory as vehicles to bring the past into dialogue with the present, to question and revise history in light of new exigencies for change and new definitions of identity. This is also true of some contemporary films in which memory itself becomes a central issue, as adult sisters harbor sometimes competing stories and visions of their lives, rendering problematic the nostalgia for a single narrative of childhood.

In his work on narration in the psychoanalytic dialogue, psychoanalyst Roy Schafer claims that we are forever telling and retelling stories about ourselves to ourselves and others, which is also the case for the histories we attribute to others. However, as much as we locate these stories in the past, they are always told in the present and thus shaped and changed by current desires and needs. "The end product of this interweaving of texts," argues Schafer, "is a radically new, jointly authored work or way of working."[3] While Schafer is primarily writing about the dialogue between psychoanalyst and analysand, this complex dynamic is easily recognizable among family members, particularly siblings, who tell each other stories about the past, creating a densely woven tapestry of reminiscences and counter-reminiscences.

In this part of the book I focus on two directors who have been influential in modern representations of female subjectivity—Ingmar Bergman and Margarethe von Trotta; both have repeatedly used adult sisters as significant subjects in their explorations of modern consciousness and memory. Both filmmakers articulate in their work a strong appreciation of the shaping power of memory and the ways in which sisters engage with the past and family history. They share a distinctly modernist perspective toward the power and value of memory in molding the present. Their films follow in the line of modernist directors of the postwar era, such as Alain Resnais and Akira Kurosawa, who explore through film the workings of memory and subjectivity.

Bergman and von Trotta are particularly concerned with how the figure of the sister can powerfully embody the link between identity and family history. Their exploration of sisterhood within the psychological dynamics of family life reveals a connection to what Helena Michie in *Sororophobia* has called the "uncanny power" of the sister, alluding to Freud's notion of the unfamiliar or strange, which always implies the repression of the familiar and familial.[4] Perhaps the power of sisterhood is so uncanny, not because it evokes idealized affiliation, but because it suggests Freud's association of the double with ambivalence.

The intense intimacy that develops between sisters in the process of growing up fosters in many such a strong feeling of mutual identification that at a psychic level they at times experience each other as mirrors or extensions of themselves. As Christine Downing notes, "For a woman the sister is the other most like ourselves of any creature in the world. She is of the same gender and generation, of the same biological and social heritage. We have the same parents; we grew up in the same family, were exposed to the same values, assumptions, patterns of interaction." Yet "this other so like myself is, ineluctably, *other*. She, more than any other, serves as the one over against whom I define myself. . . . Likeness and difference, intimacy and otherness—neither can be overcome. That paradox, that tension, lies at the very heart of the relationship."[5] It is the paradox of difference and sameness embodied in the sister that many women must contend with in their definition of self. Margarethe von Trotta alludes to the uncanniness of sister narratives when she speaks of the sister as representing "encounters with our other sides, the unknown aspects of our personae which at the same time seem so familiar. I imagine meetings with ourselves in other people's bodies, stories of mirror images."[6]

As John Orr suggests in his discussion of modern cinema, Freud's definition of the uncanny is "literally and metaphorically a homecoming, a finding of the familiar in unfamiliar circumstances, of home within a strange country, of the self within the world of the Other."[7] Many films treated in this book—and in my view, Bergman's and von Trotta's films in particular—take up this exploration of the uncanny aspects of sisterhood, bringing to light the hidden familiar secrets that have been repressed.

Two of these works, Brigitte Roüan's *Overseas (Outremer,* France, 1990) and Richard Franklin's *Sorrento Beach* (Australia, 1995) explore sisters' memories in the context of colonialism and gender relations. *Overseas* is a semiautobiographical reflection on the life of Roüan's *pied noir* family in Algeria between 1946 and the outbreak of national revolution in 1954, told through the separate but overlapping perspectives of three European sisters—Zon, Malène, and Gritte. (It recalls Kurosawa's *Rashomon* with its play on different points of view of the same past events.) Each must negotiate her relationship as a European woman to Algerian society, as the colonized country moves toward war. The opening shots of the film, in which the three vivacious sisters canoe toward the North African shore in the Mediterranean sunshine, suggest their sororal unity and adventurous spirit. Yet this image can also be read as an ironic commentary on the "arrival" of Europeans in North Africa. The young women refuse to acknowledge the oppression and exploitation French colonialism has wrought upon Algeria. "Driven inexorably by sexuality and politics into tragic outcomes, the sisters' narratives . . . move from marital or colonial rule to an illusory liberation whose site of struggle is women's bodies and female subjectivity," comments Catherine Portuges.[8]

Overseas's representation of memory from the three sisters' perspectives also suggests the differences between the women, revealing in each new segment a subtle and critical understanding of the women's particular choices and attitudes. The most conservative, eldest sister Zon lives only for her naval officer husband and fully submits to the myths of heroism, colonialism, and male dominance. The middle sibling, Malène, frustrated with her passive, bookish husband who leaves all responsibilities to her, practically manages their farm by herself. The youngest sister, Gritte, secretly rebellious and more ambivalent about her social and gendered position, carries on a short-lived, clandestine love affair with an Arab rebel who is killed at the end in the revolution. In the film's ironic coda, which takes place in a cathedral in France after Algeria's independence, Gritte, the only surviving sister and the sibling most hopeful for change, is about to be married to a traditional Frenchman. Looking up, she sees in her mind's eye the smiling faces of Zon and Malène superimposed on the high screens behind the altar, an image that celebrates the ties between the sisters. Sadly, it also links Gritte's fate to that of her sisters, women who were trapped in traditional marriages and rigid codes of class and gender.

In the Australian feature film *Sorrento Beach*, three sisters reunite in their childhood home to deal with sexual betrayal in their past. The catalyst for the confrontation is a thinly disguised autobiographical novel and family memoir, *Melancholy*, written by the middle sister, Meg. Hillary, the eldest, has remained at home in the bayside resort of Sorrento, Australia, caring for her widower father and her sixteen-year-old son. The others, Meg and Pippa, live as expatriates in England and the United States respectively. Each sister represents a facet of modern Australia and its search for a national identity and postcolonial independence from British cultural influence and American economic domination. They also attempt to carve out a viable identity in relation and opposition to the traditional Australian masculine culture represented by their father. Cinematically, *Sorrento Beach* is, as some critics have noted, fairly uninspired; adapted from a play by Hannie Rayson, the film allows dialogue to carry the meaning, and the characters often remain static within the frame.[9] However, the film's self-referential use of the family memoir underlines the role of sororal memory in the construction of family history.

Pippa, who has returned to Australia to open up a sandwich franchise and tries to convince Hillary to give up her domestic role, turns out to have had an affair with Hillary's husband. She blames Meg, the writer, for "raiding" their childhood for literary fame: "It's as if our memories aren't ours anymore." The history of sexual betrayal is compounded by Meg's emotional betrayal of her sisters through the publication of her novel. The memoir, in effect, reflects Meg's belief that in order to transcend the limitations placed on women by Australian culture, she is forced to betray her sisters. Accused of plagiarizing her memoir, Meg must defend and reexamine her writing and its reception. Marge, the family's neighbor and a long-time resident of Sorrento Beach, mediates between the two sisters' positions—Hillary's commitment to family and her survival in Australian culture and Meg's insistence on artistic freedom and self-definition. The tensions among the sisters are ultimately unresolved at the end. After selling the family home in the wake of their father's sudden death, the three sisters are shown framed by the windows of the house, looking out silently onto the open sea, each isolated by her own emotions.[10]

Jane Campion's *Sweetie* is another film that portrays the relationship between adult sisters in the context of fragmented memory, uncertain identities, and family breakdown. Campion's first feature film attracted intense criticism and debate upon its release for its supposedly callous representation of the grotesque sister, Sweetie, and its stylistic mannerisms.

Conversely, John Orr reads *Sweetie*'s surreal tragicomedy as an important contribution to contemporary Australian cinema's exploration of
suburban entropy.[11] The film exemplifies what critic Adrian Martin has
called Australian cinema's "unyielding gaze at the ghastliness, the
'muckiness' of suburban family life," infused with "sudden flights of
fancy or surrealism, as well as a certain rhetoric of deflation or laconic
sense of humor."[12]

Both her shy, introverted sister, Kay, and the excessive, out-of-con-
trol Sweetie struggle with a suburban life-style that further destabilizes
a family in disarray. Sweetie represents only a more extreme manifes-
tation of Kay's fragmented self—an identity precariously held together
by vague secular rituals of meditation and prognostications of the future
as well as by an affectionate but shaky love relationship. Sweetie is associated with images of nature wildly out of bounds, and her behavior
destabilizes Kay's carefully organized routine. Kay's neurotic fear of
trees—repeatedly visualized in time-lapse photography of plants shooting through the ground—seems to imply a fear both of phallic pene-
tration and of nature run rampant. There is a suggestion here that
Sweetie's unrestrained narcissism and illusion of omnipotence tap primal emotions far too unruly and powerful for the artifices of modern
society to tame. Campion's decentered, even surreal, cinematic style
underscores the film's concern with fragile family bonds, conveying the
menace and anarchy beneath the placidity of everyday life—visions of
disturbing memories that never quite rise to the surface of consciousness. When Sweetie falls out of a treehouse, her death seems to temporarily reunite the family and return them to precarious normality.
However, the final image belongs to Sweetie, a haunting memory of her
childhood self, isolated among the garden bushes, struggling to win her
father's attention.

Ulu Grosbard's *Georgia* (1995) explores the rivalry between two adult
sisters, both artists (a theme dramatized in a very different context in
Little Women). The elder, Georgia, is a folk singer in the Seattle neo–folk
music scene and a conventional mother and wife; the younger, Sadie, is
a struggling punk-rock singer who has never found success and lives in
the shadow of her sister's talent and fame. Jennifer Jason Leigh's performance as the strung-out, vulnerable Sadie captures all the nuances of the
younger sister's ambivalent desire to emulate and be recognized by her
older sister, and her equally strong need to stake out her own terrain as
a musician who challenges conventional images of female singers.[13]

A different take on adult sisters as artist-performers is suggested by African American independent director Ayoka Chenzira's first feature film, *Alma's Rainbow* (1993). It concerns the triangular relationship between Alma, a practical, responsible beautician, her sister, Ruby, a Josephine Baker-like dancer and singer who abruptly returns from Paris to visit, and Alma's daughter, Rainbow, who is struggling to define her identity and sexuality in the midst of adolescent confusion. Alma and Ruby appear to represent opposite personalities—and different role models for Rainbow—but a flashback reveals that they were in their youth a performance duo, the Fabulous Flamingo Sisters, who became estranged when Ruby left for Paris. Ruby's energy colorfully transforms the mise-en-scène in Alma's and Rainbow's brownstone apartment and sparks a sensual awakening in mother and daughter. More importantly, in the process of finding their sensual and erotic capacities for pleasure, mother and daughter also grow closer to each other (a departure from earlier melodramas that generally link the daughter's sexual maturity with her alienation from the mother). Chenzira includes numerous forms of performance in this episodic film, from hip hop to earlier black women's traditions of singing and dancing, to suggest their significance in African American female identity formation and a female tradition of sensual self-expression.

Rare representations in cinema of sisters in old age who return to their memories of the past are Lindsay Anderson's *The Whales of August* (1987), starring screen legends Bette Davis and Lillian Gish, and Gabriel Axel's *Babette's Feast* (1987), based on Isak Dinesen's story about a pair of Danish sisters who in a sumptuous meal find themselves experiencing the pleasures they have missed throughout their lives. Like the films I have already mentioned, Anderson's and Axel's dramas portray the psychological encounters that ensue between adult sisters as their memories return to the uncertain ground of their familial pasts, to shadowy landscapes where in a reversal of time characters search for self-recognition through their sisters.

In the following chapters I examine the films of Ingmar Bergman and Margarethe von Trotta. Revisiting Bergman's early modernist films that feature biological sisters, *The Silence* and *Cries and Whispers*, I take into account the male director's problematic representation of the female body but also his depiction of intersubjective relationships between women, and sisters in particular, inscribed in his preoccupation with the themes of human isolation and alienation in the modern world and his characters' attempts to find grace, human connection, and affection. In the words of John Orr, "[Bergman] explores the collisions of intimacy, of beings wrapped in mutual or collective solitude."[14]

Bergman's focus on the painful and complicated relationships between adult sisters has had enormous influence on later, very different directors concerned with this theme, notably Woody Allen and Margarethe von Trotta. *Interiors* (1978) is Allen's most candid homage (or imitation, depending on one's point of view) to *Cries and Whispers*, with its thematic echo of three sisters' ambivalent relationship with their genteel, suicidally depressed mother and its careful attention to color in the mise-en-scène. In *Hannah and Her Sisters* (1986) Allen reprises his focus on three sisters in a more comedic vein, although as Lefkovitz has convincingly argued, the film is concerned less with the sisters' bond than with their relationships with men. One can even detect allusions to Bergman's films about sisters in such works as Nancy Meckler's *Sister My Sister*, which recalls *The Silence*; and in Susan Streitfeld's postmodern, postfeminist *Female Perversions* (1996), which features a pair of sisters and a seductive though rejecting father (who stands in for patriarchal structures that "pervert" female behavior). The film visually quotes Bergman's *Cries and Whispers* when one sister mutilates her own body in imitation of her mother, much as the cold and self-destructive Karin does in Bergman's film.

It is, however, German director Margarethe von Trotta who most rigorously and effectively takes up Bergman's concern with memory and family history and the role of the sister in the retrieval of a personal and cultural past, as I establish in the final chapter of this book in my analysis of her three sister films: *Sisters, or The Balance of Happiness, Marianne and Juliane*, and *Paura e amore*.

The director's own life story and discovery as an adult of an unknown half sister is, in her own words, nothing short of "amazing from a psychoanalytic point of view."[15] Margarethe von Trotta was born in 1942 in Berlin to Elizabeth von Trotta, a déclassé German noblewoman born in Moscow. After the war, von Trotta and her mother fled to the Rhineland but remained stateless persons. Von Trotta's mother never married her father, the painter Alfred Roloff, and mother and daughter lived alone in poverty throughout most of von Trotta's childhood, creating an intimate bond intensified by their dislocation and exile. In 1979, when von Trotta had completed her second film, *Sisters, or The Balance of Happiness*, her older half sister, given up for adoption at birth, contacted her. The discovery of a sister whose existence she had never suspected was a shock to Margarethe von Trotta's image of her mother, with whom she had always shared everything. In retrospect, von Trotta believes that her mother communicated to her the fact of her sister nonverbally:

> I think I knew unconsciously that I had a sister because my mother often thought very intensely about her, especially around holidays and on my sister's birthday. I think she conveyed that to me telepathically. Freud wrote a nice article about the relationship between mother and child, a case history in which a female patient tells Freud her dream about a coin. When this woman went home, her four-year-old son brings her this coin. On the basis of this case, Freud developed his theory about the special bond between mother and child that relies on a deep inner connection and is internalized by the child in the prelinguistic phase. I think that was the case with me and my mother. I was deprived of some of my mother's love on my sister's birthday. She loved me terribly and showed me so much affection, but on that day I sensed that she was absent-minded and wasn't there for me.[16]

The phantasmagorical presence of an absent sister in the director's unconscious and her intrusion into the preoedipal bond between mother and daughter surfaced in von Trotta's early film work: von Trotta used her own and her sister's middle names, Maria and Anna, for the two sister characters in *Sisters, or The Balance of Happiness,* and in the 1972 film *A Free Woman,* which she coscripted, she played the central character undergoing a divorce, adopting her mother's first name and unconsciously choosing her sister's exact birth date.

The biographical details of von Trotta's experiences form a rich psychological picture of the space occupied by the absent, unknown sister in von Trotta's films, which demonstrate the connection of self-knowledge and the intersubjective communion with a sister who is both similar and different from the self. For the discovery or recovery of a sister must surely initiate a revision of one's life narrative, a journey for Margarethe von Trotta always related to history and politics as shaping and constituting forces of identity. My purpose in closely reading von Trotta's sister films is to highlight this process as political: the retrieval and recognition of a sister signifies the possibility of creating a new relationship between two subjects, a recognition of the self in the sibling who is different that might lead to a politics of intersubjectivity.

The Internal World of Sisters

Ingmar Bergman's The Silence *and* Cries and Whispers

O f all the male filmmakers associated with the advent of the European art cinema in the late 1950s and 1960s, Ingmar Bergman is arguably the director most consistently engaged with the exploration of female subjectivity. The hallmark of his work is his inquiry into the interrelationships between men and women, parents and children—their struggles for recognition and love, their inability to connect with one another, and the ways in which their failures of intimacy result in pain and violence. These themes inform Bergman's two films about adult sisters, *The Silence* (1963) and *Cries and Whispers* (1972), which mark the beginning and close of his most innovative period as a writer-director. Among the nine feature films Bergman made in those years, five are especially daring and experimental: *The Silence, Persona* (1966), *Hour of the Wolf* (1968), *A Passion (The Passion of Anna,* 1969), and *Cries and Whispers.* Bergman has been recognized for stretching the properties of the cinematic apparatus in order to scrutinize both the complexities of the human personae and the elusive interior worlds of his characters—all signify Bergman's departure from the strong theatrical influences and the rather conventional plot structures apparent in the realist films and allegories he made in the 1950s. In these five films, Bergman self-consciously experiments with cinematic time, point of view, memories, fantasies, and dreams; indeed, critic John Orr considers Bergman's fusion in one image of the imaginary, the real, and the dream state to be the director's greatest contribution to cinematic modernism.[1]

Bergman's modernist films invite a psychoanalytic reading because they so insistently probe the unconscious connections between his characters. *Cries and Whispers* is centrally preoccupied with two adult sisters' response to the death of a third, the painful transience or absence of affectionate relationships, and the reunion of adult sisters confronted with their childhood and their relationship with their deceased mother, who continues to play a major role in their internal lives. *The Silence* prefigures *Cries and Whispers* in its focus on two symbiotically intertwined sisters whose agonized struggle is influenced by the haunting presence of their dead parent, in this instance a cold and perfectionistic father.[2]

The animosity between the sisters raises the issue of how women's relationships are represented in Bergman's work, an issue that has been more frequently addressed with respect to *Cries and Whispers*. His depiction of female attachment is often considered problematic, especially from a feminist perspective. The inscription of male perspectives in the visual and aural codes of the cinema over its history, coupled with the self-avowed "confessional" nature of Bergman's work, has tended to throw into doubt his ability to film across gender lines.[3] On the one hand, Robin Wood, in his 1969 study of Bergman's films, called him one of cinema's greatest directors of women, tracing his development from early stereotypical representations of women as virginal innocents to an increasingly complex depiction of female subjectivity in *The Silence* and *Persona*. On the other hand, feminist critics after the 1960s have largely argued that Bergman's films reflect his essentialist conception of women, and they have analyzed how his female characters appear to function as projections of his own spiritual and artistic conflicts. Bergman himself professed in an interview that his "ceaseless fascination with the whole race of women is one of [his] mainsprings. Obviously such an obsession implies ambivalence; it has something compulsive about it."[4]

Bergman's varied and often contradictory comments about his female characters reveal his very complicated and ambivalent attitude toward women. *Cries and Whispers*, which was made in 1972 in the midst of the women's movement, sparked an especially virulent controversy. When the film appeared, critics conceded its haunting beauty and dreamlike intensity, but many feminists rejected the film as "furtively misogynist."[5]

At the time, feminist critics were mainly upbraiding Bergman, a male director, for dramatizing the interrelationships between the four central female characters as painful, conflicted, and estranged instead of presenting more positive, celebratory images of modern, liberated women. These critics largely dismiss Bergman's work for what they regard as his malicious stereotypes of women, or they interpret his films symbolically as "subjective metaphors" for his own fears and frustrations.[6]

Bergman's films have always invited autobiographical readings, preoccupied as they are with an exploration of his own dreams and the "family romance": "I take up the images from my childhood, put them into the 'projector,' run them into myself, and have an entirely new way of evaluating them," he once told an interviewer, Torsten Manns.[7] Many of his films, and certainly his last one—the quasi-autobiographical *Fanny and Alexander*—can be seen as a reworking of the oedipal scenario, with his female characters cast as mother figures.

Critics in the 1990s such as Mark Sandberg and Marilyn Johns Blackwell, however, have called for a more nuanced evaluation of Bergman's representation of gender.[8] Sandberg has argued in his revisionist study of Bergman's films that the director's work after *The Seventh Seal* shifts increasingly from a masculine discourse to a focus on female subjectivity and alternative modes of cinematic narrative. Blackwell offers a full-scale analysis of Bergman's most prominent works about women, considering the ways in which they embody certain feminist sensibilities, particularly in his critique of the social and cultural hierarchies in which women are subordinated and imprisoned. Interestingly, Blackwell, who deplores *Cries and Whispers* for its retrograde depiction of women's subjectivity as rooted in biology, sees in *The Silence* a criticism of male ideology and discourse and argues that the film unmasks the violence of patriarchal structures.[9]

The Silence is indeed a pivotal work in Bergman's oeuvre. The last in his trilogy of films (which includes *Through a Glass Darkly* and *Winter Light*) that are overtly or implicitly concerned with the viability of Christian morality and the spiritual meanings of faith and suffering in the modern world, the film reveals the overlap between his existential questioning and his interest in women as the victims of repression. Depicting a modern wasteland ruled by God's silence and the collapse of patriarchal values, *The Silence* emphasizes the alienation that ensues from the sisters' psychological internalization of their father's authoritarian control.

Cries and Whispers locates the source of women's repression in a specific historical and cultural milieu—the repressed Victorian world of the

Swedish high bourgeoisie.[10] The film's meticulous mise-en-scène, its use of objects and clothes as symbols of the constricting bourgeois household, not only operates on a psychological level but also represents Bergman's critique of a system of relationships that imprisons and isolates women from each other and from positions of power and independence. Although Bergman has been justly criticized for generalizing social and political conflicts in his films—that is, for exploiting images of war, civil unrest, and political injustice as symbolic correlatives of psychological alienation—in *Cries and Whispers* he is delineating a social world with which he is very familiar.[11] As in *Fanny and Alexander* as well as in his screenplay for *Best Intentions* (based on the courtship and marriage of his parents), Bergman discloses a keen historical comprehension of Victorian gender roles and the ways in which they were influenced by Protestant morality and even by class divisions. The father is conspicuously absent in *Cries and Whispers*, and the other male characters—the sadistic doctor, the sisters' repulsive husbands, and the ineffectual priest—are marginalized, yet they serve as important reminders of male power. In this microcosmic upper-class world, the "absent presence" of patriarchal authority has profound impact on the sisters' conflicts and on their self-involved and melancholy mother; all the women have internalized the era's strictures on female identity.

Bergman is by no stretch of the imagination a feminist filmmaker: nowhere in his cinematic universe does he champion women's rights nor does he present an alternative female realm where, to use Marianne Hirsch's words, the subject/object dualism and power relationships might be challenged and redefined;[12] rather the pull of desire and the clash of difference between women are, in Bergman's view, the products of "the unreasonable and never-satisfied longing for fellowship, the clumsy attempts to do away with distance and isolation."[13] But *The Silence* and *Cries and Whispers*, like Bergman's other modernist films, are nevertheless deeply critical of the patriarchal logos—the realm of the authoritarian father and of an unresponsive God.

The Silence

Throughout his career Bergman has repeatedly examined the psychological anguish and alienation created by compliance to conventional social roles. This theme becomes increasingly central in his films of the 1960s and early 1970s, which focus on characters undergoing existential crises of faith and trust in religion, work, love, and family relationships. Touched by death, illness, violence, or failures of intimacy, his characters experience a loss of self when they can no longer convince themselves that the social conventions they live by have any meaning. *Persona* is the most famous of Bergman's dramas of the self's dissolution, psychological merger, and the unsuccessful struggles for intersubjectivity. But *The Silence*, made several years earlier, anticipates *Persona*'s exploration of psychic breakdown. The two sisters in *The Silence*, Ester and Anna, whom critics often see as opposites, both wear social masks that the film suggests are at variance with their own feelings yet continue to influence the organization of their personalities. The film, as elusive and unspecific as it is about the prior history of the sisters' relationship, visualizes the instability of what Winnicott calls the "false self," the persona each sister has adopted unconsciously to comply with social expectations and norms.[14]

As the film opens, Ester (Ingrid Thulin), an unmarried translator who is dying of tuberculosis, her married sister, Anna (Gunnel Lindblom), and Anna's ten-year-old son, Johan, are traveling through a strange foreign country that is in the grip of an unexplained military conflict. In the middle of the night tanks roam the empty streets, and during the day women and children are strangely absent from the cafes and sidewalks of the sweltering city. The film's psychological focus oscillates between the tense relationship of the two sisters and the boy, Johan, who is often caught between the women's needs. Both the object of his mother's capricious seductive affection and the victim of her casual neglect, Johan is caught in the painful orbit of his dying aunt's yearning for love. Johan is also repeatedly shut out from the world of his mother and aunt. He strays through the desolate corridors of the dimly lit, almost empty Victorian hotel where they have come to rest from their journey because of Ester's illness. The hotel's labyrinthine pathways suggest a psychic landscape where any notion of a stable self must be abandoned. Johan's encounter with a grotesque group of dwarfs, who for fun clothe him in a girl's dress, and Anna's later surreptitious observation of a copulating couple in a theater are just two of a number of events in the film that suggest a preoccupation with fantasy scenarios and the performance or masquerade of gender identities and sexuality. Disconnected from familiar cultural signposts, unable to understand the local language, and facing the reality of Ester's impending death, the sisters are forced to confront their common history of paternal domination and repression.

From the very beginning of *The Silence*, Bergman captures the estrangement and hostility but also the intense homoeroticism between the sisters. Anna feels compelled to leave the hotel soon after they have arrived, searching for and finding a sexual encounter that she will later consummate with a waiter from a cafe. Meanwhile, Ester, confined to her bed by her debilitating illness, drinks alcohol, smokes, and seeks sexual release through masturbation to assuage her loneliness and her feelings of humiliation over both her physical condition and, more importantly, her rejection by her sister, whom she loves with great intensity. Separated yet connected by adjoining hotel bedrooms, the sisters are engaged in a psychic battle that goes back in time and memory: their arguments reveal that the proud and efficient Ester has always identified with their father, while Anna has felt dominated and controlled by both her father's and her sister's intellectualism and what she perceives to be Ester's prying involvement with her life. For her part, Ester observes her sister longingly from afar, finally imploring Anna not to leave her alone in the hotel room for her sexual tryst. Their conflict reaches the breaking point when a dejected Ester enters the room where Anna is engaging in loveless intercourse with the waiter from the cafe. By the time Anna and her son leave Ester behind in the hotel to resume their train journey, Johan has transferred his affection to his aunt and, unlike his mother, empathizes with her pain. In the train compartment, Johan reads a message from Ester, who has translated a few words she has learned in the foreign language, notably the words "hand" and "face," which connote her attempt to establish intimacy and connection, to communicate meaning beyond the walls of silence.

The Silence has been analyzed largely in symbolic terms. The film's enigmatic and menacing setting has invited allegorical readings that extend to the relationship between the two sisters. Critics have seen Anna's compulsive need to seek gratification in anonymous sexual encounters and Ester's intellectualism and rejection of the heterosexual act of intercourse as evidence of the film's stark opposition of body and soul, or of stereotypical femininity and masculinity.[15] As Robin Wood and more recently Marilyn Blackwell have pointed out, however, Bergman's characterizations of Anna and Ester are hardly schematized and he endows their relationship with nuanced psychological shadings.[16]

While Ester and Anna are partly presented through Johan's visual perspective, the sisters never function as mere objects of fantasy in the boy's developing consciousness. Bergman foregrounds the difficult interdependent sister relationship in its own right and gives Ester and Anna authority and presence through many close-ups of their faces. While he codes Anna and Ester as opposites through their different dress and hairstyle Anna wears low-cut feminine dresses and loose hair, Ester prefers simple suits and masculine pajamas—the film is ultimately more concerned with examining their attachment and psychological interdependency.

Ester is deeply, even homoerotically attached to Anna: early in the film, we see her contemplating a sleeping Anna and Johan and tenderly touching their hair; then she returns to her room and, after obtaining more drink from the hotel servant and listening to Bach on the radio, masturbates in bed. This sequence establishes an emotional continuity between Ester's frustrated longing for her sister's love and her sexual self-gratification. For her part, Anna feels both afraid and overwhelmed by Ester's love and control, resorting to increasingly desperate measures to assert her difference and independence from her older sister.

Bergman often frames Anna and Ester in deep focus shots that emphasize both their inescapable emotional bond and their distance, their fascination for and repulsion by each other. In a particularly complex shot arrangement, Anna is washing herself in front of a bathroom mirror and observes Ester watching her through double doorways. The sisters' gazes meet in the mirror, and this composition suggests the degree to which both Ester and Anna are caught in a prison of mutual projections: Anna appears to be simultaneously soliciting her sister's gaze, displaying her naked body to both her son and her sister, and rejecting her sister's desire as controlling and manipulative, or as too intrusive. The mirror shot is repeated when Anna returns from her excursion in the city and undresses in the bathroom; Ester appears in the doorway, picks up Anna's dress, and inspects it. Furious at her prying, Anna later disturbs Ester working at her desk and accuses her of "spying." "To think that I was afraid of you," she sneers, and leaves Ester, whose face in close-up is contorted in anger and humiliation.

The most expressionistic arrangement of the sisters' faces occurs during their argument over Anna's leaving the hotel room for her tryst. Ester tells her to leave if her conscience allows her to, and Anna turns away from the door and waits by a window to confront her sister with the time Ester forced her to share the intimate details of a sexual affair. Now Anna turns the tables by flaunting her sexuality and inventing an encounter that is designed to humiliate Ester. In this chiaroscuro scene,

Ester faces the camera while half of her visage is covered by Anna's profile, which is illuminated by the moon and streetlights—a composition of two women's faces that would eventually become Bergman's signature shot, one he elaborated to great effect in *Persona*. Hubert Cohen has interpreted this mise-en-scène as a visualization of each sister's desire for and rejection of the other's qualities[17]—Ester's fascination with and repulsion by Anna's sexual promiscuity, and Anna's desire to control her domineering sister through torturous lies about her affairs. The image conveys a merger that is fractured and about to fall apart, an overlap of two subjectivities that do not quite meet. Ester returns to her bed and asks Anna to sit by her; pleading with her not to rendezvous with her new lover, she kisses Anna repeatedly on her neck and face. The shot conveys each sister's emotional response in the same frame: Ester's need for Anna's affection and attention, and Anna's view of her sister as a kind of "vampire" whose love she experiences as a form of smothering control. (This view of Ester as a vampire is perhaps alluded to in an earlier scene between Johan and Ester, in which Johan sketches for Ester a picture of a face with fangs, clearly meant to represent Johan's unconscious projection. Bergman leaves ambiguous whether the image refers to Ester, Anna, or Anna's feelings about Esther.)

Forced and desperate, Anna's "acting out" of her sexuality in the following scenes with the waiter is arguably directed against her sister, or it can be interpreted as Anna's attempt to achieve a sense of distance from Ester's control. "How nice we don't understand each other," Anna says to her anonymous lover; shortly thereafter, she admits, "I wish Ester was dead." When Ester appears at the door, pleading to be let in, Anna stages a lovemaking scene and then berates Ester for spying on her. Anna's lover is virtually pushed to the edge of the frame or consigned to the background as the camera focuses on the sisters' explosive confrontation. Ester kneels in the foreground, hands folded almost in prayer, while Anna lunges at her, full of anger, straining against the bars at the end of the bed. Anna accuses Ester of adopting their father's authoritarian rule, of keeping her locked in a prison of moral principles, and charges Ester with hating herself as well as Anna. Yet Anna's fury and Ester's melancholy protestation that she loves her sister cast doubt on the truth of Anna's accusations, suggesting that Anna may be projecting her own fear, self-hatred, and ambivalence onto her sister.

The Silence implies that Ester's identification with the father divided her from Anna, who is left to define herself in opposition to her sister.

The sisters' mother is never mentioned except when Ester, wracked with pain on her death bed, calls out for her mother to deliver her from loneliness and agony (significantly, Ester had earlier prayed to God to let her die at home).[18] To a large extent, the back story to the sisters' relationship in *The Silence* remains elusive to the end. The father, whom Ester calls "kind," someone who "laughed and told funny stories," is described by Bergman as a man who "controlled [Ester] with . . . a despotic love . . . [and] the beginning of Death."[19] We are left with the sisters' inability to function as transitional objects for each other, to recognize each other's suffering and respond to each other's individual needs. Bergman's script suggests, I think, that Anna's denial of love to her sister contributes to Ester's death, and Ester's controlling love leaves Anna feeling alienated and guilty. Anna's failure to show compassion for her sister because she fears her dominance is as self-destructive as Ester's unquestioning identification with her father and her inability to separate love from control.

Whereas *Cries and Whispers* focuses on the power of the mother in the sisters' psyches, *The Silence* hints at the role of the father in the construction of the sisters' identities. The sense of menace and claustrophobia in the city streets outside the sisters' hotel symbolizes a patriarchal order in crisis in which women play no active role, as if pressing in upon the two rooms where Ester and Anna play out their interpersonal drama of love and rejection. Among Bergman's most apocalyptic films, *The Silence* charts a psychic journey that remains incomplete and unresolved; the sisters achieve no self-recognition through their encounter with the past and each other. Unable to free themselves from the social masks that define them, Ester and Anna remain caught in a web of relationships not of their own making.

Cries and Whispers

Cries and Whispers immerses the spectator in a dream world, a figurative womblike enclosure full of childhood memories that both engenders and problematizes female identity. A "chamber film" (Bergman's appropriation of Strindberg's term for his most intimate psychological dramas), it is set in turn-of-the-century Sweden, inside an old manor house that becomes a metaphor for the intersubjective relationships between the sisters—one of whom, Agnes, is dying of cancer of the uterus—and their faithful servant Anna. Returning to the parental house triggers memories of childhood for the sisters and returns them to a prelinguistic, presymbolic form of communication and bonding. In her distinction between oedipal and preoedipal narratives, Marianne Hirsch describes and analyzes the drive of the preoedipal—the desire to regain the original unity with the mother's body—as a fundamental characteristic of many modern and contemporary feminist plot revisions:

> Whereas for Freud the process of imagination and the activity of fabulation are motivated by loss and by the longing for liberation from familial constraints, for feminist theorists and for some feminist writers of the 1970s, the imagination is fueled either by a longing to reexperience symbiotic union with the mother (by identification with her) or by a struggle against an identification which still reveals a profound and continued closeness. The content of plot is not a process of successive distancing but, rather, is a struggle with a bond that is powerful and painful, that threatens engulfment and self-loss even while it offers the very basis for self-consciousness. . . . The pre-oedipal realm figures as a powerful mythic space, not irrevocably lost but continually present because it is recoverable in ideal(ized) female relationships. Pre-symbolic and pre-cultural, it points to an alternative to patriarchy and the logos.[20]

In retrospect, Hirsch's theorizing regarding preoedipal narratives has relevance for a reading of Bergman's depiction of the familial relations among the four women, all of whom attempt to recover maternal nurturing—at least temporarily—in their relationships with their sisters.[21] As Toni McNaron points out, since biological sisters participate in a woman-to-woman bond made even more powerful by their familial heritage, they share the potential for being each other's second love object, as their mother is their first.[22] The emotional connections between the mother and her daughters and between the adult sisters themselves in *Cries and Whispers* are often dramatized without words and set to music, in spaces located between dream and reality. The mother's boredom, anger, and frustration with the limited roles available to her in the Victorian era also comprise the emotional legacy for her daughters, who either adopt or rebel against it in self-destructive ways. Bergman's film shows sisters seeking recognition, attempting to break out of their psychological isolation and overcome their mutual feelings of rejection and humiliation in a family built on patriarchy.

Early in the film, in a revealing scene that introduces Maria, the sister who is most closely identified with the mother, the camera pans across an ornate Victorian dollhouse, and through it Bergman captures in miniature the social hierarchies and traditional gender roles that have shaped the four women's lives. The isolation of various dolls in different rooms—the maid in the kitchen at the stove, the married couple that is reminiscent of Karin and her husband Frederik in the dining room, the blond woman who resembles Maria in the bedroom, a blond man like Maria's husband in the dining room conveys the fragmented relations in *Cries and Whispers*. Much like the dolls, the sisters are decorative objects, which Bergman implies makes it supremely difficult for them to internalize one another and to relate as subjects and feeling beings. Yet as Bruce Kawin points out, there is an "ascending intimacy" between the sisters over the course of the film. Extended first-person sequences reveal how each sister attempts to connect with another and overcome the divisive psychological impact of their conflicted or ambivalent relationships with their mother.[23]

The sisters' conscious and unconscious childhood memories of their mother's erratic pattern of nurturance and neglect dominate Bergman's film; they hunger in adulthood for the maternal mirroring they never experienced as children.[24] The mother played favorites, showering affection and intimacy on Maria while excluding Agnes and Karin. She placed her daughters in a double bind, inviting their trust and love and then rejecting them, a trauma Agnes and Karin relive when they come together in the parental home.

At the beginning of the film, we see Maria and Karin dressed in white flowing nightgowns, whispering in the antechamber to Agnes's bedroom. The white robes visually link them to their long-dead mother who, in Agnes's memory, always wore an elegant white gown. The white robes express the sisters' unconscious wish to return to the "virginal" first love with their mother, much as Adrienne Rich writes in her poem "Sibling Mysteries":

> *The daughters never were*
> *true brides of the father*
>
> *the daughters were to begin with*
> *brides of the mother*
>
> *then brides of each other*
> *under a different law*

Rich's 1976 poem fantasizes a daughter's return to her mother's body through the sharing of common memories with her sister, a reunion that may foster a new language and new forms of relationships between women beyond the dictates of the "Law of the Father."[25] Rich also problematizes this retrospective journey, however, by acknowledging that sisters, by virtue of their difference, also disrupt the fantasy of a complete merger between mother and daughter; in Bergman's film this journey remains an unfulfilled desire. The fantasy of the daughter's return to the mother's body is symbolically underscored in *Cries and Whispers* through images of a white rose, which Agnes paints in watercolor and which recall for her memories of her mother and childhood.

Also significant in the film's mise-en-scène is the color red, which dominates the manor's interiors and appears in the frequent dissolves and facial close-ups Bergman uses to overlap the memories and emotions of the four female characters. Red comes to represent their shared biological and psychological bond as well as the way in which every woman acts out a facet of the others' personalities. Blood red also signifies the occasions of emotional and physical violence that the characters inflict upon each other and their own bodies, while connoting the wound of separation from the mother, which the three sisters experience with particular intensity.

The third shade that dominates the screen is black, which refers not only to Agnes's impending death but to the loneliness that accompanies the psychological and existential recognition that childhood is over.[26] The haunting sound of crying children on the sound track is a recurrent reminder of internal abandonment, of object loss, of "the fear in which that to be feared is never put into words."[27] In a sense all three sisters have become orphans. For example, a shot of an empty crib fades to a close-up of Agnes holding a white rose, triggering her memory of her lonely childhood. And in the opening sequence of the film we learn that the young child of Anna, the family servant, is dead. The sickly Agnes in her final hours of life becomes Anna's surrogate child, their bonding a redemptive act of love for both. In one of the film's most famous images, Bergman composes an archetypal tableau of Anna cradling Agnes against her naked breast, in the manner of a pietà.[28] This icon of unity between mother and suffering child appears at a moment suspended between dream, fantasy, and "reality," or in Bergman's words, "a space in the midst of a chaos of confusion and conflicting impulses, a space in which with a joint effort, imagination and the wish for form crystallize a component in my sense of being alive: the unreasonable and never ending longing for fellowship, the clumsy attempts to do away with distance and isolation."[29] Yet the child's impulse toward unity with the mother carries within it the inevitability of dissolution. The desire to return to the womb constitutes in part a death wish. The huge black Victorian bed with its luxurious white sheets and deep red covers in which Agnes spends her final days evokes women's conflicted emotional relationship to the realities of childbirth, sexuality, and death.

Cries and Whispers is structured around first-person sequences that embody each sister's subjectivity in dreams and fantasies. Significantly, the film's first major flashback is devoted to Agnes, whose idyllic memories of the lush grounds of the family's manor house on a bright summer day contrast sharply with the bleak landscape of the film's present. This idealized vision captures Agnes's desire to return to "preoedipal bliss," when the child is united with the mother. Against the flourishing greenery of the Edenic garden, Agnes's memory of her mother shows this elegant but severe woman as both strikingly beautiful and unapproachable, her white gown setting off her black hair and her distant blue eyes. Agnes recalls how she spied on her mother with childish admiration; the camera adopts her point of view as she watches the graceful figure from her hiding places behind trees and curtains. Her voyeuristic compulsion embodies an overwhelming curiosity and desire for a mother whose subjectivity remained mysterious and elusive to the child. As we see the mother seated in a garden chair, overcome by her ennui and despair, Agnes recalls in voice-over:

> Mother is in my thoughts nearly every day. I loved Mother to such a jealous extreme. Because she was so gentle and beautiful and alive—and so everlastingly present. But she could also be cold and playfully cruel. Yet I couldn't help feeling sorry for her, and now that I'm older I understand her much better. I should like so much to see her again and tell her what I have understood of her ennui, her longing and loneliness.

Only as an adult is Agnes able to comprehend her mother's despair and alienation in the stifling confines of her husband's house, but as a child she could not grasp how her own craving for love often left her mother feeling oppressed. Agnes could only experience the rejections that in time left her incapable of becoming a mother herself; she is the eternal daughter. And yet, perhaps because of this, the film focuses first on Agnes's memories, which represent a retroactive reconciliation with her mother. And through Agnes, *Cries and Whispers* at its end returns to a moment of happiness and love between the sisters. It suggests, to use Bruce Kawin's words, that "the burden of the film . . . appears to be on the side of loving, of community, and of self-knowledge."[30]

Agnes' vision is dramatized in two flashbacks. In the first, Agnes remembers the magic-lantern shows at Twelfth Night celebrations, where she always felt left out while her mother and her sister Maria shared secrets and intimacies. Tellingly, "Hänsel and Gretel" is the featured attraction of the show—a fairy tale that mirrors Agnes's experience of emotional abandonment and comments ironically on the lack of solidarity among the sisters. Moreover, the themes of oral desire for and aggression toward the mother at the heart of the fairy tale reflect the disturbed preoedipal relations among the women in *Cries and Whispers*.[31] The scene establishes the jealousy and competition between the sisters for the love of the mother, a rivalry that, as Toni McNaron observes, "predates any potential struggle over a father's attention and affection."[32] Agnes's other childhood memory involves an encounter in the red drawing room, when Agnes unexpectedly comes upon her mother in a disturbed and pensive mood. "I went up to her. Then she gave me a look so full of sorrow that I nearly burst into tears. But instead I began to stroke her cheek. She closed her eyes and let me do it. We were very close to each other that time."

The part of the film devoted to Maria and her memories expands our understanding of how her mother's adoration for her as the youngest daughter has shaped Maria's adult narcissistic personality. Not surprisingly, this sequence begins in her childhood room, with the adult Maria surrounded by her dolls and dollhouse. Bergman cuts back and forth between close-ups of Maria's childlike, self-absorbed face on the bed pillows, the dolls in the dollhouse, and a wall portrait of her mother. The intercutting suggests the resemblances between Maria and her mother (a likeness underlined by having Liv Ullmann play both parts), while the images of the dollhouse subtly hint that the mother's attachment to Maria is related to the ways in which her beautiful daughter mirrors her own grandiose self-image as a member of Sweden's upper class. For Maria as much as for her mother, social position is a source of narcissistic gratification. And other people become for Maria really no more than dolls, "subjectively arranged in her life as narcissistic tributaries."[33] Maria continually seeks fleeting sexual gratification and pleasure without emotional involvement. At one point, her former lover, the coldly intellectual doctor, speaks of her indifference toward other people as they both look into a vanity mirror. Bergman's use of the vanity mirror as a frame for this exchange suggests that the doctor is in fact projecting his own indifference and narcissism on to Maria. She ironically asks him: "Can all that be actually seen there? I think you're joking with me. You see it in yourself." Yet the mother's grandiosity has left Maria with disturbed object relations of her own, resulting in her pure pleasure seeking without intimacy.

Although Maria denies her own strong preoedipal ties to her mother by shifting her desire completely to the opposite sex, she functions as an exact double of her mother in the eyes of her two sisters, haunting them with memories of the mother's erratically impulsive displays of affection and rejection. Throughout the film Bergman alternates scenes of each sister's isolation with those in which they share rare moments of communion and togetherness, as when (in an extended take) Karin and Maria cleanse and dress Agnes, and Maria comforts her by reading from Charles Dickens's *Pickwick Papers*. At other times, Karin and particularly Maria shrink from touching Agnes and retreat into their insular selves. Two scenes toward the end of the film show them mimicking the very pattern of approach and withdrawal typical of the mother and Agnes. Following Agnes's death, Maria approaches her sister Karin after many years of estrangement and superficial communication. The camera focuses on Maria as she appeals to Karin to consider their common history as sisters:

> I want us to be friends. I want us to touch each other. After all, we're sisters. We have so many memories in common—we can talk about our childhood! Karin, my dear, it's so strange that we don't touch one another, that we talk only impersonally. Why won't you be my friend? We've been both happy and unhappy, we could go on talking for days and nights on end, we could laugh and cry together, we could hold each other tight. Sometimes as I move about here in the home of our childhood, where everything is both strange and familiar, I feel as if I'm mixed up in a dream and that we're going to be affected by something decisive, something that will change our lives once and for all.

Karin, the most alienated and repressed sister, refuses to respond to Maria's entreaties; instead of answering, she picks up Agnes's diary and reads a passage that seems to echo Maria's desire for companionship: "I have received a gift of human contact and kindness. I think it is called grace." After Maria approaches her, Karin allows her sister to touch her face and to embrace her as tears fill her eyes. But she suddenly withdraws and screams, "Don't touch me! There is no pity, no relief, no help, nothing." Her neurotic fear of merging with her sister ultimately represents the fear of a dissolution of self, a defensive response to the loss of boundaries in the preoedipal bond between mother and (female) child. "[Our mother] was nearly always impatient," writes Agnes in her diary, "mostly with Karin. I was sickly and puny as a child, but Karin was always scolded, because mother thought she was so clumsy and unintelligent."[34] Since early childhood, Agnes and Karin had offended their mother's narcissistic grandiosity, the former by her sickliness and the latter by her lack of grace. Only Maria completely mirrored their mother's beauty, perfection, and grace.

In adult life, Karin desperately desires affection but at the same time recoils from any kind of emotional connection or touch, especially with Maria, who so resembles their mother. Karin's complete severing of her emotional ties to her mother is closely related to her fear of death. Hence she stubbornly refuses to accept Agnes's death, especially its physical reality. "It's disgusting and meaningless. She has already started to decay. She has great spots on her hands." Karin refuses to acknowledge the dead child within herself and is therefore unable to comfort her dying younger sister.

There is one moment in the film where Karin allows herself to overcome her fears of death and dissolution of self and to be seduced by Maria. She guiltily pursues Maria and asks for her forgiveness after having rejected and abused her at the dinner table. What follows is another one of Bergman's "spaces in the midst of a chaos of confusion and conflicting impulses," a beautifully choreographed "ballet" of wordless touching between the two sisters, accompanied by a Bach cello piece. This nonverbal moment of connection, similar to the one between the depressed mother and Agnes, here conveys joy and exhilaration. The camera pans back and forth between Karin's and Maria's profiled faces as they cry happily and passionately stroke each other in a moment of great emotional release and forgiveness. Their meeting is one of the most erotically charged moments in the film.

Karin tries to recapture this moment as she and Maria are about to leave the manor house after Agnes's funeral. Maria refuses to acknowledge their new intimacy, regressing to a comfortably shallow level of family ritual: "Look after yourself and give my love to the children. I expect I'll see you again at Twelfth Night, as usual." The reference evokes the magic lantern shows where Maria was close to her mother while Agnes and Karin were excluded. The camera again focuses in close-up on the two women's faces, but they are not framed in the same shot: as Karin sees Maria's empty, distracted face, she accuses her of being preoccupied with her waiting husband rather than with their new-found intimacy and compassion. In this cold farewell scene (which recalls Anna's departure from Ester in *The Silence*), Maria's empty gestures suggest those of her mother, who always adopted a playfully cruel air when rejecting Agnes's pleas for affection.

In her own flashback sequence, Karin unconsciously plays out her aggression toward her mother in her antagonistic marriage to the cold, sardonic Frederik. Feminist psychoanalytic critics such as Juliet Mitchell and Nancy Chodorow have emphasized that a girl never completely separates from her mother, the first love-object, and that preoedipal conflicts often underlie male-female relationships. "Thus behind every girl's love for the father, there lurks her love for the mother; for every 'normal' woman who chooses her husband on the acceptable model of her father, the difficulties that ensue are just as likely to echo those that arose with the love and hate for the mother."[35]

In Karin's memory sequence, she is sitting at the dinner table with Frederik when she breaks a wine glass, spilling the blood red wine on the white tablecloth. The symbolic reference to defloration is obvious, especially in light of the subsequent scene when Karin mutilates herself with a sliver of the broken glass. The gesture is an unconscious expression of her hatred of her husband, her desire to "spill his blood." But the gesture is also overdetermined, since some of the aggression Karin feels toward Frederik is directed unconsciously toward her mother. Indeed, Bergman's script implies a parallel between the feelings of hatred Frederick arouses in Karin, through his condescending criticisms of her clumsiness, and those toward Karin's mother, who expresses annoyance with Karin's gaucheness as a child. Karin says to Maria: "My husband says I'm a fumbler and he's right. I'm clumsy. My hands are too big, you see." In addition, Karin compulsively repeats the act of breaking her wine glass during her dinner with Maria, the sister who intrapsychically stands in for the mother.

Karin's mutilation of her genitals in the following scene, one of the most shocking moments in modern cinema, has been heavily criticized by feminist critics. After her husband leaves the dining room, Karin fingers a shard of the broken glass, obsessively repeating the phrase, "It's all a tissue of lies." The ambiguous "it" might refer to any number of things: her feminine identity, her hypocritical marriage and perception of her husband's repulsive demands for sex, her life as a woman in a repressive society, her relationship with her distant and critical mother, or her own brittle, cosmetic social persona. Retiring to her bedroom, Karin undresses in front of a mirror that refracts her into three reflections, a visual comment on her schizoid emotional life, which will momentarily find its breaking-point. The servant Anna helps Karin to remove her heavy layers of Victorian female garments, a costume that conceals a psychic life in the process of being crushed by the weight of social pretense and by Karin's consequential anger, long repressed.

Bergman's characterization of Karin's and her family's psychological history in *Cries and Whispers* suggests to me that he is interested in tracing the perverse logic and indeed the most violent and tragic manifestations of repression in Karin. Longtime emotional inhibition transforms her passionate anger toward her mother and husband into irrational rage. Through her masochistic act of mutilation Bergman reveals how her feminine identity and her sexuality have become implicated in her thoughts as the sources of her rage and depression. As a prelude to the violence, however, Bergman demonstrates the confused and unpredictable orbit of Karin's aggression, as she suddenly strikes out in her dressing room at Anna. In a moment of tense eroticism, Karin feels Anna staring at her exposed, vulnerable body and, unable to bear the scrutiny, she abruptly slaps her. Karin's overreaction to Anna's candid looking suggests that there is more at issue here than either a violation of personal privacy or a transgression of class boundaries and etiquette. Rather, Karin's inability to endure any kind of physical or emotional closeness for fear of disparagement and rejection is a sign of her frigidity. The underlying emotional dynamic of Karin's violent reproach of Anna is not unlike that of her mother's withdrawal from Agnes's offer of affection earlier in the film. Oppressed by her social and familial relationships, Karin is equally burdened by her denial of her feelings.

A number of important elements in Bergman's rendering of the harrowing mutilation scene suggest how Karin's masochism represents an anger whose "real" object is the patriarchal system that has in fact driven her "mad with rage." First, she is dressed in a white nightgown, on one level a link to her mother but on another ironically conjuring up the male ideal of the archetypal virginal bride. Second, the scene ends with Karin entering her husband's bedroom to display to him her bloody genitals, suggesting that her action appears to be an act of rebellion as well of self-hatred. By exhibiting her bloody genitals to her husband, she mocks his fetishistic desire, if not his male fears of castration. In another sense, her act is a violent and tragic repudiation of her mother, who apparently in Karin's eyes acquiesced to the patriarchal norms of Victorian marriage.[36] Paradoxically, for Karin's mother as well as for Karin, emotional intimacy represented a disturbing intrusion through the stiff layers of their Victorian social armor.

Maria's and Karin's similar flashbacks show their confusion over intimacy and female identity, and their sense of alienation as adult women. Maria's narcissism damages others, and Karin's repression of her conflict with her mother leads to her self-destruction, but both responses relate to their impaired object relations and their injured selves. Psychoanalysts have claimed that siblings sometimes serve as "bridging or connecting object[s]" that fulfill functions similar to the ones that Winnicott attributed to the "transitional object," the familiar and present object that provides comfort to the child during the stage of separation from mother.[37] *Cries and Whispers* stages this psychological dynamic at the moment of death—the most radical instance of separation. When in Anna's dream and fantasy sequence the dead Agnes asks her sisters to comfort her, both fail her. Too psychologically fragile to empathize and merge with their sister, they cannot fulfill the role of transitional object.

Cries and Whispers ends with a nostalgic memory scene that expresses a rare moment of emotional connection and unity among the sisters. The scene is triggered by Anna's reading of a passage from Agnes's diary, the only memento she has chosen to take from Agnes's possessions. As we hear Agnes's voice-over the film dissolves into an image of a glorious, bright autumn day reminiscent of Agnes's memory of her mother walking in the summer garden. In this sequence, the three sisters are together again in the garden, walking among the fallen leaves, dressed in white like their mother and carrying white parasols. Anna, wrapped in a white shawl, is accompanying them. The three sisters sit together in a garden swing. Rocked by the mother figure, Anna, as if in a cradle, Agnes experiences a moment of intense closeness and love with her sisters: "I felt the presence of their bodies, the warmth of their hands. I closed my eyes tightly, trying to cling to the moment and thinking: Come what may, this is happiness. Now, for a few minutes, I can experience perfection."

While some critics have interpreted this scene as "cruelly ironic" or an "illusory" moment of happiness and connection,[38] it is a moment that has been prepared for, as it recalls earlier scenes in the film—Agnes's silent communion with her mother, the montage of Karin's and Maria's tender caresses, Maria's memory in the death room of her intimacy with

Agnes as children. While Agnes's vision of sororal love and happiness exists only in the memory of a dying woman, the experience of the three sisters mothering one another is a significant affirmation of life, an epiphany that momentarily redeems the feelings of alienation, aggression, and death.

The interrelations between the adult sisters reactivate the original bond with the mother, but we are not dealing with a mere maternal transference relationship here. Rather the sister bond represents a psychological space where earlier object relations of *both* a preoedipal and an oedipal nature are renegotiated. In *Cries and Whispers*, which reveals the lack of an empathic mirroring response from the original mother, the sisters do not seek contact through pleasure but in pain. Their damaged relationships with each other and with their emotionally unavailable mother are framed within a corrupted and damaging patriarchy. The sisters' psychological return to the mother's body elicits conflicted emotions that tap into the viewer's own unconscious desires and fears about boundaries and emotional needs. Bergman's film remains all the more powerfully unsettling for its refusal to offer a clear resolution of those conflicts.

In my view, Bergman's exploration of sister- and mother-daughter bonds in *Cries and Whispers* should not be dismissed as some demonization of women's psychological relationships. If Bergman fails to elaborate the possibilities of a productive and fulfilling reciprocity between women, it is not for his lack of understanding the oppressive social morality through which women in this era become divided against each other. In Margarethe von Trotta's work, as I discuss in the chapter ahead, the kinds of ambivalence between sisters that Bergman dramatizes are more fully conceptualized in respect to the social and political. In von Trotta's trilogy of sister films, the intersubjective relations between siblings reveal, as they do in *The Silence* and *Cries and Whispers*, the social and political forces that shape the past and oppressively haunt the sisters' adult identities. In contrast to Bergman's films, however, the women in von Trotta's trilogy also find in their common sororal history sources of self-understanding and new ways to connect to the world.

The Politics of Intersubjectivity

The Sister Films of Margarethe von Trotta

The women in Trotta's films regard each other. They are no longer objects, things to be seen. They are in much closer relationship to one another, and between sisters, this is almost to be expected.

H.-B. Moeller, "The Films of Margarethe von Trotta"

I automatically spin out the story of sisters or of sisters and friends—encounters with our other sides, the unknown aspects of our personae which at the same time seem so familiar. I imagine meetings with ourselves in other people's bodies, stories of mirror images.

Margarethe von Trotta

German director Margarethe von Trotta's feature films, with their introspective portraits of the psychic bonds between women, have often been compared to Ingmar Bergman's chamber dramas of the 1960s and 1970s.[1] Her second, *Sisters, or The Balance of Happiness* (1979), one of an unplanned trilogy of sister films including *Marianne and Juliane (Die Bleierne Zeit*, 1982) and *Three Sisters (Paura e amore*, 1988), is particularly reminiscent of Bergman's work: its emphasis on the emotional flow between two women, their mutual dependency and intersection of internal worlds, recalls Bergman's

147

The Silence, Persona, and *Cries and Whispers.*[2] By von Trotta's own account, Bergman and his films have been the greatest influence on her cinematic work. She credits him with introducing her to cinema when she first saw his films at the Cinémathèque in Paris in the early 1960s and then "fell in love" with the medium and its possibilities for representing inner psychic worlds. Von Trotta claims that her own and Bergman's cinematic visions are very similar, especially in their mutual emphasis on the exploration of the unconscious. "He [Bergman] sees himself in my films, and I recognize myself in him. We have an inner bond that manifests itself in our respective films."[3] Bruce Kawin, who describes Bergman's "mindscreen" cinema as one that "merges its characters' objective and subjective worlds in a complex first-person format that is as painful in its intimacy and 'realistic' in its style as it is hallucinatory," could just as easily be writing about von Trotta's films. Her works combine dreams, visions, ambiguous flashbacks, and personal obsessions within a "realist" framework of women struggling to negotiate their place in a patriarchal society.[4]

Von Trotta has nevertheless remained skeptical about Bergman's representation of women.[5] In her films, compared to Bergman's, sisters' shared psychic experiences are much more firmly grounded in specific social and political realities, and sisters' mutual challenges to each other's memories of their childhood become an impetus for change. The theme of the death of a sister at a moment of existential crisis is present in both directors' works, but with different accents. While the sisters in *The Silence* and those in *Cries and Whispers* all remain trapped in their intrapsychic worlds, von Trotta emphasizes sisters' struggles toward intersubjectivity, toward what Jessica Benjamin calls the paradoxical balance between sameness and difference, dependence and independence. Whereas in Bergman's films the recognition process between sisters goes awry, in von Trotta's the outcome is more optimistic, largely because she more fully explores and critiques the psychology of domination in its personal and political implications.

Von Trotta combines the psychological exploration of female relationships, which often take the form of a woman's rigorous self-examination through her sister, with the social and cultural conflicts of the post-1968 period in Germany (and Italy in *Three Sisters*). Her films articulate the difficulties that women confront in late twentieth-century societies afflicted with the legacies of historical violence and environmental destruction, personal and social guilt, isolation and anxiety. Like von Trotta herself, the female protagonists in her films grow up in the conservative period of the late 1940s and 1950s but question conventional roles for women in society; rebelling against those compromised positions in the 1960s and 1970s, they reassess the achievements and losses in their personal and professional lives during the neoconservative 1980s.

Von Trotta's films have been analyzed and categorized as either political statements or as psychograms of female identity with melodramatic overtones—approaches that have rarely been seen as mutually interdependent. By contrast, fellow German director Jutta Brückner, speaking on the occasion of von Trotta's reception of the Konrad-Wolf Prize from the Berlin Academy of the Arts in 1994, has observed that:

> The archimedic point from which Margarethe von Trotta directed her look at German history was the women's experience; making political films meant for her in the first instance questioning oneself and not only the "power" or the "institution." For the definition "the personal is the political," which was correctly understood as a challenge to the public realm, also means realizing what the private is all about and from where awakening and fundamental change take place.[6]

This dialectic between the public and private realm, which from von Trotta's viewpoint are mutually constitutive, shapes her vision of women's and sisters' relationships as political. As Gretchen Elsner-Sommer suggests, "By paying close attention to these relationships von Trotta brings into question the social and political systems which either sustain them or do not allow them to exist."[7] Moreover, her films trace how her female protagonists come to a keen self-awareness of the ways in which particular histories and social arrangements have molded them, and the relationship with the sister becomes vital to remembering.

Unlike the mothers in von Trotta's films, who are separated from their daughters by their own generation's circumstances—dominated by their husbands, trapped in conventional marriages, and altogether too compromised by their complicity in Germany's fascist past—the daughters struggle to define their identities in relationship to each other, seeking personal and professional fulfillment in an era quite different from their mothers'. Oppressed by her subservient position in the patriarchal family and state, the mother falls victim to depression and is often unable to perform the role of the maternal, nurturing parent, failing to connect emotionally with her adult daughters. Her influence on her daughters' identity formation thus becomes palpable through her absence.

In lieu of the mother's affirming presence, the connection between sisters takes on primary importance in von Trotta's films, although, as Jutta Brückner has written, their connection is not necessarily harmonious or harmless. As they become a medium for mutually exploring memories and the past, their resistance to each other—as much as their desire for communication and intimacy—drives them to critically examine themselves; their intersubjective knowledge is thus linked to the "retrieval of history" in both a personal and social sense.[8]

Sisters, or The Balance of Happiness

In 1988, Barbara Quart wrote: "It is the quest for wholeness that is the preoccupation of von Trotta's entire sister series," an insight that to some extent still holds true.[9] The adult sisters in von Trotta's works are often drawn to each other because they represent opposite poles of identity, as though their complementary qualities attract each other. But their quest is not a neoromantic one for organic wholeness, but a modern one, beset with tragedy and uncertainty, and possibly reflects an awareness of the tattered fabric of relationships—even the most intimate ones—in modern German society.

Perhaps no single film in her oeuvre is more revealing in this respect than *Sisters, or The Balance of Happiness*, which von Trotta has called a "soulpainting, a story of interior life," the story of the relationships and interlocking psyches of two sisters and a female friend.[10] The central character is the older sister, Maria (Jutta Lampe), an executive secretary who lives almost solely for her work, administering to her kind but manipulative boss "like an angel." Maria financially supports her younger sister, Anna (Gudrun Gabriel), a graduate student in biology, and the siblings live together in a dark, claustrophobic apartment. All these circumstances intensify, as von Trotta has pointed out, their emotional interdependency. Anna feels isolated with her exam books, her self-doubts, and her uncertainty about the value of scientific knowledge and progress. Maria's relentless drive toward success, which is consistently linked in the diegesis of the film to other forms of social domination, leaves Anna feeling alienated and anxiety ridden. When Maria becomes involved with Maurice, her boss's son, Anna feels neglected and reproaches her sister for not spending enough time with her. All their lives the two sisters have been locked into an unhealthy balance of domination and submission, at their own psychic expense. When Anna commits suicide out of existential despair and as an act of revenge against her sister, Maria represses this knowledge and refuses to deal with her emotions. Haunted by her dead sister in nightmares and fantasies, she unconsciously turns a spirited young typist from her office, Miriam, into a substitute for her dead sister, financing her foreign language courses and inviting her to move into her apartment. However, Miriam is not as fragile as Anna was and resists Maria's attempts to control her life. After speaking to Maria's mother and discovering Anna's diary, Miriam realizes she must extricate herself from the kinds of emotional pressures with which Maria had imprisoned Anna. Suddenly alone for the first time, Maria confronts herself and begins her search for a new inner balance; she allows herself to grieve for her sister, whom she only now recognizes as an individual, albeit a sibling who had come to represent an unacknowledged part of herself. Significantly, Maria takes up Anna's diary, writing her first entry on the page where her sister had left off: "I shall try to learn to dream while I live, Anna. I shall try to be Maria *and* Anna."

There is a strong case to be made for reading Margarethe von Trotta's repeated, even obsessive, use of the sister constellation in her films in autobiographical terms (see the introduction to part 3). Her discovery of an older half sister during the production of *Sisters* provides a rich psychobiographical context for her consistent interest in female doubles, the merging and exchange of female identities, and the complex relationship between female subjectivities, a connection the director herself makes.

> I sometimes think that by unconsciously knowing I had a sister but never being able to experience that knowledge, I incorporated or internalized the "other." I internally lived a potential sister relationship that developed into a dualistic one. . . . I've always felt the duality very strongly and I've always been attracted to literature that deals with doubles, E.T.A. Hoffman's *Elixirs of the Devil* and Dostoevsky, for example, where the other becomes the mirror of the self or the self is divided. My films are always expressions of my unconscious but at the same time I think it goes back to my sister.[11]

This fixation on the theme of doubles has, to be sure, cultural as well as autobiographical roots. Critics such as Barton Byg, Lucy Fischer, and Martin Donougho have commented on von Trotta's indebtedness to the image of the double in Romantic literature and German Expressionist film, and she certainly alludes to this legacy in the diegesis of her films and in her use of expressionistic cinematic codes.[12] However, along with feminist critics such as E. Ann Kaplan and Janice Mouton,

I read her use of the sister constellation as more than a metaphor for the split inner self or a divided postwar Germany. Her nuanced psychological portraits of sisters invite an analysis of the intersubjective dimension of the bond. As Jutta Brückner astutely observes, "the motif of the double appears, not romantically coded, but rather as the opposite pole of another identity, sometimes in the harsh opposition of female and male characteristics, at other times as necessary complements of qualities that are fascinating in the other woman. For it is no longer a matter of melodramatically juxtaposing vamp and nice girl, good and evil mother."[13]

Von Trotta complicates the Romantic legacy of the double—that split-off part of the self, which Romantic and Expressionist texts typically turn into an evil other that must be destroyed, yet returns to haunt the self. In my view, her films critique the psyche's defensive posture of domination and narcissistic merging, emphasizing the need for the integration of opposites and the recognition of differences among women. Von Trotta's films represent above all a cinema of remembering rather than repression, in which self-recognition is achieved through apprehending the other's individuality.

The opening shots of *Sisters* immediately engage the viewer in what Quart calls a "fairy tale archetypal dream-like structure." As the voice-over of a young girl reads a fairy tale about two sisters lost in the woods, the camera tracks forward into a darkening, bare-trunked forest intercut with the image of two young sisters, Maria and Anna, huddled on a bed as the older reads the story to the younger one. The fairy tale world of "once upon a time" and the dark woods usher the viewer into the realms of memory and the unconscious, into the internal world of childhood that underlies the relationship between the adult sisters in the "present tense" of the film.[14]

Like a number of modern films that self-consciously allude to fairy tales about siblings lost in the forest, such as Bergman's *Cries and Whispers*, Krueger's *Manny and Lo*, and Ogrodnik's *Ripe*, the story of orphaned siblings who leave the parental home and embark on a journey through the unknown forest symbolizes the psychological development toward adulthood and individuation, fraught with fear and danger, particularly for women in a society in which power is held by men. In the fairy tale told in *Sisters*, the younger sister is tired and wants to rest from the long walk but her older sibling presses her to move on to escape the dangerous beasts lurking in the forest. This narrative within the film is not simply a return or "regression" to the imaginary state where there is no distinction between self and other (as Lucy Fischer argues): the forest itself is a site of terror and *difference*. As an intertextual moment, the fairy tale foreshadows both the extraordinary closeness of the sisters in adulthood and their problematic relationship of domination and submission. In childhood, Maria reads the tale to her frightened younger sister, Anna, who leans on her with affection and fear. As the film unfolds, Maria's attempts to protect her sister by urging her to be a successful scientist are revealed as a complicated guise for her own need to be needed and to control the relationship.

The forest image continues to mark critical junctures in the film. After an adult quarrel between the sisters, the motif triggers Anna's memory of their childhood interdependency, a sign of her increasing doubts about her ability to forge a personal identity apart from Maria's expectations for her. The image reappears after Anna's suicide as a reminder of Maria's tragic domination of her, and again at the end of the film when Maria pledges in Anna's diary that she will try to incorporate dreams into her daily life.

The image of the dark forest is linked through the mise-en-scène to Anna, the melancholy and introverted sister, who is closely identified with nature, imagination, and intuition. The opening shots of the woods fade into the dark room filled with plants and terrariums that contain Anna's iguanas and lizards. Maria, on the other hand, is allied with the masculine world of commerce and competition—brightly lit, ultramodern, and antiseptic office spaces, an alienating corporate environment that is closer to the sterile laboratory in which Anna reluctantly performs DNA cloning experiments under the watchful eye of a male professor. Anna yearns for a world where people live in harmony with nature, where inner and outer worlds remain interconnected. At one point, she sits in a large anonymous lecture hall, listening to a male science professor expound on the possibilities of genetic engineering. She is terrified of the ethical consequences of science (a fear with particular historical relevance in Germany in light of the pseudo-scientific experimentation of Nazi doctors). In her diary she expresses her fears of a society that can produce genetic clones but is incapable of dealing with love.

Cloning, which in the 1990s has become a much-debated scientific reality, is the central metaphor in *Sisters* for the dangers of modern doubling and suppression of difference in the sister relationship: it refers to von Trotta's feminist critique of a society's madness and destructiveness, its exploitation of the human gene pool in the name of scientific progress. This recurrent theme in von Trotta's oeuvre links the artificial reproduction of sameness and the obliteration of difference to a male fear of death and a fascist suppression of the other. The clone also symbolizes the failed intersubjective dimension of the relationship between the two sisters—for even as Anna seeks Maria's attention and approval, she is afraid of her sister's domineering attempts to turn her into her "double," a clone of her success-oriented and corporate ethos.

After Anna returns from the lecture about genetic manipulation, she asks Maria whether she thinks copies of herself exist, which leads into a discussion about whether people are replaceable, particularly in the workplace. Anna's fears of the consequences of artificial reproduction as well as her anxiety about losing her identity are linked to the sisters' discussion of the role of women in the corporate world, where they may be made obsolete at any time by computers or more efficient, cheaper labor. The fear of the double is here both a fear of the dominating psychic other and a political anxiety of being destroyed in the capitalist system. Maria admits to her sister in a moment of fatigue that "everyone is replaceable"; however, later she insists to Miriam that qualified secretaries will always be needed.

Numerous other scenes critically reference the theme of doubling and underline Anna's struggle to forge her own identity while remaining connected to her sister. For example, when Anna decides to become more independent from Maria and goes to work for an elderly blind woman, she is confronted with an ominous image of sisterhood in old age. Hearing the blind woman's older sister scolding her sibling, Anna is confronted with a mirror image of her own symbiotic relationship with Maria. Moreover, early in the film, we see Anna taking three Polaroid snapshots of herself in the mirror. As she watches her ghostly image slowly developing on the photographic paper, she appears to be seeking confirmation of her separate existence through a triple exposure of her face; however, the scene also subtly foreshadows the transference relationship between Anna, Maria, and Miriam.

A similarly overdetermined use of the mirror occurs when Anna remembers a joyous childhood scene: Maria and Anna as children are trying out their mother's lipstick and kissing each other in front of a three-way mirror that refracts the sisters into multiple doubles of each other. Janice Mouton has rightly seen this scene as an important intersubjective moment in the sisters' childhood relationship, as a sign of their ability to together discover, create, and inhabit an imaginary space of play, which only Anna is able to maintain in adulthood.[15] The multiple images in the mirror should not be seen only as an "infinite regression suggestive of a retreat to the imaginary," as Lucy Fischer has claimed. Rather, they throw the intersubjective moment into question: at what point does creative mutuality and recognition between siblings become overshadowed by the possibility of domination and defensive insistence on "oneness"? Significantly, Anna later recalls this scene in a flashback when she is working in the science laboratory conducting genetic experiments, suggesting that her doubts about cloning are explicitly linked to her vexed symbiotic relationship with her sister. The juxtaposition of those scenes also once again raises the ethical question in a social context: when do the creative possibilities of science turn into destructive forms of control? The lipstick-mirror scene is a linchpin in the sisters' psychic history wherein sharing and difference coexist in a "balance of happiness." The scene is cinematically and dramatically echoed and developed in the relationship between Maria and Miriam, who first meet in the office bathroom in front of a mirror as Miriam asks Maria for a lipstick. The intersubjective potential of Maria's and Miriam's friendship is, however, overshadowed by Maria's later attempts to recreate Anna in Miriam.[16]

Another overdetermined instance of play between the sisters occurs when Anna and Maria visit their mother in the country: Anna gets out of the car, a red dot in the landscape, and walks along the road as Maria drives behind her in a teasing way. Maria then bumps her and Anna turns, laughing. The scene shows a more light-hearted moment between the sisters but also offers a visual correlative to Maria's efforts to push her sister along a professional path Anna does not choose for herself, which ultimately results in Anna's suicide. During the visit to their mother, the sisters quarrel over Maria's date with her boss's son, whose intrusion makes Anna feel abandoned. Maria, overwhelmed by her sister's emotional demands and jealous attacks, recalls that as a child she was playing with a friend when Anna stepped on a piece of glass to attract her attention.[17] Again, the childhood memory comments on their interdependent adult relationship: Maria's involvement with a man triggers Anna's jealousy and increasing self-destructive behavior. Significantly, Anna kills herself on the night that Maria decides to make love to Maurice.

Clearly, the suicide is more than a masochistic act of self-destruction; it is, as von Trotta has said, a positive act of rebellion against a society

that is "the byproduct of the hierarchical, patriarchal system based on effi-
ciency, merit, and obedience" that first draws rigid boundaries between
public and private spheres and then privileges the public persona over
imagination and the inner life.[18] As Maria's friend Fritz gently tells her
after Anna's death, "To not want success can be a sign of life." When
Maria reads Anna's diary, she finds a poem addressed to her: "Drive a stake
into my chest./So that I don't haunt you./Cut off my hand/when I am
dead,/bury it at the crossroads,/so that I don't return/to torture you. . . .
I killed myself/in opposition to *you*." This and other references to vam-
pirism and haunting ghosts as well as the expressionist style of Maria's
nightmares and fantasies are, according to Lucy Fischer, typical codes
from psychological suspense films, including Hitchcock's work and the
"female twin films" such as *Dark Mirror* (1946) and *A Stolen Life*
(1939/46).[19] (They also, of course, recall the German Expressionist cinema of Murnau's *Nosferatu*, Wiene's *Cabinet of Dr. Caligari*, and Ingmar
Bergman's later use of those tropes in *Persona* and *Hour of the Wolf*.) These
codes take on a particular psychological coloration in *Sisters*, since Anna,
who had felt dominated by Maria's attempts to turn her into a double,
returns as a "vampire" in Maria's dreams to devour her. Images of Anna's
ghost appearing Dracula-like in Maria's doorways and eating at the table
reinforce the theme of psychic incorporation, for they signify Anna's
vengeful reversal of Maria's own desire for control.

Maria consciously denies her role in Anna's suicide: "I shared everything with her," she claims. "Her death was the highest expression of her
selfishness." But her fantasies tell another tale. In a revealing mirror
shot, she sees not her own reflection but Anna dressed in Maria's business suit and pinned-up hairstyle. This mirror vision contrasts with the
earlier flashback to childhood, where the sisters take pleasure in gazing
in the mirror at their refracted, multiple selves; for now their twinlike
sameness is embodied in grotesque images—Anna has indeed finally
become Maria's double. H.-B. Moeller has analyzed these optical reflections in the same frame in terms of how the sisters' exchange of roles
leads to a merging of personal polarities.[20] However, this exchange also
foreshadows Maria's growing self-recognition and eventual acceptance
of Anna's individuality and difference.

Drawing on the trope of the double as a split identity, Lucy Fischer
views the relationship between Anna and Maria primarily as embodying stereotypical female and male characteristics: Anna is cinematically
coded as highly feminine in her dependency on the more "masculine"

Maria. Fischer also sees the sensual intimacy between the sisters in a number of scenes as further evidence of their resemblance to a heterosexual "couple."[21] Maria is not always confined to the "masculine" position, however, as numerous scenes in the film suggest: not only is she often shown wearing a sheer, feminine blouse with her suits and skirts; she also clearly plays a maternal figure, if an ambivalent one, to her younger sister, at one point holding a distraught Anna to her breast to comfort her (not unlike the motherly servant Anna holds Agnes in Bergman's *Cries and Whispers*). (After Anna's death, we see Miriam cradling a grieving Maria in her arms in bed, in much the same posture. The reversal of roles—that of mother and child—prefigures Miriam's role as a catalyst for change in Maria.) Moreover, after Anna's suicide, Maria and her mother, in an almost wordless choreography of bodies that recalls scenes from *Cries and Whispers* and *Persona*, wear identical black sweaters as they pack up Anna's belongings. At one point, Maria's and her mother's bodies overlap into one, connecting mother and daughter in their shared grief despite their differences, foreshadowing Maria's eventual need to work through her sister's death and accept her melancholia and dreams.

Maria's ambiguous gender position is underscored by von Trotta through the connections she draws between Maria's maternal solicitude toward Anna, her severe demand for perfection, and her subservient role vis-à-vis her own male superior. An early sequence in the film cuts from Maria cooking dinner for Anna to her preparing a morning snack for her employer. It is precisely Maria's identification *as a woman* with the values of the patriarchal order that comes under scrutiny in *Sisters*. Despite her ambition and assertiveness, she is ultimately a mere servant to her boss, fulfilling a stereotypically female role by meeting his every demand, even to the point of volunteering to type his son's dissertation without pay. Her behavior is thus just as "masochistic," perhaps even more insidiously so, than her "visibly" softer, feminine sister, and Anna challenges Maria when she hears of Maria's decision to take on additional work. Miriam, whom Maria later sponsors to become a foreign language secretary so she can obtain a higher-paying position, also questions Maria's belief in "professional advancement" for women in the corporate world. For Miriam, this merely means performing the same kind of secretarial work on a higher level. Von Trotta carries over her critique of women's ambivalent positions of success in a man's world to *Marianne and Juliane*, where the politically more radical sister Marianne is shown making coffee for her fellow male terrorists. Von Trotta's feminist critique is not limited to the binary oppositions between masculinity and femininity but is also critically concerned with deconstructing women's different and sometimes contradictory ways of responding to inequality and struggling for their place against opposition.

In *Sisters* as in *Marianne and Juliane*, the death of one sister initiates the surviving sibling's inner voyage of critical self-evaluation and self-discovery and opens a path toward integration of different modes of being in the world. It is only in the last act of *Sisters* that Maria is finally able to work through the mutual dependency that Anna had described earlier: "You only need me to need you." In the transference relationship with Miriam, whom Maria takes in and supports, she is at last forced to confront those aspects of her relationship with Anna that have remained unresolved. For Miriam, who is free of Anna's childhood dependencies, comes to understand the family dynamics after discovering Anna's anguished diary and visiting Maria's and Anna's mother. She breaks away from Maria, who has unconsciously attempted to make her into Anna's "double." Significantly, Maria takes away Miriam's lipstick during their final violent confrontation over her desire to live her own life. This scene deliberately echoes in a contrapuntal manner the earlier flashback of the young sisters sharing their mother's lipstick in front of the mirror. It is precisely Miriam's resistance to Maria, her demand to be recognized by Maria as different from Anna, that prompts Maria to find a balance in herself between the doer and the dreamer.

After Miriam leaves Maria alone in her apartment, two contrasting scenes conclude the film and highlight Maria's understanding that she must change. In the first, her employer dictates a perfunctory message of condolence to Maria, treating death as just another formality. Maria's loss of her sister is here both evoked by and summarily dispensed with in the public world of business. In the following and final scene, the camera moves into a close-up of Maria writing in Anna's diary and then cuts to the dark forest of the childhood fairy tale, signifying Maria's act of remembering and mourning her sister, her movement toward greater psychic equilibrium, and her journey into the familiar but unknown heart of herself.

Marianne and Juliane

The act of remembering and mourning a sister as an other—or what Thomas Elsaesser has called "identification across difference"—is also the central preoccupation of Margarethe von Trotta's third film, *Marianne and*

Juliane, her most critically acclaimed but most controversial work.[22] More explicitly concerned than *Sisters* with radical politics in the 1970s and the consequences of Germany's refusal to confront its fascist past after the war, the film remains von Trotta's most rigorous investigation of the ways in which the intertwining discourses of nationhood and patriarchy shape, indeed distort, the personal and political development of two sisters.

Marianne and Juliane is loosely based on the lives of the Ensslin sisters. Gudrun Ensslin was a member of the radical leftist Baader-Meinhof terrorist group in West Germany in the 1970s and died under suspicious circumstances in the Stuttgart-Stammheim maximum security prison in 1977. After Gudrun's death, her sister, Christiane, embarked on a campaign to disprove the government's claim that Gudrun and the other inmates had committed suicide. Gudrun and Christiane Ensslin were born during the bombings of World War II and grew up in the authoritarian family of a Lutheran minister in the repressive 1950s. That decade—the "leaden times," referred to in the film's German title and taken from a Hölderlin poem—was characterized by a national repression of guilt over Nazism. Like many other women of that generation, including von Trotta herself, the sisters became politically active in the 1968 student movement. Ultimately, however, they pursued different political directions: Christiane became a feminist journalist with *Emma* (the German equivalent of *Ms.*), while Gudrun turned to terrorism and violence against the dominant order, revolting against the remnants of fascism in the German government.

Despite *Marianne and Juliane*'s reference to this explosive political climate, it is less a "documentary biography" of the Ensslin sisters than a film about the need to remember and confront one's own history, in this instance the psychological and political costs of the failure of Germans to come to terms with their Nazi past. According to von Trotta, the Ensslin sisters were only "a point of departure" for a film more accurately described as a composite portrait of the postwar generation, which by 1968 was challenging the crimes of their parents' generation. This statement should caution against too literal an interpretation of *Marianne and Juliane* as a film "about" terrorism. Several critics, including Charlotte Delorme and Ellen Seiter, have faulted the film for a skewed representation of the terrorist sister. Conversely, the U.S. critic E. Ann Kaplan has deemphasized the specific political context in favor of a psychoanalytic interpretation of the film's family relationships. Despite her generally favorable review, however, Kaplan claims that von Trotta's cinematic realism diminishes the feminist potential of her films. Susan Linville's nuanced study of the "retrieval of history" in the film is, in my view, the only critical essay that seriously engages with its reflexive cinematic structure and von Trotta's aim to foreground the interdependency of the psychological and the sociohistorical.[23]

A reason for the controversial critical reception of *Marianne and Juliane* was, no doubt, the film's reference to recent political events that had divided political progressives over the "correct" approach to social and political change. That von Trotta developed its stocktaking of Germany's political development primarily through Juliane's perspective, the sister who is not at the radical center of terrorist activism in the 1970s, was considered evidence of her revisionist and conciliatory approach to the political conflicts between conservatives and the New Left. In retrospect, however, the director's "personal" approach to history—her dramatization of contemporary events through the complex history of two sisters—takes into account the fact that people do not experience their times according to the neat schemas of historical interpretation but instead act and react to events in a fragmentary and personal fashion.[24] It is precisely the film's depiction of the explosive relationship between sisters within a political context that highlights the debates between women over responses to violence, responsibility toward others, and women's work in the private and public realm, or what Kaplan has termed the intersecting "discourses of politics, feminism, and the family." The complex bonding and differentiation between the two sisters in *Marianne and Juliane* is a central psychological correlative for the political need to revisit the past from a critical vantage point. According to Linville, "the sisters' prison meetings paradoxically promote an intersubjectivity that lays the ground for Juliane's most interiorized self-reflection in relation to history: the self-reflection that evolves from processes of bonding and identity formation."[25] The contentious but intensely intimate relationship between the sisters thus represents the very medium through which the connection between past and present, the intersection of public and private, are explored.

In the beginning of the film, the sisters see themselves as polarized in their life-styles and their approach to politics. Juliane, the older (Jutta Lampe), works as a journalist with a feminist journal and tries to initiate empowerment for women and social change by "doing the unglamorous dirty work"—grassroots organizing from within the system, fighting antiabortion legislation, and educating women in the media. She lives with her empathic and liberal boyfriend, Wolfgang, with whom she has decided not to have children. Marianne (Barbara Sukowa), on the other hand, married and a mother, lived a normal bourgeois life until she left her family to join a left-wing terrorist group to fulfill her political vision. Yet early in the film other characters emphasize the sisters' similarities and point out the contradictions in their lives. For instance, Marianne's husband claims that his wife's radical critique of society reflects his and Juliane's own ideology, but that they are simply too cowardly or too sensible to act on their beliefs. Furthermore, Juliane's female doctor friend comments to Juliane: "You two are indeed strange women. You don't want any children, and Marianne abandons her child in order to save so-called humanity." Not to adopt the nurturing role of the mother is for both sisters a political choice, later linked to their ambivalent, "matrophobic" relationship with their own mother, who had never questioned her husband's authoritarian behavior and values. Marianne stands in radical opposition to her family history and her mother, refusing to allow her mother to visit her in prison, whereas Juliane attempts to reconnect with both her mother and her sister, appreciating both their positions. Juliane's more nuanced understanding of women's contradictory history in patriarchal societies is prefigured in an early self-reflexive scene, when she is shown composing a commentary on the paradoxical role of mothers in Nazi ideology, surveying a number of photographs that depict mothers and children in the Third Reich as both idealized supporters of Hitler and as abjected others, complicit participants and victims.

Throughout the film, the sisters live out and confront the contradictions of the older generation. *Marianne and Juliane*'s main narrative and mise-en-scène are structured confrontations and discussions between the sisters, particularly after Marianne is captured and imprisoned and Juliane spends much of her time visiting her and taking care of her needs. The camera repeatedly frames them sitting across from each other at tables in the prison's visiting room, arguing their different positions even as they strain to connect across the ideological divide that politically separates them.

Before Marianne is imprisoned, the sisters' first reunion occurs at a museum, where we see Marianne at the end of a long row of crumbling stone statues of male political and religious leaders, which embody the weight of an oppressive yet challenged historical past. Marianne stands in front of a stone angel, which recalls both her Christian upbringing and symbolically characterizes her as the "wild avenging angel" of her parents' generation's failed resistance to fascism.[26] The bitter confrontation between the sisters at the museum over Marianne's violent politics and her abandonment of her family and son eventually gives way to a temporary sense of solidarity when the skin that has formed on their untouched cups of cocoa triggers a shared childhood memory: it is 1947, and the young sisters are sitting next to each other at the family breakfast table with their parents. Their authoritarian father, a Lutheran minister, is delivering the morning prayer, emphasizing the German people's unexpiated, self-inflicted guilt. The two small girls meanwhile wait to drink their cocoa as it cools, exchanging glances of mock disgust as their father drones on.

This symbolically rich scene is the first of a series of visual statements that links the patriarchal family to national history, suggesting an inherent cultural association between familial and state authority in the correlation between the father's domination and the oppressive phalanx of stone memorials of the nation's political and spiritual fathers. Moreover, this flashback in the museum underlines the family history shared by Marianne and Juliane and its influence on their adult development. Finally, the young sisters' suppressed smiles suggest an emotional bond that, despite the sisters' adult differences, is played out in the rest of the film. This silent bond includes the mother, who sees her daughters' faces and does not admonish them. The flashback thereby serves to emotionally reconnect the adult sisters during their museum encounter by evoking their common history, reminding them of their mutual resistance to their strict, authoritarian upbringing in a society ruled by the German *Vater*.

Marianne and Juliane, told from Juliane's point of view, foregrounds the importance of personal memory in coming to terms with the past. Juliane actively seeks continuities between the present and past, whereas Marianne denies her personal history as bourgeois false consciousness. Juliane also investigates her sister's death in prison and prepares a counternarrative to the official demonization of her sister by the mainstream press. Linville has argued that the main body of the film can be seen as a giant flashback or a "mindscreen." Von Trotta herself claims that flashbacks in her films do not so much signal a conscious return to the past as the synchronicity of all time levels in a person, from past to present, from dreams to premonitions—a statement confirmed by Linville's insightful analysis of ambiguous time structures in von Trotta's films.[27]

Like Maria in *Sisters*, Juliane is the central consciousness in this film, the sister who must reidentify with and understand herself and her history through her sister; at the same time, she challenges Marianne to reexamine her own personal history which, in Juliane's view, cannot be divorced from her political identity. This trajectory is emphasized by repeated flashbacks to their childhood and adolescence. Juliane's memories prepare the viewer for her increasing identification with Marianne, as she tries to integrate her sister within her own psyche and understand their mutual development. In the conservative 1950s the young Juliane is the family rebel, while Marianne is submissive, her father's favorite daughter. As teenagers, Marianne plays classical music on the cello and dreams of devoting herself to relief work in Africa, while Juliane reads Sartre and mocks her sister for naive idealism and docile behavior. Juliane rebels at home and in school, defying her father and provoking his anger by wearing American "black jeans" instead of a skirt to school, a conflict that almost turns violent. When Juliane responds, "Why don't you hit me if you can reconcile that with your Sunday sermons!" the viewer is once again reminded of the "discipline and punishment" that links family and state—a theme that runs through the entire film. It is Marianne who sits on her father's lap to persuade him to allow Juliane to go to a school dance after he had forbidden it, as punishment for her defiance. Marianne dutifully recites poetry by Rilke during a German lesson at school, while Juliane suggests reading poems about anti-Semitism and concentration camps, such as Brecht's "Ballad of the Jewish Whore" or Paul Celan's "Death Fugue"; she is harshly reprimanded by the teacher for her provocations. The school building, which is reminiscent of the prison where the adult Marianne is later incarcerated, represents another site of repression—personal and historical—much as von Trotta herself experienced it in the 1950s.

In time, as Juliane and Marianne become young adults, the film reveals how they exchange roles and attitudes. Marianne adopts a more radical critique of patriarchal authority than Juliane's, rebelling against her bourgeois life-style and her parents as much as against the Vietnam war and imperialistic atrocities in the Third World. In many ways, Marianne's outrage at suffering and oppression in the world grows out of her Christian upbringing and echoes her father's moral righteousness—a connection underscored by images of the young Marianne and Juliane juxtaposed against a large painting of Christ's crucifixion, an icon of suffering that inspired both awe and fear in the girls.

Marianne's memory image of herself and Juliane as young girls, buttoning up each other's identical undershirts "even when they hated each other like poison," discloses the sisters' powerful childhood bond. Huddled in bed together, they each experience fear during the nighttime air bombings of World War II. As teenagers, they react to Resnais's documentary about Nazi concentration camps, *Night and Fog* (1955), by crying and vomiting in the bathroom as they attempt to deal with a guilt that is never discussed or worked through collectively.[28] These flashbacks enrich the conflicted relationship between Marianne and Juliane as adults. Intercut with the scenes of Juliane's visits to Marianne in prison, the memories emphasize Juliane's growing consciousness of the important psychological roles each sister has played in the other's life. As Janice Mouton writes, "Each is who she is because of her connection with the sister. Each is enabled, because of her involvement in the shared space of the relationship, to expand her definition of who she is."[29]

One of the central debates between the sisters—and one of the most politically controversial statements in the film—occurs after Juliane writes a personal portrait of her sister for the feminist journal for which she works in an attempt to counter the public's perception of the terrorists. Marianne categorically rejects Juliane's attempt to describe and understand her life from the perspective of her family history:

> Marianne: My story only begins with the others [the Baader-Meinhof group].
> Juliane: Why do you remember our nightshirts then? Why did you remember that?
> Marianne (dismissive): For your sake . . . damn it. The important thing is reality not words, you understand.
> Juliane: As if our childhood wasn't real. I also don't think we can liberate ourselves from our personal history.
> Marianne: I proved it.
> Juliane (sharply): What did you prove? A generation earlier . . . and you would have joined the BDM [Hitler's youth organization for girls] . . . I left that out of the article . . . for your sake, too.[30]

Juliane clearly sees the connections between their personal lives and experiences and their political choices, whereas Marianne refuses to acknowledge the painful familial and historical forces that shaped her personality and identity, and which thus affected her political commitments.

Both Susan Linville and Marc Silverman have pointed to *Marianne and Juliane*'s allusions to Sophocles' *Antigone*, which portrays political conflict between siblings and the state.[31] But von Trotta characteristically provides her own spin on *Antigone* by focusing on the siblings' relationship. Tellingly, she had collaborated with director Volker Schlöndorff on his segment of the anthology film *Germany in Autumn* (1977), which shows a television production of *Antigone* being canceled during the burials of members of the radical Red Army Faction because of its "inflammatory content." The segment shows the confrontation between Oedipus's daughters Antigone and Ismene over Antigone's defiance of Creon's patriarchal law so they can bury their brother, Polynices. The play dramatizes the conflict between Antigone's loyalty to family bonds and Ismene's submission to the law and politics of the state, represented by Creon. The transcription of political history into family drama in Schlöndorff's *Antigone* episode must have appealed to von Trotta's sensibilities. Indeed, the confrontations between Marianne and Juliane in the film's prison scenes may put the viewer in mind of the bitter quarrels between Antigone and Ismene, as Marianne attempts to draw her sister into joining the "revolutionary cause." But the film represents an important departure from that classical model of opposed sisters: indeed, von Trotta destabilizes the correlations between Marianne and Antigone and between Juliane and Ismene. In its second half, Juliane's empathy with her radical sister reconnects her to her own rebellious past and transforms her into another "Antigone," as she defends her sister's honor and presses for a thorough investigation of her death.

Numerous visual and narrative cues indicate Juliane's deepening appreciation of Marianne's political and personal dilemmas. Early in the film Juliane had dreamed that her boyfriend was betraying her with her sister—a dream that incorporates both their competition and intimacy. As the memory scenes and dreams bring more and more repressed and unconscious material to the surface, Juliane engages with her sister in a more conscious way. E. Ann Kaplan suggests that the flashbacks become unnecessary after Marianne's death and after Juliane confronts her relationship to her sister directly.[32] At the end of one of the prison visits, they exchange sweaters; Juliane experiments with her own body to recreate Marianne's experience of being force-fed in prison and anxiously wonders for how long her sister can endure this procedure psychologically.

The most poignant scene, however, takes place when Juliane visits her sister in the new ultramodern high security prison and the reflection of her face in the glass divider is superimposed on Marianne's. Reminiscent of Bergman's composite picture of Elizabet and Alma in *Persona* and

Ester and Anna in *The Silence*, this image is a highly modernist cinematic metaphor for psychological merging or fusion with the other, here Juliane's important identification with her sister to "continue her work." Yet the incongruence of the image also visualizes the resistance to complete merging, to the dissolution of identity. The psychic identification between Juliane and the incarcerated Marianne also creates anxiety about the loss of self and the other through merging, as some of the mirror shots in *Sisters* suggest as well. Juliane nervously says: "Your face is blurry . . . I can't see you very clearly anymore." She pulls away from the glass divider, the reflection of her face no longer overlapping Marianne's, as if to confirm their separate existence and maintain the space between them. Juliane's dream of rescuing her sister and Marianne's resistance to her efforts ("You wouldn't come with me") serves as a premonition of Marianne's death in prison, but the dream also evokes the ambivalent dance between intimacy and opposition that has characterized the sisters' relationship since childhood.

The ambiguous image of the merging face is picked up again in the diegesis of the film after Marianne has died when Juliane is away on vacation with Wolfgang in Italy. Confronting her sister's contorted face in the coffin, Juliane suffers a breakdown and cries hysterically: "You'll never see such a face again. I must continue her work." The camera cuts to Juliane lying on a hospital bed, and then to her dream of the sisters as little girls buttoning one another's undershirts. The screen is suffused in red light as the girls look up at a grim picture of a bleeding, crucified Christ and then, in an extreme low-angle shot, see their father as he preaches fervently and furiously from his pulpit. Representing the wrath of the Old Testament God rather than Christ's love and forgiveness, the father is again explicitly linked in Juliane's consciousness to the oppressiveness of the patriarchal state and, in the context of this sequence, to Marianne's political persecution and death. As Marianne's mother once says of her husband's hard stance against Marianne's politics, "If she was dead he could love her again."

As Juliane becomes more deeply involved in investigating her sister's unexplained "suicide," she incorporates her sister's psyche in a process of mourning. Her recovery of the "inner sister" counteracts what Alexander Mitscherlich has called German society's "inability to mourn," the nation's psychic disavowal of its crimes in the Adenauer years of reconstruction after the war.[33] Revealingly, Juliane's pursuit of "the truth" of Marianne's death comes to resemble Marianne's own single-minded revolt against the state. When Juliane finally has the evidence that Marianne could not have killed herself, the editor she contacts to report the story considers the political upheaval of the 1970s "old news" and consigns the story to the "dungheap of history." This repression of Marianne's story drives home the danger of forgetting history, for it ironically reenacts the nation's amnesia over its responsibilities for allowing the Nazis to build their murderous police state.

At the close of the film, Juliane decides to take care of Marianne's orphaned son, Jan, who has suffered serious burns in an arson attack by a person who sought to retaliate against Marianne's terrorist acts. Juliane's assumption of his care is not intended to imply a rejection of political action for the sake of motherhood, but is for all intents and purposes a symbolically and politically meaningful act in itself. Jan's anger at his dead mother mirrors Marianne's and Juliane's rebellion against their parents. When he tears up Marianne's photograph, Juliane responds: "You are wrong; your mother was an extraordinary woman," and then tells him Marianne's life story. Unlike her mother, who "always trusted people and never asked questions," Juliane acknowledges Jan's demands to know everything. But she also confesses the inherent limits of her knowledge and reminds him of the partiality of all truths, a clear reference to the deliberately subjective structure of *Marianne and Juliane* as a whole. Juliane's willingness to embrace Jan and to answer his questions not only signifies an integration of her own and her sister's point of view ("Marianne is no longer either a threatening Other or an imaginary Same," notes Susan Linville), but her actions also represent her desire to fulfill her responsibility to the next generation, to face the recent history of Germany in all its tragic contradictions.[34]

Three Sisters/Paura e amore

Just as Marianne and Juliane recall Antigone and Ismene, the sisters in Margarethe von Trotta's sixth feature film, *Three Sisters* (*Paura e amore*, 1988), are based on the Prozorov sisters, Olga, Masha, and Irina, in Anton Chekhov's *The Three Sisters* (1901). (I will use the original Italian title, *Paura e amore*, for von Trotta's film to avoid confusion with Chekhov's title.) Co-written with Italian novelist Dacia Maraini, this contemporized version of Chekhov's play is set in 1980s Pavia, a small northern Italian university town on the banks of the Po. Von Trotta uses the character constellation from *The Three Sisters* to articulate her feelings and concerns about the contemporary situation of women and the conservative political climate of the time. Her "update" carries its own particular ironies: the dissolution of the family and collective values, the uncertainty of love, job competition, nuclear threat, and terrorism are all far removed from Chekhov's prerevolutionary era. The vision of hope that the Prozorov sisters express at the end of Chekhov's play for the accomplishments and changes of the twentieth century—which was paralleled to some degree by the political activism and optimism of von Trotta's student generation—is negated by the disasters, disillusionments, and missed opportunities of the twentieth century. The director has commented on the difference in tone between her film and the play:

> Chekhov saw the future as a beacon of hope. He thought that he was responding to suffering and that he was creating new values. He believed that times would change and make people happier whereas the characters in my film are afraid of the future. Our century has brought so many hopes and disillusionments that their conscience is more acute. Even if they are intellectuals who ask themselves these questions, the real message in my film lies in that difference.[35]

Set in the world of academia, *Paura e amore* focuses on the three sisters' relationships with each other and the men they are involved with, their search for meaning in their personal and professional lives. The film presents a melancholy portrait of women of von Trotta's generation, who in their forties have lived through the political challenges and personal disappointments of the 1980s and face a world in the midst of ecological disasters and a politically conservative backlash against the progressive social changes initiated in the 1960s and 1970s. Contemporary Europe now privileges success, wealth, and technological progress at the expense of personal happiness and creative expression. Anna's warning in *Sisters* about a society that can manipulate genes but cannot deal with love resonates strongly in this film too, in which the youngest sister is concerned with the human ravaging of the natural landscape and the irresponsible use of science. In fact, *Paura e amore* resembles *Sisters, or The Balance of Happiness* in many ways. Its constellation of three women with different personalities—the competent, duty-bound older sister; the melancholy middle sister; and the more ebullient, life-loving youngest sibling—represent three faces of female identity.

Velia, the eldest (Fanny Ardant), is a former political activist and now a university professor of literature specializing in women mystics. She has been repeatedly passed over for promotion and tenure and criticized for her close relationship with her students. Velia falls in love with Massimo, a physics professor who was her father's star student and protegé, and who has just returned to Italy from the United States with his wife. Maria (Greta Scacchi), the melancholy, bored middle sister, married to television comedian Federico, is psychologically adrift, searching for a place in life. She begins a love affair with Massimo after he retreats from Velia's overpowering need for love. Expecting to spend the rest of her life with him, she finds herself rebuffed when he decides to return to the United States with his wife. Sandra (Valeria Golino), the eighteen-year-old "baby" sister, is a premedical student worried about her chances of becoming a doctor. An environmental activist, she attempts to engage her sisters and Massimo in her campaign to halt environmental damage. She too is disappointed in her romantic life, when the biology professor she has fallen in love with is killed in a car accident at the end of the film. A brother, Roberto, like Andrei in Chekhov's play, is a gifted musician and the object of adoration for his sisters. However, he neglects his music and becomes a clerk and investment adviser at a bank after marrying his pregnant, somewhat vulgar girlfriend, Sabrina. The only character who does not become disillusioned in love is the old doctor, a family friend, who has long idealized the sisters' mother and still desires her. (The middle sister, Maria, resembles her mother, and Greta Scacchi plays both Maria and the mother as she appears in a black-and-white home movie, much as Liv Ullmann plays the roles of mother and daughter in *Cries and Whispers*.)

At the beginning of the film, the legacy of the father—both literally and figuratively—looms large over the sisters' lives. Velia is first seen walking along the arches of the university, past rows of male statues reminiscent of those in *Marianne and Juliane*. Sandra's eighteenth birthday party also marks the first anniversary of their father's death, and it is on this occasion that Massimo, their father's favorite student, meets the sisters. Von Trotta borrows from Chekhov's play the theme of the sisters' fixation on their father, but the film makes their psychological relationship to the father less explicit. During the birthday dinner, the old doctor toasts the three sisters, announcing, "Since the French revolution, nothing has been more important than the women's movement. The future belongs to you." Despite this note of optimism, *Paura e amore* depicts the sisters' search for love as a struggle to find meaning in a life marked by betrayal, death, and uncertainty.

An overarching theme of the film is the concern for the future and the fragility of life, visually captured by the mise-en-scène of the fog-enshrouded Italian landscape in the Po valley surrounding Pavia. The festive moment at the party turns to a bleak reflection on a future threatened by environmental destruction; in fact, only Massimo is optimistic that the planet is a living organism able to care for itself. Sandra vehemently protests that human beings have a responsibility to nurture the environment, while Massimo contends that "death does not exist in physics—it is something that poets have invented," hence admitting his fear of life. The film clearly links Massimo's repression of the experience of death—his scientific detachment from life—to his inability to understand the depth of Velia's and Maria's love and his refusal to take responsibility for his careless attitude.

Velia, who as the oldest sister has always put the needs and demands of her siblings and family before her own, confesses to Sandra after the birthday party that she feels old. With Massimo she experiences—for the first time, it seems—the all-consuming love that she finds articulated in the thirteenth-century mystic Angela de Follinion. Massimo, after listening to Velia's lecture on de Follinion's views on the power of love, suddenly realizes the depth of her feelings for him and recoils from her passion, transferring his affections to what he thinks is a safer object, Velia's sister Maria. Velia witnesses Maria's and Massimo's budding attraction through a small window in an old empty farmhouse. The next shot reveals Maria's and Massimo's exchange of looks in a reflection in a well. The specular illusion of perfect love—a major theme of *Paura e amore*—is reemphasized when, in the following shot, Massimo and Maria exchange glances in the rearview mirror of the car. Having found a person whom she fantasizes will provide her with an identity she lacks, Maria projects her entire wish for happiness upon Massimo: "I want to share everything with you. You are my only happiness." He replies, "Only the *desire* for happiness is real"—a statement on the impossibility of complete love, which for him belongs to the realm of what Jacques Lacan would call the Imaginary.

This fantasy of reexperiencing "the mirror phase" in romantic love is activated by the cinematic apparatus itself, for several self-reflexive scenes in the film reveal von Trotta's understanding of how the screen serves as a mirror of primary identification.[36] In a revealing intertextual moment, for instance, Maria watches on television the famous cigarette-lighting scene from the 1942 American romantic melodrama *Now, Voyager,* starring

Bette Davis and Paul Henreid. The film foreshadows Maria's desires: just as Bette Davis's Charlotte Vale imagines Henreid's character's marriage to be unfulfilling, Maria will fantasize that Massimo's marriage is an unhappy one. Maria searches for her own identity, which means separating from the powerful image of her dead mother as well as from Velia, a mother substitute. At the same time she attempts to overcome her romantic ennui and sense of loss through a complete merging with Massimo.

For her part, Sandra seeks, like Anna in *Sisters*, a connection with the world around her, although she is less melancholy than Anna and more engaged and resilient. At a meeting of environmentalists, her eyes fill with tears as she watches film footage of a dying forest. Later, she climbs a solitary tree in a field and perches in the womblike enclosure of its branches, protected from the outside world. In another scene, she shares her shelter with her boyfriend, who remarks, "You taught me that to love a tree can be a political gesture." For Sandra, nurturing nature means a reparation of the self—a process becoming increasingly difficult at the end of the twentieth century.

All three sisters are shown undergoing pain, separation, and suffering. Unlike their male counterparts, they realize that even the greatest scientific progress cannot eliminate human anguish or the existential reality of death. In a particularly revealing juxtaposition of scenes, the camera cuts from Massimo's and Maria's blissful lovemaking to a museum laboratory that contains rows of jars preserving twin fetuses. Here Sandra's new lover, a doctor, is discussing advances in artificial reproduction, excitedly expounding on the possibility of preserving sperm to impregnate future generations of women. Meanwhile, Sandra clearly recognizes his narcissistic desire to symbolically defy death and eliminate the uncertainties of life. The sisters' loss of romantic love represents a more primal loss of love that precedes all other disillusions, expressed in the scene in which Velia and the elderly doctor watch home movies of the sisters' mother and their brother as he plays the violin. The doctor, who never found again the love he had felt for the sisters' mother, fantasizes that she was really in love with him, and that she is gazing from the screen directly at him, thus confirming his existence. Velia reminds him that in the home movie her mother is fact looking at her husband, who holds the camera. This moment in the film comments on the connections between cinema and fantasy through their similar play on the illusion of plenitude. The absence of the camera allows the doctor to fantasize the imaginary relationship between himself and the sisters' mother. The search for absolute romantic love recaptures the desire for fusion but is necessarily disillusioned in the lived relationship. The theme of the fragility of self and subjectivity is highlighted again when Velia and the doctor discuss the question of whether one exists only if one has loved.

Paura e amore is an elegiac film about love and its loss, expressing the fragility of the environment and the self in a tone of great urgency. Velia plays the role of surrogate mother as did Maria in *Sisters* and Juliane in *Marianne and Juliane*. She helps Sandra with her anxiety about her future career and supports Maria through her depression and aimlessness. She provides a mirror for her brother, listening admiringly to Roberto's music as did their mother. In the course of the film, she develops a close friendship with Massimo's melancholy wife, Erika, a significant departure from Chekhov's play, in which Vershinin's wife never appears on stage. Indeed, von Trotta often portrays women's relationships and friendships as a counterpoint to heterosexual bonds, but she does so without minimizing their complexity. Velia's and Erika's friendship is, in fact, an integral part of the film, since Erika's increasing independence provokes Massimo's jealousy and ultimately causes him to break off with Maria.[37] Velia is in many ways the most complex and passionate sister of the trio despite her composed and reserved appearance. Only once does she lose control, when Maria happily announces her love for Massimo to her two sisters. Unaware of Velia's innermost feelings, Maria accuses her of knowing nothing about love, for all her commitment to women and feminism.

The conclusion of the film seems to suggest that the sibling bond is the only relationship capable of surviving the turmoil of betrayal and loss, a source of stability and continuity, however tenuous. The final scene finds the sisters and their friends reunited as in the beginning, this time in celebration of their brother's promotion to manager of a branch of his bank. Massimo and Erika are returning to the United States, as he has "satisfied his nostalgia for Europe." It is a scene of momentary redemption and reconciliation. Velia has forgiven Massimo, noting wryly that he will fit in well with his colleagues in the United States who have "such an infantile belief in technological progress." Maria accompanies Roberto on the piano for the first time in years, while her family looks on. The old doctor admires her as he once admired her mother, and the film turns from color to monochrome as if to freeze the scene in memory. It is significant that the transfiguration of Maria in this scene occurs in the eyes of a male character who never had the chance to live his love and hence has never experienced its loss. The future remains uncertain, and so do the characters' identities and relationships, weighed down as they are by their fantasies, needs, and expectations. As in Chekhov's play, there is a suggestion that only in the future will the present seem happier. Unlike *Sisters* and *Marianne and Juliane*, both of which are open-ended but still indicate the sister's moment of awakening and change, *Paura e amore* concludes on a strangely nostalgic note, even if this nostalgia is the product of male desire and illusion.

Of the three sister films, *Paura e amore* is the most indebted to the codes of melodrama with its emphasis on emotion and suffering, even though it is infused with von Trotta's contemporary political concerns. In contrast to the other two, it seems more conventional, perhaps because it was a commissioned film, and perhaps because Chekhov's classical play may have constrained von Trotta's imagination. Nevertheless, it remains an interesting coda to the series and a revealing self-analysis in the director's late forties. As such, it is concerned less with topical or political issues than with existential questions of love, life, and death, and with von Trotta's view of gender differences with regard to these issues.

All three sister films explore the subject of bonds between sisters in a decentered modern society faced with self-destruction—concerns that situate von Trotta within the thematic body of the New German Cinema. Thomas Elsaesser, in his psychoanalytic essay on Rainer Werner Fassbinder's films and German history, argues that "German directors seem to be preoccupied with questions of identity, subjectivity, estrangement," given their faithfulness "to a persistent Romantic tradition"; that in German cinema "identity appears negatively, as nostalgia, deprivation, lack of motivation, loss"; and that filmic "characters only know they exist by the negative emotion of anxiety—the word that in the German cinema has become a cliché." Elsaesser locates this anxiety about identity in the political context of a conformist postwar West German society. Citing Mitscherlich's psychoanalytic studies of German fascism and post–World War 2 reconstruction, he suggests that the New German Cinema's obsession with mirroring, doubling, and illusory self-images expresses the search for a lost national and individual identity. He mentions von Trotta's film *Sisters* as an example of the ways in which the configuration of two sisters is used as a "symptom of the split subject," the theme of self-alienation so prominent in films of the New German Cinema.[38]

Like Fassbinder, who is commonly identified as the most prominent if controversial of the New German filmmakers, von Trotta views the political and social reality of postwar and contemporary Germany through the lens of personal relations and family dramas. For Fassbinder, too, politics and power relationships begin at home and are negotiated in interpersonal relations rather than in abstract political debates or historical conflicts. Both directors frequently employ melodramatic techniques to portray their characters' inner contradictions and growing self-awareness, in a conscious attempt to engage the viewer in the emotional drama. While von Trotta is much less self-conscious in her cinematic style than Fassbinder, who created a more Brechtian blend of artifice and realism, her films are nonetheless modern versions of what Jutta Brückner has called a self-reflexive realism. Despite von Trotta's allegiance to the New German Cinema and its postwar thematic obsessions, her treatment of the sister motif sets her apart from other German filmmakers' uses of doubling and splitting. Her vision of the dynamics between women, altogether more complicated, is related, I think, to her articulation of women's ambivalent position in private familial and public spheres.

Women looking through windows or waiting at windows frequently appear in von Trotta's films at key moments in characters' psychological development and their attempts to relate to an other—a sister or a friend. Mary Ann Doane writes of the motif's importance in the "woman's film" of the 1940s "in terms of the social and symbolic position of the woman—the window is the interface between inside and outside, the feminine space of the family and reproduction and the masculine space of production." Given von Trotta's indebtedness to the codes of domestic melodrama in her depictions of personal anguish and her analysis of the imprisonment of women in domestic and public spaces, her symbolic use of windows should not come as a surprise. However, in her films the separation described by Doane between the private and the public, the personal and the political, is not so clearly demarcated. The motif of the window, much like her frequent use of mirrors, suggests "threshhold" spaces of introspection and engagement, of reconstructed memory and the return of the repressed, as well as potential pathways to new possibilities and a better future. Windows represent meeting places for potential connections between women, which enable them to recognize themselves and each other. In her book on transference in literature, Laura Tracy cites Evelyn

Keller's work on gender identity and knowledge, arguing that windows in women's writing define

> "potential space" between self and other—the "neutral area of experience" that, as Winnicott . . . describes it, allows the temporary suspension of boundaries between "me" and "not me" required for all empathic experi-ence—experience that allows for the creative leap between knower and known. It acknowledges the ebb and flow between subject and object as the prerequisite for both love and knowledge.[39]

Of course, for von Trotta, this potential space is never "neutral" but profoundly political and is never given but attained through intersubjective engagement with an other. This form of identificatory knowledge between two subjects is particularly relevant for von Trotta; like other German artists of her generation, she is preoccupied in all her work with the question of self-knowledge and its relation to cultural experience—a concern that inevitably leads her to a confrontation with the memory of the past. Her sister films articulate her view that this self-knowledge is achieved through intersubjectivity, through the encounter and iden-tification with an other, in the confrontations and intimacy with a sister who frequently initiates a psychological journey to the past and a process of self-transformation. In von Trotta's cinema, the sister relationship connotes another of Winnicott's "potential spaces"—a third psycholog-ical space, so to speak, in which an individual and shared reality converge and boundaries between self and other are negotiated. The sister bond is unique because it involves women who have shared a personal history and frequently the internal spaces of childhood consciousness. It thus permits a process of self-reflection and identity formation that involves empathy and female bonding, bridging inner and outer worlds.

Conclusion

From Gillian Armstrong's popular 1990s adaptation of *Little
Women*, I have traveled to Margarethe von Trotta's political
cinema about sisters, which exemplifies, in the larger argument of this study, modern narrative cinema's probing of the
sister bond. In *Little Women*, the visual trope of windows
functions as a seductive frame for the spectator to nostalgically return to childhood memory and nineteenth-century
domestic feminism, to recreate or redeem a lost, unified sisterhood. In contrast, the frequent appearance of windows in
von Trotta's sister films solicits a more critical, nuanced look
at women's ambivalent positions in private and public spaces,
and sisters' conflictual relation to each other and the past.
There windows become metaphoric liminal sites of separation and connection between sisters who actively negotiate
their similarities and differences, their shared, yet sometimes
conflicting experiences and views of family history and cultural identity.[1]

In examining in cinema the dynamic role of a sister in a woman's self-definition, I have largely drawn on Jessica Benjamin's
psychoanalytic concept of intersubjectivity in identity formation.
Her theory takes into account not only the workings of the
intrapsychic realm—"the inner world of fantasy, wish, anxiety
and defense; of bodily symbols and images whose connections
defy the ordinary rules of logic and language"—but also the
capacities for recognition and exchange that originate in the
interrelation between self and other. The films I have discussed take up this topic of intersubjectivity in the context of

sisterhood, and I believe they represent what Jackie Stacey terms "a dialectical interplay of multiple feminine identities."[2] In doing so, these films provide provocative cultural inflections on modern (especially post-1960s) cinema's challenge to more conventional images of either idealized sisters or the split between "good" and "evil" female siblings.

The feminist scholarship on mother-daughter and female friends that proliferated during the 1980s and after curiously omitted the sister relationship. Feminist film scholars, while paying serious attention to the representation of motherhood in cinema, have surprisingly shown a certain "amnesia" about sisterhood.[3] Not only does the sister bond represent one of the most significant and lasting relationships in women's lives, but "sisterhood" has become an image of solidarity and identification between women of our era. Paradoxically, the neglect of sisters' relationships in feminist scholarship may in fact be explained by the understandable need of women to construct only positive images of "sisterhood" as a kind of political rallying cry for female solidarity and as a defense against gender stereotypes that have oppressed women for generations. Critic and journalist Barbara Mathias argues that scholars' failure to devote more attention to the extremely complex and intricate connections between biological sisters "is mainly due to the plodding growth of women's psychology, but ironically, it is also a product of the feminist movement, which typically glorified the sisterhood of women, thus discouraging a more realistic look at the ambivalent, sometimes wretched condition between biological sisters."[4] In the absence of a systematic psychoanalytic or feminist theory of sisterhood, the films discussed in this book provide an intriguing and nuanced understanding of the sister relationship.

In my critique, I have grouped modern and contemporary films not chronologically but according to their portrayal of sisters in adolescence and in adulthood. While the coming-of-age film is indebted to the literary tradition of the bildungsroman, that genre's paradigm of progressive development toward a coherent identity and integration into the social order has always been highly problematic for women. I was more interested in precisely those films about sisters that question a cohesive identity and complicate female subject formation through the relational, ongoing intersubjective relationship and search for recognition between sisters through adulthood. This framework allows for an exploration of the films' frequent preoccupation with memory, in these cases a nonnostalgic return to childhood and the role of sisters in shaping and remembering family history. *An Angel at My Table*, *Eve's Bayou*, the autobiographical films of Diane Kurys, and the works by Margarethe von Trotta and Ingmar Bergman show sisters "coauthoring" family history for the spectator as their experiences and visions clash or create a more complex tapestry of the past. Sisters, as Emily Gwathmey and Ellen Stern so aptly put it, help (but also sometimes hinder) each other to remember, interpret, invent, and reinvent family history, and modern films about sisterhood have effectively addressed this facet of sororal intersubjectivity.

Sisterhood has long been an appealing metaphor for women's power and solidarity; conversely, it has signified a convenient trope for the split female self as evil double. Cinema and popular culture at the end of the twentieth century have reimagined the sister relationship as both an important intersubjective bond in women's lives and a marketable visual icon of postfeminist "girl power." The current plethora of representations of sisters in popular media range from the sentimental to the more subversive. Photographs inspired by the success of Carol Saline's and Sharon Wohlmuth's national bestseller coffee-table book about sisters, often framed in affectionate poses, have been marketed as calendars, photo frames, notecards, and other ephemera.[5] The contemporary Warner Brothers television series *Charmed*, about three sisters who are present-day witches, and the recent Hollywood film *Practical Magic* (1998), based on Alice Hoffman's novel, recall Shakespeare's "weird sisters" but with a 1990s feminist twist: young sororal witches use their subversive magic powers to do battle with various, often male, villains; they protect each other from harm, mediate romantic entanglements and tempt fate, and affirm their female power.

In a different vein, biographical films continue to explore the sister's complex and contradictory role in female artist's lives, such as Anand Tucker's recent *Hilary and Jackie* (1998), a dual portrait of the gifted British cellist Jacqueline du Pré and her older sister, Hilary, whose symbiotic, yet competitive relationship was shaped by the narcissistic demands of artistic genius. *Marvin's Room* (1996), an updated Hollywood melodrama, treats two estranged sisters who clash over caring for their old, bed-ridden father but ultimately reconcile. One is a self-sacrificing caretaker who eventually becomes terminally ill with cancer herself; the other left home and avoided taking responsibility for her family. The film reinvokes the dichotomy of "good" and "bad" sisters to argue for the value of daughterly sacrifice for the parent and asks us to judge the sisters by which one has reconciled her oedipal attachment to the father. By contrast, the playful avant-garde Hungarian film *My Twentieth Century* (1989) employs the trope of twin sisters separated as young girls—one becomes a revolutionary anarchist, the other a courtesan—to comment critically on how radical social and technolog ical changes in the early part of the twentieth century have both liberated and circumscribed women's roles.[6] The final visual tour-de-force reunion of the twin sisters in a funhouse full of mirrors suggests the need for integration of women's split social identities, and thus it represents a provocative response to the Hollywood twin melodramas of the 1940s that Lucy Fischer has written about. The role of sisters in genres such as the melodrama, the thriller, and the horror film, as well as in specific national cinemas or periods in cinema history, might in addition point toward fruitful avenues of investigation.

Sisters have long commanded the attention of the cultural imaginary, often in the form of a problematic and ideological metaphor for women's conflicted relationship to culture and society at large. Modern and contemporary filmmakers, especially women directors, have responded to these images but also elaborated on the pleasures and ambivalences of sisterhood with both a critical and sympathetic camera eye. The wide variety of modern, edgy, and bold films about the sister bond suggests that there is indeed more than one story to tell about sisters on screen.

Appendix
Filmography

Alma's Rainbow (USA, 1994). Produced by Howard M. Brickner, Ayoka Chenzira, Geri Jasper, and Charles Lane. Director and screenplay: Ayoka Chenzira; cinematography: Ronald K. Gray. Featuring Kim Weston-Moran, Mizan Nunes, Victoria Gabriella Platt, Jennifer Copeland, Lee Dobson, Roger Pickering, Isaiah Washington. Color. 85 minutes.

An Angel at My Table (New Zealand, 1990). A production of Bridget Ikin for Hibiscus Films, in association with the New Zealand Film Commission, Television New Zealand, the Australian Broadcasting Corporation, Channel 4. Director: Jane Campion; screenplay: Laura Jones, based on the autobiography by Janet Frame; cinematography: Stuart Dryburgh. Featuring Kerry Fox, Alexia Keogh, Karen Fergusson, Irish Churn, K. J. Wilson, Melina Bernecker, Glynis Angell, Sarah Smuts-Kennedy, Andrew Binns, Colin McColl, Martyn Sanderson. Color. 160 minutes.

Babette's Feast (Denmark, 1987). Produced by Just Betzer and Bo Christensen. Director and screenplay: Gabriel Axel. Based on the short story by Isak Dinesen. Cinematography: Henning Kristiansen. Featuring Ghita Nørby, Asta Esper Andersen, Gert Bastian, Viggo Bentzon, Vibeke Hastrup, Therese Hojgaard Christensen, Pouel Kern. Color. 102 minutes.

Cries and Whispers [Viskningar och Rop] (Sweden, 1972). Produced by Ingmar Bergman for Cinematograph, in cooperation with Svensk Filmindustri. Director: and screenplay: Ingmar Bergman; cinematography: Sven Nykvist. Featuring Harriet Andersson, Kari Sylwan, Ingrid Thulin, Liv Ullmann, Erland Josephson, Henning Moritzen. Color. 95 minutes.

Daughter-Rite (USA, 1978). Director, editor, and screenplay: Michelle Citron; cinematography: Michelle Citron with assistance from Sharon Bement, Barbara Roos. Featuring Penelope Victor, Anne Wilford, Jerri Hancock. Distributed by Iris Films. Color. 48 minutes.

Double Happiness (Canada, 1995). Produced by Steve Hegyes and Rose Lam Waddell for Fine Line Features, a First Generation Films Inc./New Views Films production. Director and screenplay (English and Cantonese with English subtitles): Mina Shum; cinematography: Peter Wunstorf. Featuring Sandra Oh, Alannah Ong, Stephen Chang, Frances You, Johnny Mah, Callum Rennie, Donald Fong, Claudette Carracedo, Barbara Tse, Nathan Fong, Greg Chan. Color. 87 minutes.

Eve's Bayou (USA, 1997). Produced by Caldecot Chubb and Samuel L. Jackson for Trimark Pictures. Director and screenplay: Kasi Lemmons; cinematography: Amy Vincent. Featuring Jurnee Smollett, Samuel L. Jackson, Lynn Whitfield, Debbi Morgan, Diahann Carroll. Color and B/W. 109 minutes.

Female Perversions (USA, 1996). Produced by Mindy Affrime, Janine Gold, Zalman King, Rainer Koelmel, Gina Resnick, Rena Ronson for Mindy Affrime/Transatlantic Entertainment. Director: Susan Streitfeld; screenplay: Julie Hebert, Susan Streitfeld; cinematography: Teresa Medina. Featuring Tilda Swinton, Amy Madigan, Karen Sillas, Francis Fisher, Clancy Brown, Laila Robins, John Diehl, Paulina Porizkova, Dale Shuger. Color. 110 minutes.

Gas Food Lodging (USA, 1992). Produced by Daniel Hassid, William Ewart, Seth M. Willenson for Cineville Partners II; Seth Willenson Inc. Director and screenplay, based on the novel *Don't Look and It Won't Hurt* by Richard Peck: Allison Anders; cinematography: Dean Lent. Featuring Brooke Adams, Ione Skye, Fairuza Balk, James Brolin, Robert Knepper, David Lansbury, Jacob Vargas, Donovan Leitch. Color. 100 minutes.

Georgia (USA, 1995). Produced by Barbara Turner, Jennifer Jason Leigh, and Ulu Grosbard for Miramax. Director: Ulu Grosbard; screenplay: Barbara Turner; cinematography: Jan Kiesser. Featuring Jennifer Jason Leigh, Mare Winningham, Ted Levine, Max Perlich, John Doe, John C. Reilly, Jimmy Witherspoon, Jason Carter. Color. 117 minutes.

Hannah and Her Sisters (USA, 1986). Produced by Robert Greenhut for Orion Pictures. Director and screenplay: Woody Allen; cinematography: Carlo di Palma. Featuring Woody Allen, Michael Caine, Mia Farrow, Carrie Fischer, Barbara Hershey, Lloyd Nolan, Maureen O'Sullivan, Max von Sydow, Dianne Wiest. Color. 107 minutes.

Heavenly Creatures (New Zealand, 1995). Produced by Jim Booth for Wingnut Films, coproduced with Fontana Film Productions GmbH in association with the New Zealand Film Commission. Director: Peter Jackson; screenplay: Peter Jackson and Fran Walsh; cinematography: Allun Bollinger. Featuring Melanie Lynsky, Kate Winslet, Sarah Peirse, Diana Kent, Clive Merrison, Simon O'Connor, Jed Brophy, Peter Elliott, Gilbert Goldie. Color. 98 minutes.

Hilary and Jackie (U.K., 1998). Produced by Guy East, Ruth Jackson, and Nigel Sinclair for British Screen and Intermedia Films, in association with the Arts Council of England and the Oxford Film Company. Director: Anand Tucker; screenplay: Hilary du Pré, Piers du Pré, and Frank Cottrell Boyce, based on *A Genius in the Family*; cinematography: David Johnson. Featuring Emily Watson, Rachel Griffiths, James Frain, David Morrissey, Charles Dance, Celia Imrie, Rupert Penry-Jones. Color. 125 minutes.

Hotel Sorrento [a.k.a. *Sorrento Beach*] (Australia, 1995). Produced by Richard Franklin. A Castle Hill Productions release of a Bayside Pictures production in association with Horizon Films/Australian Film Finance Corporation. Director: Richard Franklin; screenplay, based on a play by Hannie Rayson: Richard Franklin and Peter Fitzpatrick; cinematography: Geoff Burton. Featuring Caroline Goodall, Caroline Gillmer, Tara Morice, Joan Plowright, Ray Barrett, Nicholas Bell, Ben Thomas, John Hargreaves. Color. 112 minutes.

The Last Days of Chez Nous (Australia, 1990). Produced by Jan Chapman for Jan Chapman Productions, with assistance of the Australian Film Commission/Australian Broadcasting Corporation/Australian Film Finance Corporation. Director: Gillian Armstrong; screenplay: Helen Garner; cinematography: Geoffrey Simpson. Featuring Lisa Harrow, Bruno Ganz, Kerry Fox, Miranda Otto, Kiri Paramore, Bill Hunter. Color. 97 minutes.

Little Women (USA, 1994). Produced by Denise DiNovi for Columbia Pictures and DiNovi Pictures. Director: Gillian Armstrong; screenplay, based on the book by Louisa May Alcott: Robin Swicord; cinematography: Geoffrey Simpson. Featuring Winona Ryder, Gabriel Byrne, Trini Alvarado, Samantha Mathis, Kirsten Dunst, Claire Danes, Christian Bale, Eric Stoltz, John Neville, Mary Wickles, Susan Sarandon, Florence Paterson. Color. 115 minutes.

Manny and Lo (USA, 1996). Produced by Marlen Hecht and Dean Silvers. Sony Pictures Classics. Director and screenplay: Lisa Krueger; cinematography: Tom Krueger. Featuring Scarlett Johansson, Aleksa Palladino, Mary Kay Place. Color. 90 minutes.

Marianne and Juliane/The German Sisters [Die Bleierne Zeit] (Germany, 1982). Produced by Eberhard Junkersdorf for Bioskop Filmproduktion. Director and screenplay: Margarethe von Trotta; cinematography: Franz Rath. Featuring Jutta Lampe, Barbara Sukowa, Ruediger Vogler, Luc Bondy, Doris Schade, Verenice Rudolph, Franz Rudnick, Julia Biedermann. Color. 107 minutes.

My Twentieth Century (Hungary, 1989). Produced by Gabor Hanak and Norbert Friedlander for Budapest Film-Studio/Mafilm, Friedlander Filmproduktion/Hamburger Film Buro, and I.C.A.I.C. Director and screenplay: Ildiko Enyedi; cinematography: Tibor Mathe. Featuring Dorothea Segda, Oleg Jankowski, Peter Andorai, Gabor Mate (X). B/W. 100 minutes.

Overseas [Outremer] (France, 1991). Produced by Serge Cohan-Solal for Paradise Productions; Lira Films; Aries Film Releasing. Director: Brigitte Roüan; screenplay: Brigitte Roüan, Philippe Le Guay, Christian Rullier,

Cedric Kahn; cinematography: Dominique Chapuis. Featuring Brigitte Roüan, Nicole Garcia, Marianne Basler, Yann Dedet, Philippe Galland, Bruno Todeschini, Pierre Doris, Monique Melinand. Color. 98 minutes.

Peppermint Soda [Diabolo menthe] (France, 1977). Produced by Alma-Alexandre Films. Director and screenplay: Diane Kurys; cinematography: Philippe Rousselet. Featuring Eleonore Klarwein, Odile Michel, Coralie Clement, Marie-Veronique Maurin, Francoise Bertin, Jacques Rispal, Anouk Ferjac, Valerie Stano, Anne Guillard, Corinne Dacla. Color. 97 minutes.

Ripe (USA, 1997). Produced by Suzy Landa, Richard Abramowitz, Michael Chambers, Patrick Panzarella for C&P Productions, Trimark Pictures. Director and screenplay: Mo Ogrodnik; cinematography: Wolfgang Held. Featuring Monica Keena, Daisy Eagan, Gordon Currie, Ron Brice, Karen Lee Gorney, Vincent Laresca, Scott Sowers. Color. 93 minutes.

The Silence [Tystnaden] (Sweden, 1963). Produced by Allan Ekelund for Svensk Filmindustri. Director and screenplay: Ingmar Bergman; cinematography: Sven Nykvist. Featuring Ingrid Thulin, Gunnel Lindblom, Hakan Jahnberg, Birger Malmsten, Jorgen Lindstrom, The Eduardini, Eduardo Gutierrez, Lissi Alandh, Leif Forstenberg. B/W. 95 minutes.

Sister My Sister (U.K., 1995). Produced by Norma Heyman. A Seven Arts Releasing release of a Film Four international presentation in association with British Screen of an NFH production. Director: Nancy Meckler; screenplay: Wendy Kesselman, based on her play "My Sister in This House"; cinematography: Ashley Rowe. Featuring Julie Walters, Joely Richardson, Jodhi May, Sophie Thursfield, Amelda Brown, Lucita Pope, Kate Gartside, Aimee Schmidt, Gabriella Schmidt. Color. 102 minutes.

Sisters, or The Balance of Happiness [Schwestern, oder Die Balance des Glücks] (Germany, 1979). Produced by Eberhard Junkersdorf for Bioskop/Westdeutscher Rundfunk/Cinema 5. Director and screenplay, based on extracts from *Traumprotokolle* by Wolfgang Bachler: Margarethe von Trotta, Luisa Francia, Martje Grohmann; cinematography: Franz Rath. Featuring Jutta Lampe, Jessica Frueh, Gudrun Gabriel, Konstantin Wecker, Rainer

Delventhal, Agnes Fink, Heinz Bennent, Fritz Lichtenhahn, Guenther Schuetz, Ilse Bahrs, Barbara Sauerbaum, Marie-Helene Diekmann. Color. 92 minutes.

Sweetie (Australia, 1989). Produced by John Maynard and William MacKinnon for Arena Film; released by Avenue Pictures. Director: Jane Campion; screenplay: Gerard Lee, Jane Campion; cinematography: Sally Bongers. Featuring Genevieve Lemon, Karen Colston, Tom Lycos, Jon Darling, Dorothy Barry, Michael Lake, Andre Pataczek. Color. 100 minutes.

Three Sisters [Fear and Love/Paura e amore] (France/Italy/Germany, 1988). Produced by Angelo Rizzoli for Erre-Reteitalia-Bioskop-Cinemax. Director: Margarethe von Trotta; screenplay: Margarethe von Trotta, Dacia Maraini; cinematography: Giuseppe Lanci. Featuring Fanny Ardant, Greta Scacchi, Valeria Golino, Sergio Castellito, Paolo Hendel, Peter Simonischek, Agnes Soral, Gila von Weitershausen. Color. 112 minutes.

Welcome to the Dollhouse (USA, 1995). Produced by Ted Skillman and Todd Solondz for Suburban Pictures. Director and screenplay: Todd Solondz; cinematography: Randy Drummond, Gabor Szitanyi. Featuring Heather Matarazzo, Victoria Davis, Christina Brucato, Christina Vidal, Siri Howard, Brendan Sexton Jr., Telly Pontidis, Daria Kalinina, Matthew Faber, Angela Pietropinto, Eric Mabius. Color. 87 minutes.

The Whales of August (USA, 1987). Produced by Carolyn Pfeiffer and Mike Kaplan for Alive-Circle-Nelson/Alive Films. Director: Lindsay Anderson; screenplay: David Berry, based on his own play; cinematography: Mike Fash. Featuring Betty Davis, Lillian Gish, Vincent Price, Ann Sothern, Harry Carey Jr., Frank Grimes, Frank Pitkin, Mike Bush, Margaret Ladd, Tisha Sterling, Mary Steenburgen. Color. 90 minutes.

Notes

Introduction

1. Emily Gwathmey and Ellen Stern, in *Sister Sets: Sisters Whose Togetherness Sets Them Apart* (New York: William Morrow and Company, Inc., 1997), quoted in the chapter epigraph, offer a lively and amusing tour through the ways in which sisters, particularly twin sisters, have been represented in popular culture, literature, film, advertising, music, performance, and family photographs.

2. The most significant discussions of sisters in literature, women's studies, and art history are: Toni A. H. McNaron, *The Sister Bond: A Feminist View of a Timeless Connection* (New York: Pergamon, 1985); Amy Levin, *The Suppressed Sister: A Relationship in Novels by Nineteenth- and Twentieth-Century British Women* (London and Toronto: Associated University Presses, 1992); Michael Cohen, *Sisters: Relation and Rescue in Nineteenth-Century British Novels and Paintings* (Madison, N.J.: Fairleigh Dickenson University Press, 1995); JoAnna Stephens Mink and Janet Doubler Ward, eds., *The Significance of Sibling Relationships in Literature* (Bowling Green, Ohio: Bowling Green State University Popular Press, 1993); Christine Downing, *Psyche's Sisters: Re-Imagining the Meaning of Sisterhood* (San Francisco: Harper & Row, 1988).

3. Lucy Fischer, "Sisters: The Divided Self," in *Shot/Countershot: Film Tradition and Women's Cinema* (Princeton: Princeton University Press, 1988), 172–215.

4. For historical overviews and critical assessments of the multiple directions and developments taken by the modern cinema from 1960 to the mid-1990s, see the following comprehensive histories of global cinema: Geoffrey Nowell-Smith, ed., *The Oxford History of World Cinema* (Oxford: Oxford University Press, 1996), 463–766; Robert Sklar, *Film: An International History of the Medium* (New York: Abrams, 1993), 364–517.

5. I discussed these films in my dissertation, "Those Precious Bonds: A Psycho-analytic Study of Sister Relationships in Twentieth-Century Literature and Film," University of Massachusetts, Amherst, 1994.

6. Three feminist works stand out for their wholesale dismissal of the film: Molly Haskell, *From Reverence to Rape* (New York: Reinhart and Winston, 1974), 315; Joan Mellen, "*Cries and Whispers:* Bergman and Women," in *Ingmar Bergman: Essays in*

Criticism, ed. Stuart Kaminsky (New York: Oxford University Press, 1975), 297–312; and Constance Penley, *"Cries and Whispers,"* in *Movies and Methods*, ed. Bill Nichols (Berkeley: University of California Press, 1976), 204–8.

7. Margarethe von Trotta, interview by the author, Munich, Germany, July 13, 1992.

8. Bruce Kawin, *Mindscreen: Bergman, Godard, and First Person Film* (Princeton: Princeton University Press, 1978).

9. Fischer, "Sisters," and Lori Hope Lefkovitz, "Leah behind the Veil: Sex with Sisters from the Bible to Woody Allen," in *Sister to Sister: Women Write about the Unbreakable Bond*, ed. Patricia Foster (New York: Anchor, 1995), 109–28.

10. Lefkovitz, "Leah behind the Veil," 124–25.

11. Ibid., 125. Lefkovitz does mention contemporary films that follow the general plot of a husband sleeping with his sister-in-law but place more emphasis on the relationship between the sisters, for example, Steven Soderbergh's *sex lies and videotape* (1989) and *Like Water for Chocolate* (1991). More recently, Australian director Shirley Barrett's deadpan ironic comedy *Love Serenade* (1997) provides an offbeat twist to the tale of two sisters who compete for and are seduced by the same man, Ken Sherry, a sleazy radio DJ from out of town; after Ken cruelly rejects one of them, the sisters kill him.

12. Louise Bernikow, *Among Women* (New York: Harmony, 1980), 77.

13. Fischer, "Sisters," 205.

14. For a critique of psychoanalytic film theory's conceptualization of active female desire in terms of masculinity, see Jackie Stacey, *Stargazing: Hollywood Cinema and Female Spectatorship* (New York: Routledge, 1994), particularly chap. 2, "From the Male Gaze to the Female Spectator."

15. Notwithstanding the considerable value of Fischer's model, her argument is based on a selective sampling of films. Even during the 1940s, the Hollywood studio system produced a number of films featuring sisters that lacked the dualistic plot conflict of good sister versus bad sister, including Anatole Litvak's *The Sisters* (1938), Vincent Sherman's *The Hard Way* (1942), Irving Rapper's *The Gay Sisters* (1942), and Irving Reis's *The Bachelor and the Bobby Soxer* (1947). Although these films were less interested in exploring the relationship between sisters than their attachment to men, they hardly conform to Fischer's model of the sister melodrama.

16. See Laura Mulvey, "Visual Pleasure and Narrative Cinema," *Screen* 16, 3 (1975): 6–18, for a discussion of the ubiquitous male gaze in classical Hollywood cinema.

17. Mary Ann Doane, "Film and the Masquerade: Theorizing the Female Spectator," *Screen* 23, 3/4 (1982): 74–87. See Elizabeth Cowie, *Representing the Woman: Cinema and Psychoanalysis* (Minneapolis: University of Minnesota Press, 1997), for a critique of Mulvey's and other feminist psychoanalytic film theorists' creation of a theoretical orthodoxy with regard to the cinematic gaze that works only to satisfy the fetishistic and voyeuristic pleasure of the masculine look. Her explicit critique of earlier conceptions of the male gaze appears in chapter 5, "The Partiality of the Drives and the Pleasures of the Look in Cinema's Voyeurism." For an elaboration on identification as always alienated, partial, and multiple, and on film as a fantasy scenario that allows for multiple points of entry for spectator positioning, see chapter 3, "Identifying in the Cinema," and chapter 4, "Fantasia."

18. Rueschmann, "Those Precious Bonds," particularly chaps. 2 and 7. Janice Mouton, "Margarethe von Trotta's Sisters: 'Brides under a Different Law'," *Women in German Yearbook* 11 (1995): 35–47.

19. Catherine Portuges, *Screen Memories: The Hungarian Cinema of Marta Meszaros* (Bloomington: Indiana University Press, 1993), 59. I am greatly indebted to Catherine Portuges for her insights into the relationship between cinema and psychoanalysis, and her important work on alternatives to Freudian and Lacanian models of cinematic analysis and spectatorship, as well as her pioneering essays on women's cinematic autobiography.

20. Sheila A. Sharpe and Allan D. Rosenblatt, "Oedipal Sibling Triangles," *Journal of the American Psychoanalytic Association* 42, 2 (1994): 491–523.

21. Stacey, *Stargazing*, 28.

22. See Daniel Stern, *The Interpersonal World of the Infant: A View from Psychoanalysis and Developmental Psychology* (New York: Basic Books, 1985); Jessica Benjamin, *The Bonds of Love: Psychoanalysis, Feminism, and the Problem of Domination* (New York: Pantheon, 1988), and *Like Subjects, Love Objects: Essays on Recognition and Sexual Difference* (New Haven: Yale University Press, 1995). In *Bonds Of Love*, Benjamin presents a precise definition of intersubjectivity: "The intersubjective view, as distinguished from the intrapsychic, refers to what happens in the field of self and other. Whereas the intrapsychic perspective conceives of the person as a discrete unit with a complex internal structure, intersubjective theory describes capacities that emerge in the interaction between self and others. This intersubjective theory, even when describing the self alone, sees its aloneness as a particular point in the spectrum of relationships rather than as the original, 'natural state' of the individual. The crucial area we uncover with intrapsychic theory is the unconscious; the crucial element we explore with intersubjective theory is the representation of self and other as distinct but interrelated beings" (20).

23. John Orr, *Cinema and Modernity* (Cambridge: Polity, 1994), 10.

24. Anthony Giddens, *Modernity and Self-Identity: Self and Society in the Late Modern Age* (Cambridge, Mass.: Polity, 1991), 19–21, 27–32; cited in Orr, *Cinema and Modernity*, 11; Orr, *Cinema and Modernity*, 57.

25. See Marshall Berman, *All That Is Solid Melts into Air: The Experience of Modernity* (New York: Simon & Schuster, 1982), 6.

26. Helena Michie, *Sororophobia: Differences among Women in Literature and Culture* (New York: Oxford University Press, 1992), 9.

Part I

1. The epigraph is from act 2 of *Man and Superman*, in George Bernard Shaw, *Seven Plays* (New York: Dodd, Mead, 1967), 570; quoted in Sigmund Freud, "The Archaic Features and Infantilism of Dreams," lecture 12, *Introductory Lectures on Psychoanalysis*, trans. and ed. James Strachey (New York: Norton, 1966), 205. Freud quotes Shaw to illustrate his views on hostile impulses between siblings as an expression of rivalry for parental love.

2. Downing, *Psyche's Sisters*, 3–4. Downing argues for the lifelong significance of the sister in the psychic life of a woman.

3. I am using Roy Schafer's interpretation of psychoanalytic theory as a "retelling of the analyst of the analysand's narratives." Schafer claims that psychoanalytic theorists have employed different narrative structures to develop ways of doing analysis and telling about it. See Schafer, *The Analytic Attitude* (New York: Basic Books, 1983), 213.

4. See Fischer's analysis in "Sisters," 172–215.

5. See Karen Hollinger, *In the Company of Women: Contemporary Female Friendship Films* (Minneapolis: University of Minnesota Press, 1998), for a critical analysis of the "mainstreaming" of feminist ideas in Hollywood women's films of the 1970s and 1980s, particularly in what she terms the sentimental female friendship films.

6. The *Künstlerroman* is generally considered a subgenre of the bildungsroman, the novel of development or initiation. Susan Fraiman asks, "Is there a female Bildungsroman?" She argues that texts that portray the education and identity formation of young women insist "less on the progress of an alienated individual than on her or his constitution by manifold social relationships—once again, attending less to the single-minded development of one character than to the tangle of conflicting notions about development and the dueling narratives that result" (*Unbecoming Women: British Women Writers and the Novel of Development* [New York: Columbia University Press, 1993], 125–26). For a classic revisionist view of gender in the bildungsroman tradition, see Elizabeth Abel, Marianne Hirsch, and Elizabeth Langland, eds., *The Voyage In: Fictions of Female Development* (Hanover, N.H.: University Press of New England, 1983).

7. Catherine Portuges, "Seeing Subjects: Women Directors and Cinematic Autobiography," in *Life/Lines: Theorizing Women's Autobiography*, ed. Bella Brodzki and Celeste Schenck (Ithaca, N.Y.: Cornell University Press, 1988), 342.

8. Abel, Hirsch, and Langland, *The Voyage In*, 12.

9. See, for example, Jean Baker Miller, *Toward a New Psychology of Women* (Boston: Beacon, 1976); Nancy Chodorow, *The Reproduction of Mothering: Psychoanalysis and the Sociology of Gender* (Berkeley and Los Angeles: University of California Press, 1978); Carol Gilligan, *In a Different Voice: Psychological Theory and Women's Development* (Cambridge: Harvard University Press, 1982).

10. See D. W. Winnicott, "Mirror-Role of Mother and Family in Child Development," *Playing and Reality* (London and New York: Tavistock, 1971), 111–18, for his analysis of the mother's face as a figurative mirror that gives back to the child his own sense of self.

11. See Stacey, *Stargazing*, 208–9.

Chapter 1

1. Besides the 1994 adaptation of *Little Women*, there was a silent film version in 1918, George Cukor's in 1933, and Mervyn LeRoy's 1949 remake. Television has hosted a short-lived U.S. series in 1978 and a British adaptation in 1970, as well as versions on CBS-TV in 1950 and 1959, NBC-TV in 1958 and 1969, and CAN-TV

in 1977. See Barbara Tepa Lupack, ed., *Vision/Re-Vision: Adapting Contemporary American Fiction by Women to Film* (Bowling Green, Ohio: Bowling Green State University Popular Press, 1996), 29, n. 6.

2. Alice Cary, "Louisa We Hardly Knew Ye," *Boston Magazine*, December 1994, p. 60.

3. Caroll Smith-Rosenberg, "The Female World of Love and Ritual: Relations between Women in Nineteenth-Century America," *Signs* 1, 1 (1975): 1–29.

4. *Little Women*'s feminist accent is reflected in the virtually all-female creative team that undertook and led the production. Mary Gaitskill traces the production history: "According to producer Denise DiNovi, the idea for the movie started with screenwriter Robin Swicord and then Columbia Pictures executive Amy Pascal, who has been trying to get it made for more than ten years, since Pascal was a lowly development girl. When they first pitched it in 1982, nobody was interested. 'People just said, "Oh, it's about women, it's a costume thing,"' said Swicord. 'It was not part of the zeitgeist at the time.' A decade later, when Pascal—now in a more powerful position—called Swicord and said she thought the moment was right for mounting a new *Little Women*. When DiNovi heard of the project, she contacted them immediately; she had already spoken to Winona Ryder about making a movie of the book years earlier, when they had worked together on *Heathers* (a film about cruel and slutty schoolgirls, arguably *Little Women*'s evil twin)." See Mary Gaitskill, "Does *Little Women* Belittle Women?" *Vogue*, January 1995, p. 38.

5. Anne Hollander, "Portraying 'Little Women' through the Ages," *New York Times*, January 15, 1995.

6. Colin McArthur, *Television and History* (London: British Film Institute, 1980), 40. Quoted in Carolyn Anderson, "Biographical Film," *Handbook of American Film Genres*, ed. Wes D. Gehring (New York: Greenwood, 1988).

7. Hollander, "Portraying 'Little Women'," 21.

8. Elizabeth Francis, review of *Little Women* (Columbia Pictures movie), *Journal of American History* 82 (1995): 1312–13.

9. In *Stargazing*, Stacey develops the idea of the film screen as a window display with which female spectators/consumers actively engage in order to fashion their identities and subjectivities. (See especially chaps. 5 and 6.)

10. The quote is from Francis, review of *Little Women*. See also David Bordwell, Janet Staiger, and Kristin Thompson, *The Classical Hollywood Cinema* (New York: Columbia University Press, 1985). Most of the film's studio scenes were shot in Vancouver, Canada, but some exterior scenes of New England village life were shot in Old Deerfield, Massachusetts.

11. Shirley Marchalonis, "Filming the Nineteenth Century: *The Secret Garden* and *Little Women*," *American Transcendentalist Quarterly* 10, 4 (1996): 284.

12. See Sandra Gilbert and Susan Gubar's seminal study of nineteenth-century women writers, *The Madwoman in the Attic: The Woman Writer and the Nineteenth-Century Literary Imagination* (New Haven: Yale University Press, 1979), for an extended discussion of "anxieties about space" in 1800s women's literature and images of women literally and figuratively trapped inside domestic enclosures. The woman waiting by the window is, of course, an iconic image of passive femininity.

192 Notes for Chapter One

13. Carolyn Heilbrun, quoted in Elizabeth Fishel, *Sisters: Shared Histories, Lifelong Ties* (Berkeley: Conari, 1997), 99–100. Nina Auerbach, *Communities of Women: An Idea in Fiction* (Cambridge: Harvard University Press, 1978), 68.

14. Released in 1979, *My Brilliant Career* resonated with reviewers and audiences hungry for a film that reflected women's changing social roles. Although Armstrong has resisted being typecast as a "woman's director," the film established her as a filmmaker with unusual respect and sensitivity for the dilemmas facing contemporary women who wished to mount professional careers rather than remain in the home as wives and mothers. According to Lizzie Francke, Armstrong acknowledges that her decision to become a filmmaker was influenced by the way in which the woman's movement forced changes in the Australian film industry's attitude toward women in the profession. Armstrong took an active role in "the Sydney Women's Film Group, formed in 1971, who encouraged the then-nascent national film and television school to be conscious about ensuring an equal female intake, whilst also putting pressure on the government to set up a separate women's film fund." Armstrong "sat on the selection panels for the fund and also had her films screened at the numerous festivals that the SWFG organised." See Lizzie Francke, "What Are You Girls Going To Do?" *Sight and Sound*, April 1995, 28–29.

15. Psychoanalyst Ethel Person comments that "the[se] more advanced pretend or make-believe games have important developmental functions: They provide a mode of mastery in response to anxiety or a solution to emotional conflicts current in the child's life; they counter unpleasant feelings and the sense of helplessness. They may also serve as life rehearsals insofar as they project the child's goals and an image of what the child wants to be." See Ethel Person, *By Force of Fantasy* (New York: Penguin, 1996), 67.

16. Stephen P. Bank and Michael D. Kahn, *The Sibling Bond* (New York: Basic Books, 1982), 61.

17. Lupack, *Vision/Re-Vision*, 2.

18. Marchalonis, "Filming the Nineteenth Century," 224. To characterize the self-denial and self-sacrifice in *Little Women* as anachronistic may underestimate its enduring power for many women in the 1990s. However, this fundamental aspect of Alcott's novel must have posed a difficult ideological hurdle for Armstrong and Swicord, just as it has for modern readers whose views have been shaped by "mainstream" or more radical feminist thought.

19. For a recent discussion of this theme of self-denial, see Greta Gaard, "Self-Denial Was All the Fashion: Repressing Anger in *Little Women*," in *Papers on Language and Literature* 27 (1991): 3–19.

20. Louisa May Alcott, *Little Women* (New York: Signet/New American Library, 1983), 187–88.

21. Madelon Bedell, introduction to *Little Women*, in *Critical Essays on Louisa May Alcott*, ed. Madeleine Stern (Boston: Hall, 1984), 145–50; first published in Alcott, *Little Women* (New York: Random House, 1983). Nina Auerbach, "*Little Women* and *Pride and Prejudice*," in *Critical Essays on Louisa May Alcott*, 129–40; first published in Auerbach, *Communities of Women*.

22. Gilbert and Gubar, *Madwoman in the Attic*; see particularly pages 69–77 for an explication of "palimpsism," or female duplicity, as a literary strategy.

23. Contemporary feminist criticism of nineteenth-century women's fiction in the United States has been divided over the cultural meanings and ideologies of the sentimental novel. For two extended and opposing critiques, see: Ann Douglas, *The Feminization of American Culture* (New York: Knopf, 1977), and Jane Tompkins, *Sensational Designs: The Cultural Work of American Fiction, 1790–1860* (New York: Oxford University Press, 1985).

24. Auerbach, *Communities of Women*, 36. Film adaptations of novelistic fiction are only rarely "documentary" in the sense of adhering to the historical actualities informing original source materials. In spite of the predilections of some literary or historical analysts who argue for "authenticity" in film adaptations of either classic works of fiction or the genre of historical novels, I regard adaptations as dramatic fictions in their own right and see them as creative interpretations. For insightful discussions of creative adaptations in film, see John Orr and Colin Nicholson, eds., *Cinema and Fiction: New Modes of Adapting, 1950–1990* (Edinburgh: Edinburgh University Press, 1992), and Millicent Marcus, "Introduction: Film and Literature," in *Filmmaking by the Book: Italian Cinema and Literary Adaptation* (Baltimore: John Hopkins University Press, 1993), 1–24.

25. Marchalonis, "Filming the Nineteenth Century," 290.

26. Donna M. Campbell, "Sentimental Conventions and Self-Protection: *Little Women* and *The Wide, Wide World*," *Legacy* 11, 2 (1994): 123. Descriptions of Jo March are taken from Alcott, *Little Women* (New York: Signet, 1983), 205.

27. For biographical information on the Alcotts and critical studies of Louisa May Alcott's writing and life, see Ednah Cheney, ed., *Louisa May Alcott: Her Life, Letters, and Journals* (Boston: Roberts Brothers, 1890); Joel Myerson, Daniel Shealy, and Madeleine Stern, eds., *The Journals of Louisa May Alcott* (New York: Little, Brown, 1987); Sarah Elbert, *A Hunger for Home: Louisa May Alcott and Little Women* (Philadelphia: Temple University Press, 1984); and Charles Strickland, *Victorian Domesticity: Families in the Life and Art of Louisa May Alcott* (Tuscaloosa: University of Alabama Press, 1985).

28. Cited in Cary, "Louisa, We Hardly Knew Ye," p. 94.

29. Francis, review of *Little Women*, 1312, 1313. Terrence Rafferty, "American Gothic," review of *Little Women* (Columbia Pictures movie), *New Yorker*, January 9, 1995, p. 84. For an articulation of positions within feminist theory, see Marianne Hirsch and Evelyn Fox Kellner, eds., *Conflicts in Feminism* (New York: Routledge, 1990).

30. Francke, "What Are You Girls?" 29.

31. For an autobiographical account by Helen Garner of her relationship with her sisters, see "A Scrapbook, An Album," in *Sisters: Six Australian Writers Explore the Joys and the Frustrations of Being a Sister*, ed. Drusilla Modjeska (New York and Sydney: Angus & Robertson, 1993), 77–110.

32. Orr, *Cinema and Modernity*, 10.

Chapter 2

1. The opening quotation is from Janet Frame, *An Autobiography* (New York: Braziller, 1989), 131. Frame's thoughts on modern autobiography are strikingly similar to Margaret Atwood's vision of time and memory in her novel *Cat's Eye* (New

York: Doubleday, 1988), 3: "You don't look back along time but down through it, like water. Sometimes this comes to the surface, sometimes that, sometimes nothing. Nothing goes away." The extract is from Virginia Woolf, "Modern Fiction," in *Collected Essays*, vol. 2 (London: Hogarth, 1966–67), 106.

2. Walter Benjamin, *Illuminations* (New York: Schocken, 1969), 156–59.

3. Patricia Mellencamp interprets the film as a case study of domestic abuse denial, reading its oblique fantasy scenes as evidence of the "doddering" father's abuse of the destructive daughter, Sweetie. See Mellencamp, *A Fine Romance: Five Ages of Film Feminism* (Philadelphia: Temple University Press, 1995), 173.

4. Freda Freiberg, "The Bizarre in the Banal: Notes on the Films of Jane Campion," in *Don't Shoot Darling: Women's Independent Filmmaking in Australia*, ed. Annette Blonski, Barbara Creed, and Freda Freiberg (Richmond, Australia: Greenhouse, 1987), 328–33. Quoted in Mellencamp, *A Fine Romance*, 174.

5. Mellencamp, *A Fine Romance*, 175.

6. Winnicott, "Mirror-Role of Mother"; Stern, *Interpersonal World of the Infant*; Benjamin, *Like Subject, Love Objects*.

7. See Pam Cook, review of *An Angel at My Table* (Fine Line Features movie), *Monthly Film Bulletin* October, 1990, p. 315.

8. See the analysis of *An Angel at My Table* in Mellencamp, *A Fine Romance*, 174–77.

9. Fishel, *Sisters*, 179.

10. Louise Kaplan, *Adolescence: The Farewell to Childhood*(New York: Touchstone, 1984), chaps. 8 and 9; for the quote, 235.

11. George Pollock, "Childhood Sibling Loss: A Family Tragedy," *Annual of Psychoanalysis* 14 (1986): 32.

12. Frame, *An Autobiography*, 110.

13. See, in particular, Michel Foucault, *Discipline and Punish: The Birth of the Prison* (London: Penguin, 1979).

14. Frame, *An Autobiography*, 191–92.

15. I paraphrase Elizabeth Fishel here. See *Sisters*, 208.

Part II

The epigraph is from Fishel, *Sisters*, 249–50.

1. Kaplan, *Adolescence*, 16.

2. Some of the most critically celebrated films in the neorealist and modernist canon have adapted many of the characteristic themes and formal elements of the prose initiation tale or the literary bildungsroman, inflected by national and ethnic differences. Among the more notable: Satyajit Ray's Apu trilogy (*Pather Panchali*, 1954; *Aparajito*, 1957; *The World of Apu*, 1969); François Truffaut's *The 400 Blows* (1959); Nicholas Roeg's *Walkabout* (1971); Bill Douglas's childhood trilogy (*My Childhood*, 1972; *My Ain Folk*, 1973; *My Way Home*, 1978); and Agnieszka Holland's *Europa Europa* (1991).

3. For comparison, the generic "teen film" produced by Hollywood is treated in the following studies: David M. Considine, *The Cinema of Adolescence* (Jefferson,

N.C.: McFarland, 1985), Thomas P. Doherty, *Teenagers and Teenpics: The Juvenilization of American Movies in the 1950s* (Boston: Unwin Hyman, 1988); and Jon Lewis, *The Road to Romance and Ruin: Teen Films and Youth Culture* (New York: Routledge, 1992).

4. Inez Hedges, *Breaking the Frame: Film Language and the Experience of Limits* (Bloomington and Indianapolis: Indiana University Press, 1991), 103. Quart mentions a number of films that focus on the bonds between mothers and daughters, including Diane Kurys's *Peppermint Soda*, Marta Meszaros's *Diary for My Children* (Hungary, 1984), Margarethe von Trotta's *Marianne and Juliane* (Germany, 1981), and Joyce Chopra's rendering of American teen culture in *Smooth Talk* (USA, 1985). See particularly the introduction in Barbara Koenig Quart, *Women Directors: The Emergence of a New Cinema* (New York: Praeger, 1988), 1–15.

5. In a more experimental vein, Su Friedrich's work stands out, such as her autobiographical *Sink or Swim* (1990), which recounts memories of growing up with her father, or *Hide and Seek* (1996), a film that mixes documentary and fiction to create a portrait of lesbian childhood. See also Jennifer Montgomery's *Age 12: Love with a Little L* (1990), for an experimental construction of lesbian adolescent identity, and Jane Campion's early work, *A Girl's Own Story* (1983) and *Two Friends* (1986), for sharply drawn portraits of growing up and adolescent female friendship.

6. Elaine (played by Mary Kay Place), the maternity shop clerk, spends most of the film in shackles but finds herself attached to the girls as their self-appointed guardian, an ironic treatment of the meaning of family bonds and home through the play on "bondage."

7. See the Internet, http://www.trimarkpictures.com/screening/ripe/makeof.html. Cited May 18, 1997.

8. Stacey, *Stargazing*, 175.

9. Carol Gilligan, Annie Rogers, and Deborah Tolman, eds., *Women, Girls, and Psychotherapy* (New York: Haworth, 1991).

10. Marian Sandmaier, *Original Kin: The Search for Connection among Adult Sisters and Brothers* (New York: Plume, 1995), 94.

11. For detailed discussion of the daughter-father relationship in psychoanalytic and cultural terms, see the anthology *Daughters and Fathers*, ed. Lynda E. Boose and Betty S. Flowers (Baltimore: Johns Hopkins University Press, 1989).

12. Terri Apter, *Altered Loves: Mothers and Daughters during Adolescence* (New York: St. Martin's, 1990), 173.

13. For a discussion of dual narrative in cinema, see Hedges, *Breaking the Frame*, 78.

14. See Stacey, *Stargazing*, 208–9.

Chapter 3

1. Paula Gallant Eckard, "The Prismatic Past in *Oral History* and *Mama Day*," *MELUS* 20, 3 (Fall 1995): 121–35.

2. In "Seeing Subjects," Catherine Portuges has written about intergenerational autobiographical films, which seem to have a particular appeal for women directors. She concentrates on the relationship between mothers and daughters, and the

ways in which autobiographical films sometimes fulfill a reparative function for the filmmaker who wishes to reconnect to the experiences of her mother or speak to the next generation. I suggest that the horizontal relationship between sisters offers an additional perspective to the mother-daughter relationship in autobiographical film, and that its complexity is often rooted in adolescence. See Portuges, "Seeing Subjects," 338–50.

3. Michelle Citron, "Women's Film Production: Going Mainstream," in *Female Spectators: Looking at Film and Television*, ed. E. Deidre Pribram (London and New York: Verso, 1988), 52.

4. For a more extensive analysis of Citron's *Daughter-Rite*, see E. Ann Kaplan, "Mothers and Daughters in Two Recent Women's Films: Mulvey/Wollen's *Riddles of the Sphinx* (1976), and Michelle Citron's *Daughter-Rite* (1978)," in *Women and Film: Both Sides of the Camera* (New York/London: Methuen, 1983), 171–88.

5. Catherine Portuges has extensively theorized the psychological underpinnings of cinematic autobiography, arguing that the autobiographers often feel impelled to offer "reparation" to those they have presumably harmed or disappointed and are searching to be reconciled with powerful "objects" from the past. "Representation of such internal experience, reconstructed and fantasized in visual and auditory registers, may permit the subject of cinematic autobiography (who may also simultaneously be narrator/director/actor), to rework object loss and hence reconstruct identity." See Portuges, *Screen Memories*, 20, and Portuges, "Seeing Subjects," 338–50.

6. See Laurie Halpern Benenson, "A Director's Life Fuels Her Film," *New York Times*, July 26, 1992.

7. Alice Cross, "Surviving Adolescence with Dignity: An Interview with Todd Solondz," *Cineaste* 22, 3 (1996): 25.

8. Sandmaier, *Original Kin*, 12.

9. Louise Kaplan, *Adolescence*. Kaplan uses the term "love dialogues" to capture the preoedipal relationship between infant and mother and infantile narcissism.

10. Dan Yakir, "Mlle. Kurys," *Film Comment* 19 (1983): 66.

11. Ibid.

12. Ibid.

13. See D. W. Winnicott, *Deprivation and Delinquency* (London and New York: Tavistock, 1984), in particular "Some Psychological Aspects of Juvenile Delinquency," "The Antisocial Tendency," "Struggling through the Doldrums," and "Dissociation Revealed in a Therapeutic Consultation."

14. This erotically charged exchange of looks between two adolescent girls ironically takes place on the grounds of a convent that Frederique and her class visit during a school outing, signifying not only the presence of female sexuality in a space devoted to religious, chaste sisterhood but also the Jewish girls' identity as outsiders in a predominantly Catholic country. *Entre Nous*, which Kurys dedicated to her mother, explores Kurys's mother's intense friendship with her female friend, which ended her marriage.

15. See Marcy Pally, "Family *Affaires*," *Vanity Fair*, November 1990, p. 150.

16. Henry Parens, "Siblings in Early Childhood: Some Direct Observational Findings," *Psychoanalytic Inquiry* 8, 1 (1988): 49.

17. Kaplan, *Adolescence*, 15–26. See particularly her introduction.

18. Benenson, "A Director's Life." My analysis of the film disagrees with Patricia Mellencamp's characterization of it as belonging to the tradition of women's obsession with romance, "the one they are socially sanctioned to seek and to which they constantly 'return in imagination'." She criticizes it for promoting marriage and relationships with men as the only goal for women, ignoring a number of important aspects of the film that I address in my discussion (see Mellencamp, *A Fine Romance*, 101). In contrast, Kathleen Rowe sees *Gas Food Lodging* as one of a number of explicitly feminist texts that "invite us to look at melodrama through the lens of comedy" and in this case positing "to varying degrees other forms of family and community where passion, play, and love can thrive, especially among women." This reading coincides with my analysis of the film as a more complex text that questions melodramatic modes in Hollywood cinema. See Rowe, *The Unruly Woman: Gender and the Genres of Laughter* (Austin: University of Texas Press, 1995), 243, n. 8.

19. Feminist critics of the Western frontier myth such as Annette Kolodny have written about European men's fantasies about the American Western landscape as a virginal wilderness to be explored, ravaged, and mastered, in contrast to European women's images of it as a garden to be tended and nurtured. See Kolodny, *The Land Before Her: Fantasy and Experience of the American Frontiers, 1630–1860* (Chapel Hill: University of North Carolina Press, 1984), and *The Lay of the Land: Metaphor as Experience and History in American Life and Letters* (Chapel Hill: University of North Carolina Press, 1975); Melody Graulich, "'O Beautiful for Spacious Guys': An Essay on the 'Legitimate Inclination of the Sexes'," in *The Frontier Experience and the American Dream*, ed. David Mogen, Mark Busby, and Paul Bryant (Texas A & M University Press, 1989), 186–201.

20. For a deployment of Winnicott's theory of "potential space" and play in cinema, see Portuges, *Screen Memories*, 59–60, and Mouton, "Margarethe von Trotta's *Sisters*," 35–47.

21. Kaplan, *Adolescence*, 173–74.

22. For further elaboration of Benjamin's discussion of recognition and difference, see "The Omnipotent Mother: A Psychoanalytic Study of Fantasy and Reality," in *Like Subjects, Love Objects*.

23. See Louise Kaplan, "Narcissism II: Ars Erotica and Dreams of Glory," in *Adolescence*, 213–46, for a discussion of narcissism in adolescents, their fantasies of omnipotence and dreams of glory that must be negotiated with a deidealization of parents. Trudi's continual arguments and confrontations with her mother—her love-hate relationship with her—reveal her attempt to hold onto a narcissistic, omnipotent self that is being assailed by multiple losses. As Shade says in voice-over, Trudi interprets her life as one of decreasing options.

24. The mise-en-scène of this shot evokes countless Western films, but in its focus on adolescents in the modern West it alludes to Peter Bogdanovich's *The Last Picture Show*, a male coming-of-age story that symbolizes the closing of the Western frontier and its codes of masculinity by a decaying Texas town and the closing of a local movie theater.

25. For a thorough discussion of the role of the desert landscape in O'Keeffe's painting and Willa Cather's writing, see Judith Freyer, *Felicitous Space: The Imaginative*

Structures of Edith Wharton and Willa Cather (Chapel Hill: University of North Carolina Press, 1986).

26. David Desser and Lester Friedman, eds., *American-Jewish Filmmakers: Traditions and Trends* (Urbana and Chicago: University of Illinois Press, 1993), particularly chap. 1, "Traditions of American-Jewish Art."

27. Bernard Sherman, *The Invention of the Jew: Jewish-American Education Novels, 1916–1964* (New York: Yoseloff, 1969), 19. Cited in ibid., 6.

28. Stan Schwartz, interview with Todd Solondz, Internet, http://www.desires.com/2.2/Performance/Welcome/Docs/interv2.html. Cited July 7, 1997.

29. Among the critics was Lizzie Francke; see her review of *Welcome to the Dollhouse* (Sony Pictures Classics movie), *Sight and Sound* 7, 2 (1997): 60.

30. Cross, "Surviving Adolescence with Dignity," 26.

31. Stan Schwartz, review of *Welcome to the Dollhouse*, http://www.desires.com/2.2/Performance/Welcome/welcome.html. Cited July 7, 1997.

32. D. W. Winnicott, "The Use of an Object and Relating through Identifications," in *Playing and Reality* (London and New York: Tavistock, 1971), 86–94.

33. Sandmaier, *Original Kin*, 94.

34. Cross, "Surviving Adolescence with Dignity," 25.

35. Cowie, *Representing the Woman*, 117.

36. Cross, "Surviving Adolescence with Dignity," 25.

37. Ibid., 26.

Chapter 4

The epigraph is from "Director's Note," Fine Line Films, Internet, http://www.flf.com/double/synopsis.htm. Cited July 7, 1997.

1. For an expanded analysis of these texts, see Fishel, Sisters, 123–42. Lynda Boose presents an overview of the cultural history and ideology of father-daughter relationships in Western texts in "The Father's House and the Daughter in It: The Structures of Western Culture's Daughter-Father Relationship," in *Daughters and Fathers*, ed. Boose and Flowers, 19–74.

2. Ibid., 21.

3. For a representative selection of feminist critiques of Freudian and Lacanian psychoanalysis, see Dorothy Dinnerstein, *The Mermaid and the Minotaur: Sexual Arrangements and Human Malaise* (New York: HarperCollins, 1976); Chodorow, *The Reproduction of Mothering*; Gilligan, *In a Different Voice*; Luce Irigaray, *Speculum of the Other Woman* (Ithaca: Cornell University Press, 1985) and *The Sex Which Is Not One* (Ithaca: Cornell University Press, 1985); Jane Gallop, *The Daughter's Seduction: Feminism and Psychoanalysis* (Ithaca: Cornell University Press, 1982); Sarah Kofman, *The Enigma of Woman: Woman in Freud's Writings* (Ithaca: Cornell University Press, 1985); and Teresa Brennan, ed., *Between Feminism and Psychoanalysis* (London and New York: Routledge, 1989).

4. Boose, "The Father's House," 39, 33.

5. Rocio G. Davis, "Identity in Community in Ethnic Short Story Cycles: Amy Tan's *The Joy Luck Club*, Louise Erdrich's Love Medicine, Gloria Naylor's *The*

Women of Brewster Place," in *Ethnicity and the American Short Story,* ed. Julie Brown (New York and London: Garland, 1997), 7.

6. In "The Chinese American Family," Morrison G. Wong writes that the traditional Chinese family placed the father and eldest son in the dominant roles. Because of a tradition of patrilocal residence, daughters were considered less valuable and important than sons, and in cases of extreme poverty in rural areas, female infanticide was sometimes practiced. See *Ethnic Families in America: Patterns and Variations,* ed. Charles Mindel, Robert Habenstein, and Roosevelt Wright Jr. (New York: Elsevier, 1988), 230–57. Chinese American women writers such as Maxine Hong Kingston, Amy Tan, and Fae Myenne Ng have responded to this patriarchal legacy in their work, as well as to the many stereotypes of Asian women in the West, affirming the voices of Chinese American women through the mother-daughter bond, for example. Mina Shum's *Double Happiness* is one of the few *feature* films that have addressed Asian American women's complicated relationship to their traditional heritage. Wayne Wang's screen adaptation of Tan's *The Joy Luck Club* (1993) and Kayo Hatta's *The Picture Bride* (1995) are other examples of narrative films that have dramatized Asian immigrant women's bicultural experience. Wang's earlier film *Eat a Bowl of Tea* (1989) satirizes the patriarchal values of the older male immigrant generation and reveals the changes in gender roles spearheaded by a younger generation of Chinese American men and women at the end of World War 2.

7. Kasi Lemmons told Annie Nocenti in an interview that *Eve's Bayou* was "an experiment in creating a form. I'd written screenplays before, and I knew how to write them, but I guess I'm very much a frustrated novelist. *Eve's Bayou* had the feeling of a hybrid of a novel and a screenplay. The dialogue is very operatic, it has a certain rhythm, it's heightened, it's like poetry to me" ("Writing and Directing *Eve's Bayou:* A Talk with Kasi Lemmons," *Scenario* 4, 2 [Summer 1998]: 193).

8. Hortense J. Spillers, "'The Permanent Obliquity of an In[phall]ibly Straight': In the Time of the Daughters and the Fathers," *Daughters and Fathers,* ed. Boose and Flowers, 159.

9. "David Henry Hwang," in *Modern and Contemporary Drama,* ed. Miriam Gilbert, Carl H. Klaus, and Bradford S. Field Jr. (New York: St. Martin's, 1994), 811.

10. See Wong's discussion of the practice of female infanticide in "The Chinese American Family," 232.

11. David Henry Hwang has commented on the intersections of race and sex in Western imperialist visions of Asian women as exotic, obedient, mysterious others. His play *M. Butterfly,* about the love affair between a French diplomat and a Chinese man masquerading as a woman, deconstructs stereotyped notions of the relationship between East and West, female and male identities. Gina Marchetti's *Romance and the "Yellow Peril": Race, Sex, and Discursive Strategies in Hollywood Fiction* (Berkeley: University of California Press, 1993), analyzes, among other images, the Western male fantasy of submissive, exotic Asian women in Hollywood cinema. Jade breaks with the stereotype of female Asian docility through her complex, independent persona, initiating a sexual relationship with Mark, then leaving him without a word in the morning after they have made love.

12. Sandmaier, *Original Kin*, 95.

13. The screenplay of *Eve's Bayou* published in *Scenario* (4, 2 [Summer 1998]) sets the story in 1966; however, the fashion, cars, and general mise-en-scène of the film suggest the 1950s instead. A great critical success and the highest grossing independent film of 1997, the film won Best First-time Director from the National Board of Review, the Independent Spirit Award for Best First Feature, and seven NAACP Image Award nominations. Lemmons is one of the few African American female directors to succeed with a mainstream audience. For informative interviews with her, see Erika Muhammed, "Kasi Lemmons: The Woman behind *Eve's Bayou*" (*Ms.*, March/April 1998, pp. 74–75); and Nocenti, "Writing and Directing *Eve's Bayou.*"

14. On Lemmons's debt to Williams and Lee, see Nocenti, "Writing and Directing *Eve's Bayou*," 197. On Morrison's fiction, see Bernard Bell, *The Afro-American Novel and Its Tradition* (Amherst: University of Massachusetts Press, 1987), 269. For an excellent discussion of Southern Gothic elements in fiction and their cultural meanings, see Claudia Durst Johnson, *To Kill a Mockingbird: Threatening Boundaries* (New York: Twayne, 1994), especially chap. 5, "The Gothic Tradition."

15. Toni Morrison, "Rootedness: The Ancestor as Foundation," in *The Woman That I Am: The Literature and Culture of Contemporary Women of Color*, ed. D. Soyini Madison (New York: St. Martin's, 1994), 492–97. Muhammad, "Kasi Lemmons," 75.

16. Muhammad, "Kasi Lemmons," 75.

17. In *Eve's Bayou's* use of a slightly fantastical perspective, the incorporation of psychic divinations, and a syncretic mix of Christian faith and African animist magic, the film resembles the Mexican magic realist film *Like Water for Chocolate* (directed by Alfonso Arau, 1991; screenplay by Laura Esquivel), in which the youngest of three sisters uses her magical cooking skills as a comically subversive means of revenge against her older sister. Lemmons herself draws comparisons between that film and her own use of African American folklore, myth, and belief in *Eve's Bayou*: "In *Like Water for Chocolate*, the whole story is a fantastical memory; it's like interpreting your past and making it folklore." See Nocenti,"Writing and Directing *Eve's Bayou*," 196.

18. Notable examples of mirror shots include the scene in which Mozelle tells Eve about her relationship with her husbands and lovers. Taking Eve into the past, the camera tracks forward into the mirrored door of a large armoire, where the jealous confrontation between Mozelle, her husband Menard, and her lover Hosea is acted out. Mozelle's narration and the staging of the scene emphasize the subjective nature of memory, where past and present are interconnected. Distancing the viewer from the events, the mirror shot foregrounds the storytelling. Mozelle reveals to Eve that only at the moment that he was willing to die at her lover Hosea's hands did she realize her husband's love for her and her need to remain with him. The memory foreshadows Eve's (and Cisely's) complicated relationship with her father: she comes to understand her love for him when he is killed and she grieves for his loss. Another instance of the mirror shot occurs in the memory scene of Cisely's and her father's ambiguous kiss, reflected in the frame of a similar mirrored door.

19. For an elaboration on broken kinship and filiation in African American literature as shaped by forced displacement and enslavement, see Spillers, "Permanent Obliquity," 157–76.

20. Muhammad, "Kasi Lemmons," 75.
21. Another contemporary film about sisters that represents the same events from their different perspectives is Brigitte Roüan's *Overseas (Outremer)*, which explores the role of women in the familial and a larger cultural and historical matrix.
22. Nocenti, "Writing and Directing *Eve's Bayou*," 196.

Chapter 5

The epigraph is from Kaplan, *Adolescence*, 174–75.
1. My reading of the two films is informed by Person's psychoanalytic discussion in *By Force of Fantasy*: "Shared fantasies are not unusual; they form part of the very ground of human relationships. We imbue our significant relationships with fantasy, and intimate relationships provide the ideal medium in which shared fantasies can proliferate. Sharing fantasies intensifies the emotional and psychological connections between people. In fact, the deepest emotional ties generally occur between people who have congruent or complementary fantasies, whether explicitly shared or communicated through subliminal cues" (123).
2. For the complex political (mis)readings of the Papin sister crime, see Christopher Lane, "'The Delirium of Interpretation': Writing the Papin Affair," *differences: A Journal of Feminist Cultural Studies* 5, 2 (1993): 24–61.
3. Thelma Adams, in her review of *Sister My Sister*, claims that "the fact that it's about incestuous lesbian killers, always titillating, adds torrid tabloid appeal" (*New York Post*, June 23, 1995). John Anderson reduces the film to the message "Turn Lesbian, Turn Lethal" (*Newsday*, June 23, 1995).
4. On the representation of female criminality and sexuality on film, see Lynda Hart, *Fatal Women: Lesbian Sexuality and the Mark of Aggression* (Princeton: Princeton University Press, 1994), and Helen Birch, ed., *Moving Targets: Women, Murder, and Representation* (Berkeley: University of California Press, 1994). See also Lynda Hart, *Between the Body and the Flesh: Performing Sadomasochism* (New York: Columbia University Press, 1998).
5. This is an allusion to Michie's *Sororophobia*, which examines textual and cultural representations of the ways in which women negotiate their desire for and recoil from identification with other women.
6. Luisa Ribeiro, review of *Heavenly Creatures* (Wingnut/Miramax/Fontana Productions movie), *Film Quarterly* 49, 1 (Fall 1995): 33.
7. Kaplan, *Adolescence*, 163, 173.
8. Tod Lippy, "Writing and Directing *Heavenly Creatures*: A Talk with Frances Walsh and Peter Jackson," *Scenario* 1, 4 (Fall 1995): 224.
9. John D. Porter, a professor at Berkeley University, maintains an extensive website on *Heavenly Creatures* (www.666.org/heavenly/hfaq2.html), which contains background on the real people and events that inspired the film, among other information, and a summary of critical appraisals of these materials. Porter elucidates the film's complex visual and narrative details and discusses the case itself. He repeatedly addresses the question of Peter Jackson's representation of Pauline's and Juliet's relationship.

10. Rowe in *The Unruly Woman* employs the term "denaturalize" to indicate the ways in which certain contemporary films simultaneously use and subvert melodramatic forms.

11. Ribeiro, review of *Heavenly Creatures*, 33. Ribeiro provides one of the most sophisticated and insightful analyses of the film, focusing not only on the representation of female sexuality and gender roles but the ways in which Peter Jackson establishes the important religious and spiritual dimensions of Pauline and Juliet's intense friendship, specifically their romantic longing or yearning for life through death.

12. See Hedges, *Breaking the Frame*, 77–82, for dual narration in film.

13. Sigmund Freud, "Family Romances," in *The Standard Edition of The Complete Psychological Works of Sigmund Freud*, vol. 9, ed. J. Strachey (London: Hogarth, 1953–1974), 237–41.

14. The Brontë sisters as children also collectively created an intricate fantasy world of imaginary kingdoms, which provided them with not only a shared sense of identity and an outlet for their creative energies but also the material for their later Gothic fiction.

15. Susan Sontag points out that tuberculosis has been considered since the nineteenth century a sign of artistic sensibility and refinement through suffering. *Illness as Metaphor* (New York: Vintage, 1979).

16. Julia Kristeva, *Powers of Horror: An Essay in Abjection* (New York: Columbia University Press, 1982), 13, quoted in E. Ann Kaplan, *Motherhood and Representation: The Mother in Popular Culture and Melodrama* (New York: Routledge, 1992), 117.

17. Ribeiro, review of *Heavenly Creatures*, 37.

18. Kaja Silverman, *The Acoustic Mirror: The Female Voice in Psychoanalysis and Cinema* (Indianapolis: Indiana University Press, 1988), 39–40.

19. Lynda Hart offers a similar line of interpretation in "'They Don't Even Look Like Maids Anymore': Wendy Kesselman's *My Sister in This House*," in *Making a Spectacle: Feminist Essays on Contemporary Women's Theater*, ed. Lynda Hart (Ann Arbor: University of Michigan Press, 1989), 131–46.

20. The staircase plays a significant role as a space of anxiety and erotic encounter throughout the film. Significantly, it links the small attic room where the Papin sisters live and the Danzards' spacious apartment. Christine remembers only being able to descend the stairs in the convent on one leg by holding onto the railing. Lea drops a pewter pitcher while cleaning the stairs and has a hysterical fit of anxiety. Isabelle spies on the two sisters as they exchange intimacies on the stairs. Running up and down the stairs is clearly linked to sexual excitement. And the staircase is also the site where the final confrontation between the Danzards and the Papin sisters takes place.

21. Hart, "'They Don't Even Look,'" 143.

22. Bette Mandl, "Disturbing Women: Wendy Kesselman's *My Sister in This House*," in *Modern American Drama: The Female Canon*, ed. June Schlueter (Rutherford, N.J.: Fairleigh Dickenson University Press, 1990), 246–53.

Part III

The epigraph is from Sandmaier, *Original Kin*, 95–96.
1. Sandmaier, *Original Kin*, 196.
2. Gayle Greene, "Feminist Fiction and the Uses of Memory," in *The Second Signs Reader: Feminist Scholarship, 1983–1996*, ed. Ruth-Ellen Joeres and Barbara Laslett (Chicago: University of Chicago Press, 1996), 184–215.
3. See Schafer, *The Analytic Attitude*, 218–24; the quote is on p. 219.
4. Michie, *Sororophobia*, 8.
5. Downing, *Psyche's Sisters*, 11.
6. "Interview with Margarethe von Trotta," Fine Line Features (Cited November 27, 1996).
7. Orr, *Cinema and Modernity*, 38.
8. Catherine Portuges, "*Le Colonial Feminin*: Women Directors Interrogate French Cinema," in *Cinema, Colonialism, Postcolonialism: Perspectives from the French and Francophone World*, ed. Dina Sherzer (Austin: University of Texas Press, 1996), 87.
9. Among the critics was Nick James, review of *Sorrento Beach*, *Sight and Sound* (August 1996): 51.
10. This shot is a purposive visual reference to earlier films about sisters who reunite in the childhood home only to confront old rivalries and resentments, primarily Woody Allen's *Interiors* (1978) and Ingmar Bergman's *Cries and Whispers* (1972).
11. John Orr, *Contemporary Cinema* (Edinburgh: Edinburgh University Press, 1998), 92.
12. Adrian Martin, "More Than Muriel: Adrian Martin Reports from Australia," *Sight and Sound* 5, 6 (June 1995): 32.
13. On Grosbard's film and its critique of the representation of female musicians, see Felicia Feaster, review of *Georgia* (CiBy 2000/Miramax movie), *Film Quarterly* 50, 4 (Summer 1997): 32–34.
14. Orr, *Cinema and Modernity*, 115.
15. Von Trotta interview by the author.
16. Ibid.

Chapter 6

1. Orr, *Cinema and Modernity*, 97.
2. Hubert Cohen elaborates on the thematic connections between *The Silence* and *Cries and Whispers* in *Ingmar Bergman: The Art of Confession* (New York: Twayne, 1993), 209: both films involve "a caring servant, a child hungering for the love of an unpredictable, narcissistic mother, and a character whose sacrifice enlarges the protagonist's awareness."
3. See the recent comprehensive critique of Bergman's work, *Ingmar Bergman*, by Hubert Cohen, who takes the "confessional" approach. See also Frank Gado,

The Passion of Ingmar Bergman (Durham, N.C.: Duke University Press, 1986), which consistently reads Bergman's films as elaborations of the director's projections of his artistic and existential dilemmas onto his characters.

4. Stig Björkman, Torsten Manns, and Jonas Sima, *Bergman on Bergman* (New York: Touchstone, 1973), 188.

5. Haskell, *From Reverence to Rape*, 38. Three respected feminist film critics have dismissed *Cries and Whispers* as misogynist, arguing that Bergman always treated female actors as extensions of his own self or as the ultimate other threatening his artistic sense of control. Molly Haskell, in *From Reverence to Rape* (315): "Bergman seems to have turned Harriett Andersson, Liv Ullmann, and Ingrid Thulin into parody-composites of their previous selves (or personae), in a setting that rigorously and pretentiously excludes all signs of idiosyncratic life, and Bergman the artist controls them like puppets, abusing them for being what he has made them . . . and frustrating any attempts at interrelationships by silencing their conversations and aborting sensual overtones between them." Joan Mellen (*"Cries and Whispers,"* 312): "Bergman stands in the way of a liberated image of women in film through a rigidity that ought not to escape notice because it is rooted in a pseudo-philosophical determinism which passes as profundity." Constance Penley (*"Cries and Whispers,"* 204) emphasizes Bergman's "near morbid interest in the suffering of women": "The experience of *Cries and Whispers* was one of being emotionally and physically raped as, once again, a man uses women driven to the edge of experience as sacrifices for his own salvation and then calls it Art."

6. Birgitta Steene, "Bergman's Portrait of Women: Sexism or Subjective Metaphor?" in *Sexual Strategems: The World of Women in Film*, ed. Patricia Erens (New York: Horizon, 1979), 100.

7. Björkman, Manns, and Sima, *Bergman on Bergman*, 147.

8. Mark B. Sandberg, "Rewriting God's Plot: Ingmar Bergman and Feminine Narrative," *Scandinavian Studies* 63, 1 (Winter 1991): 1–29; Marilyn Johns Blackwell, *Gender and Representation in the Films of Ingmar Bergman* (Columbia, S.C.: Camden, 1997).

9. Although Sandberg argues that male characters become increasingly marginalized as women's relationships are correspondingly enlarged until they stand as the central subject of Bergman's later films, he claims that Bergman ultimately cannot relinquish his control and containment of his female protagonists. He cites Bergman's use of a male voice-over (in *Cries and Whispers*) and the unseen male interviewer (in *A Passion*) as well as other cinematic devices that turn his work into a form of male "ventriloquism" through the female body. Of course, this criticism could be applied to a very wide range of male filmmakers. Marilyn Blackwell is equally skeptical about the representation of women in *Cries and Whispers*. She detects an impressionistic fluidity of characterization and visual rhythm that has the potential to contribute to a feminist reading of female subjectivity; however, she ultimately deplores Bergman's relentless emphasis on women's bodies and biology. She focuses particularly on the film's association of the female body with disease and decay, and Bergman's supposed shift to blaming the mother rather than the alienating legacy of God as father for the guilt and self-destructiveness of the daughters. According to Blackwell, "the equation between female illness and female biology, as so often in male discourse, infects the entire diegesis" (*Gender and Representation*, 172).

10. At one point in the film, Karin and Maria are reading to the dying Agnes from Charles Dickens's *Pickwick Papers*, whose bleak Victorian world of orphans and cruel adults mirrors the themes of abandonment and loneliness in the film.

11. See Peter Harcourt, *Five European Directors* (Baltimore: Penguin, 1974), for a critique of Bergman's use of political references.

12. Marianne Hirsch, *The Mother/Daughter Plot: Narrative, Psychoanalysis, Feminism* (Bloomington: Indiana University Press, 1989), 133.

13. Ingmar Bergman, *Four Stories*, trans. Alan Blair (New York: Anchor, 1977), 86.

14. "The Concept of the False Self," in D. W. Winnicott, *Home Is Where We Start From* (New York: Norton, 1990), 65–70.

15. For an overview of early critical responses to *The Silence*, see Carol Brightman, "The Word, the Image, and *The Silence*," in *Ingmar Bergman: Essays in Criticism*, ed. Stuart Kaminsky (London and New York: Oxford University Press, 1975), 239–52.

16. Robin Wood, *Ingmar Bergman* (New York: Praeger, 1969), 123–38; "*The Silence:* Disruption and Disavowal in the Movement beyond Gender," in Marilyn Blackwell, *Gender and Representation*, 98–132.

17. Cohen, *Ingmar Bergman*, 220.

18. "*The Silence*" (screenplay), in *Three Films by Ingmar Bergman: Through a Glass Darkly, Winter Light, The Silence*, trans. Paul Britten Austin (New York: Grove, 1963), 141. This piece of dialogue does not appear in the subtitles of the film and may not have been translated.

19. Derek Prouse, "Ingmar Bergman: The Censor's Problem-Genius," *Times* (London), March 15, 1964, quoted in Cohen, *Ingmar Bergman*, 220.

20. Hirsch, *The Mother/Daughter Plot*, 133.

21. Erik Bork suggests a similar idea in his comparison between Woody Allen's *Interiors* and Bergman's "melodramas," particularly *Cries and Whispers, Face to Face*, and *Autumn Sonata* ("Rejection and Nurturance in Woody Allen's *Interiors* and Bergman's Melodramas," *Filament* 5 [1986]: 13).

22. McNaron, *The Sister Bond*, 6.

23. Bruce Kawin, *Mindscreen*, 15.

24. Bruce Sklarew presents a similar psychoanalytic reading of *Cries and Whispers:* "Bergman reveals how difficult it is for each sister to establish intimacy, a cohesive self, and a mature feminine identity because of preoedipal struggles to survive an inconsistent, narcissistic mother." See Sklarew, "Ingmar Bergman's *Cries and Whispers:* The Consequences of Preoedipal Developmental Disturbances," in *Images of Our Souls: Cavell, Psychoanalysis, Cinema*, ed. Joseph Smith and William Kerrigan (Baltimore: Johns Hopkins University Press, 1987), 169–82. In my reading of the film I place greater emphasis on the cinematography and situate Bergman's psychological exploration of the sisters' experience of maternal deprivation in a historical and cultural context.

25. Adrienne Rich, "Sibling Mysteries," in *The Dream of a Common Language: Poems 1974–77* (New York: Norton, 1978), 58. For a more detailed analysis of Rich's sister poems and their expression of "an anxiety about female difference," see "Writing Lesbian Difference" in Michie, *Sororophobia*, 123–30.

26. Julian Rice, "*Cries and Whispers:* The Complete Bergman," *Massachusetts Review* 16, 1 (1975): 149.

27. Bergman, *Four Stories*, 59.

28. Pauline Kael, "Flesh," *New Yorker,* January 6, 1973, 92. Bergman's idealized portrait of the servant, Anna, as a maternal archetype associated with primal female attachment and nature and as a madonna figure are open to criticism. When Bergman offers Anna as a counterpoint to Karin and Maria, who represent the repression and narcissism of the Swedish upper classes, he misses an opportunity to more authentically explore Anna's subjectivity as a working-class woman.

29. Bergman, *Four Stories*, 86.

30. Kawin, *Mindscreen*, 15.

31. See P. Adams Sitney, "Viskningar Och Rop," review of *Cries and Whispers* (movie), *Dictionary of International Films and Filmmakers*, vol. 1: *Films* (St. James, 1990), 957. Sitney points to the many scenes in the film that suggest oral gratification and aggression. See also his article, "Color and Myth in *Cries and Whispers*" (*Film Criticism* [Spring 1989]: 40), in which he quotes psychoanalyst Bruno Bettelheim with regard to Hänsel and Gretel.

32. McNaron, *The Sister Bond*, 6.

33. Rice, "*Cries and Whispers*," 151.

34. Bergman, *Four Stories*, 66. This scene is not included in the film but seems an important piece of Karin's psychological history that directly relates to a later response to her husband.

35. Juliet Mitchell, *Psychoanalysis and Feminism* (New York: Vintage, 1975), 111.

36. This mutilation scene evokes a similar image in *Persona*, where Alma, the nurse who resents the superiority and cruelty of the actress and mother-figure Elizabet, accidentally drops a glass on the terrace, then leaves one piece of glass for Elizabet to cut herself on. While Alma watches triumphantly, the camera creates suspense that culminates in Elizabet's graphic physical pain. In *Cries and Whispers* Karin's act of self-mutilation is clearly overdetermined, as she is expressing her self-hatred as well as her unmet needs to her mother and husband.

37. See Parens, "Siblings in Early Childhood," for an application of Winnicott's conception of the transitional object to sibling relations. See also D. W. Winnicott, "Transitional Objects and Transitional Phenomena," in *Playing and Reality* (London: Tavistock, 1971), 1–25.

38. See Barbara McManus, "A Failure of Transformation: The Feminine Archetype in Bergman's *Cries and Whispers*," *Florida State University Conference on Literature and Film 6* (1981): 57–68, and Mellen, "*Cries and Whispers*," 297–312.

Chapter 7

The epigraphs are from H.-B. Moeller, "The Films of Margarethe von Trotta: Domination, Violence, Solidarity, and Social Criticism," in *Women in German Yearbook*, vol. 2, ed. Marianne Burkhard and Edith Waldstein (Lanham, N.Y.: University Press of America, 1986), 137, and "Interview with Margarethe von Trotta," Fine Line Features.

1. In addition to her three sister films, von Trotta's feature films include *The Second Awakening of Christa Klages* (*Das Zweite Erwachen der Christa Klages*, 1977), *Sheer*

Madness (*Heller Wahn*, 1983), *Rosa Luxemburg* (1986), *The Return* (*L'Africana*, 1990), *The Long Silence* (*Il lungo silenzio*, 1993), and her critically acclaimed film about the years of the Berlin wall, *The Promise* (*Das Versprechen*, 1994). For comparisons to Bergman, see Gottfried Knapp in *Süddeutsche Zeitung*, September 22, 1979: "In order to compare this film in its aims you need to reach high. Bergman's conflicts between siblings and mothers and daughters or Woody Allen's extraordinary family psychogram 'Interiors' which have been compared to each other, come to mind" (quoted in Ministry of Culture of Munich, *Margarethe von Trotta* [Ministry of Culture of Munich,1985], 28). See also Wolfram Schütte: "Some critics have compared *Schwestern* with Ingmar Bergman's *Autumn Sonata* and Woody Allen's *Interiors*, both 1978, and it's true that a number of thematic connections exist among these drawing room dramas." But Schütte finds the films by Allen and Bergman "more psychologically textured," faulting von Trotta for presenting characters that are schematic types meant to represent specific social conditions and historical situations. I think Schütte reads the opposition between the sisters on a rather superficial level; both Maria and Anna are complex individuals rather than types. See Schütte, "An Editing Room of One's Own," *Artforum* 24 (November 1985): 66–72.

2. Von Trotta's description of *Sisters* as a film more preoccupied with "the emotional flow" between the characters than with narrative is remarkably similar to Bergman's characterization of *Cries and Whispers:* "What the film most resembles is a dark flowing stream—faces, movement, voices, gestures, exclamations, light and shade, moods, dreams" (Bergman, *Four Stories*, 59).

3. Von Trotta interview by the author.

4. Kawin, *Mindscreen*, 199, n. 7.

5. During my interview with her in 1992, Margarethe von Trotta said: "Bergman as a man has a female soul but he looks at women from a male point of view nonetheless. I often don't agree with his view of women."

6. Jutta Brückner, "Für Margarethe von Trotta," in Peter Schneider and Margarethe von Trotta, *Das Versprechen oder Der lange Atem der Liebe: Filmszenarium* (Berlin: Verlag Volk und Welt, 1994), 152. My translation.

7. *International Dictionary of Films and Filmmakers*, 2d ed., s.v. Von Trotta, Margarethe.

8. I am here referencing Susan Linville's excellent analysis of *Marianne and Juliane;* against the grain of many feminist critics, she points to the reflexive, deconstructive strategies employed in the film to present the political dimensions of public and private worlds. "Retrieving History: Margarethe von Trotta's *Marianne and Juliane*," *PMLA* 106, 3 (May 1991): 446–58.

9. Quart, *Women Directors*, 133.

10. Willi Bär and Hans Jürgen Weber, eds., *Schwestern oder die Balance des Glücks* (Frankfurt: Fischer, 1979), 7. Von Trotta interview with the author.

11. Von Trotta interview with the author.

12. Barton Byg writes about *Marianne and Juliane:* "The subtle interweaving of two sisters' images carries on a long German tradition which was prominent in Romantic literature as well as in Expressionist film: the image of the doppelgänger. This adds another dimension to von Trotta's variation on 'genres'—Marianne represents the forbidden other self of Juliane; her transgressions reveal Juliane's shallowness or point to

her real (repressed) desires. This 'Other' in literature as well as film often possesses ideal traits that become evil when taken to the extreme, and in order to preserve the integrity of the narrative and the narrating subject, it must be destroyed or sacrificed so that its energies can be harnessed for good once more" ("German History and Cinematic Convention Harmonized in *Marianne and Juliane*," in *Gender and German Cinema*, vol. 2, ed. Sandra Frieden et.al. [Providence/Oxford: Berg, 1993], 267). Lucy Fischer comments that "like the Hollywood twin films and the Mulvey/Wollen video, *Sisters* also highlights the figure of the double, using myriad visual and narrative strategies. Recurring iconic two-shots are invested with a sense of the doppelganger" ("Sisters," 207). And Martin Donougho traces the Romantic dilemma—"either the self can identify with another in a shared world of objects and projects or else it will find itself dissolved, in schizophrenia or death"—in von Trotta's films preoccupied with women's quests for themselves in relation to others ("Margarethe von Trotta: Gynemagoguery and the Dilemmas of a Filmmaker," *Literature/Film Quarterly* 17, 3 [1989]: 149–60).

13. Brückner, "Für Margarethe von Trotta," 158. Von Trotta's films do also lend themselves to an allegorical reading. In an interview with the director, Carol Bergman commented: "You seem to use the theme of sisterhood in your films as a metaphor for exploring the divided self of modern Germany. In the symbolic system you create, the dark characters with biblical names, such as Miriam in *Sisters* and Ruth in *Sheer Madness*, represent the unconscious, repressed past of Germany. These 'Jewish' women are juxtaposed with the Aryan, efficient types such as Olga in *Sheer Madness* and Maria in *Sisters*" ("*Sheer Madness:* An Interview with Margarethe von Trotta," *Cineaste* 13, 4 [1984]: 47). Von Trotta confirmed that symbolism functions on both a political and personal level in her films; still, it would be simplistic to reduce her complex characters and their conflicts to allegorical oppositions. The spectral haunting of the past, symbolized by the dead sister who returns to challenge the surviving sister, moves beyond the tradition of the split self as evil double.

14. Quart, *Women Directors*, 102. According to Bruno Bettelheim: "Since ancient times the near-impenetrable forest in which we get lost has symbolized the dark, hidden, near-impenetrable world of our unconscious" (*The Uses of Enchantment: The Meaning and Importance of Fairy Tales* [New York: Vintage, 1977], 94). In von Trotta, the forest is a complex site of ambivalence and contradictions, which Brückner compares to the home, in these films another site of the uncanny: "In the depth of the forest the scream happens that can't be uttered and resolved within society, the dream, the suicide and near fatal attempt to set fire to a child. It is the place where the suffering in society can be expressed because society no longer reaches here" ("Für Margarethe von Trotta," 153).

15. Mouton, "Margarethe von Trotta's *Sisters*," 38.

16. There are shades of Hitchcock's *Vertigo* in the latter part of *Sisters* as Maria tries to "replicate" Anna in Miriam, much as Scottie Ferguson, unable to work through his guilt and grief over not having saved Madeleine Elster from death, recreates the real Judy Barton in the imaginary Madeleine's image. In *Vertigo*, Madeleine and Judy are the same woman, and Scottie's "scopophilic" drive to turn the imaginary into the real is particularly relevant for a discussion of the "male gaze" that fetishizes the female body.

17. This story recalls scenes in other films by Bergman in which self-mutilation and aggression are ways to gain attention.

18. Bergman, *"Sheer Madness,"* 47.

19. Fischer, "Sisters," 172–92.

20. Moeller, "Films of Margarethe von Trotta," 140–41.

21. We also hear from her mother that Maria was her father's favorite daughter and stepped into his role as the breadwinner after his death. To support her thesis that the sisters represent masculine and feminine personae, Fischer cites von Trotta: "Maria is the efficient one who works, makes money, is tired in the evening; Anna is like a housewife waiting for her husband." Fischer's analysis remains highly problematic—the film itself presents a more complicated picture of the interrelationship between the sisters, and von Trotta's use of traditional gender codes in relation to Maria is much more ambiguous than Fischer allows. To be fair, Fischer concedes that the female characters are more complex than her comparison of *Sisters* with Hollywood melodramas might suggest, and she notes that "the opposition of gender poles through the relationship between two women" in *Sisters* "demonstrates how masculine and feminine roles are socially constructed, not biologically determined." However, by overemphasizing gender difference in the film, Fischer undercuts von Trotta's more radical exploration of the relationship between two women who position themselves differently in a man's world.

22. Thomas Elsaesser, *New German Cinema: A History* (New Brunswick, N.J.: Rutgers University Press, 1989), 234.

23. Charlotte Delorme, who wrote an influential review of *Marianne and Juliane* in *Frauen und Film* in 1982, accuses von Trotta of dividing the sisters along the stereotypical good sister/bad sister axis and labels the film politically reactionary and antifeminist because it supposedly collapses distinctions between the Right and the Left; Susan Linville has pointed out numerous factual errors in Delorme's interpretation. Ellen Seiter criticizes the film for presenting an important political debate within the narrative discourse of melodrama (Delorme, "On the Film *Marianne and Juliane* by Margarethe von Trotta," trans. Ellen Seiter, *Journal of Film and Video* 37 [1985]: 47–51; trans. of "Zum Film, *Die Bleierne Zeit* von Margarethe von Trotta," *Frauen und Film* 31 [1982]: 52–55). Seiter, "The Political Is the Personal: Margarethe von Trotta's *Marianne and Juliane,*" in *Films for Women,* ed. Charlotte Brunsdon (London: British Film Institute, 1986), 109–16). Barton Byg expands this critique of von Trotta's use of conventional cinematic structures in "German History and Cinematic Convention," arguing that they lead to a "manipulation of the image of women and the false harmonization of German history." See Linville, "Retrieving History," 446–58, for a more detailed critique of feminist critics' negative responses to von Trotta's film and a more accurate and nuanced assessment of von Trotta's cinematic strategies and narrative aims; the quote is from p. 456.

24. Pauline Adamek, *"The Promise*—Interview with Margarethe von Trotta," Cited November 27, 1996.

25. See E. Ann Kaplan, "Discourses of Terrorism, Feminism, and the Family in von Trotta's *Marianne and Juliane,*" in *Women and Film,* vol. 4, ed. Janet Todd (New York: Holmes & Meier, 1988), 258–70. Linville, "Retrieving History," 455.

26. Quart, *Women Directors,* 113.

27. Linville uses Bruce Kawin's term "mindscreen" to describe the subjective flashback that makes up the body of *Marianne and Juliane*. Von Trotta said in our interview: "I just think so much happens inside a person at the same time. You live in the present yet the past always plays a role; the present, past, dreams, it's all simultaneous. We live in the now, which incorporates things from the past, certain ideas or expectations or perhaps premonitions. We don't just live on one time level. And I show those different time levels in my films. I don't really go back in time because the flashbacks are part of the present in the film."

28. Linville has provided an analysis of the film's representation of women's "bodily reaction" to guilt and the gender-related differences in spectatorship that account for male and female perceptions of documents of the past. See "Retrieving History," 453.

29. Mouton, "Margarethe von Trotta's *Sisters*," 43.

30. My translation. Hans Jürgen Weber, ed., *Die Bleierne Zeit: Ein Film von Margarethe von Trotta* (Frankfurt am Main: Fischer Taschenbuch Verlag, 1981), 58.

31. In a review of *Marianne and Juliane*, Marc Silberman claims that "the classical Antigone/Ismene conflict begins to surface" in the film when Marianne becomes a terrorist and demands from her sister that she join "the revolutionary cause" ("Women Filmmakers in West Germany: A Catalog (Part 2)," *Camera Obscura* 11 (1983): 144). See also Moeller, "Films of Margarethe von Trotta," 132, and Linville, "Retrieving History," 456.

32. Kaplan, "Discourses of Terrorism," 266.

33. See Alexander and Margarethe Mitscherlich, *Die Unfähigkeit zu Trauern* (München/Zurich: Piper Verlag, 1967).

34. Linville, "Retrieving History," 455.

35. Review of *Three Sisters* (Erre Produzioni/Bioskop/Cinemax movie), *Sequences* 135/136 (1988): 30.

36. I refer here primarily to two articles by Jean-Louis Baudry on the power and fascination of the cinema in its appeal to the unconscious, "Ideological Effects of the Basic Cinematographic Apparatus" and "The Apparatus: Metapsychological Approaches to the Impression of Reality in Cinema" (both reprinted in Philip Rosen, *Narrative, Apparatus, Ideology: A Film Theory Reader* [New York: Columbia University Press, 1986], 286–98 and 299–318). Baudry's theories on the cinematic apparatus and Lacan's specular imaginary as well as the cinematic screen's appeal to the spectator's primary identification have been widely used by film theorists.

37. Von Trotta explores women's friendships and their impact on marriage in greater detail in *Sheer Madness* (1983).

38. Thomas Elsaesser, "Primary Identification and the Historical Subject: Fassbinder and Germany," in *Narrative, Apparatus, Ideology: A Film Theory Reader,* ed. Philip Rosen (New York: Columbia University Press, 1986), 540. See also Elsaesser, *New German Cinema*, 232–38.

39. See Doane's discussion of the meaning of space in "women's films" of the 1940s in Mary Ann Doane, "The 'Woman's Film': Possession and Address," in *Re-Vision: Essays in Feminist Film Criticism*, ed. Mary Ann Doane, Patricia Mellencamp, and Linda Williams (Frederick, Md.: University Publishers of America/AFI, 1984), 67–82. Evelyn Keller, *Reflections on Gender and Science* (New Haven: Yale University Press,

1985), 99, quoted in Laura Tracey, *"Catching the Drift": Authority, Gender, and Narrative Strategy in Fiction* (New Brunswick, N.J.: Rutgers University Press, 1988), 23.

Conclusion

1. Again I am indebted to Elizabeth Francis's very perceptive review and discussion of *Little Women*. I have mentioned other films that employ the visual trope of windows, such as Woody Allen's *Interiors*, Richard Franklin's *Sorrento Beach*, Ingmar Bergman's *Cries and Whispers*, and Lindsay Anderson's *The Whales of August*. Von Trotta, unlike her male colleagues, specifically questions the conventional division between private and public spaces as separate gendered sites of identity construction.

2. See Stacey, *Stargazing*, 173 (in which she quotes Benjamin, *Bonds of Love*, 20), 227.

3. More recent critical works on motherhood and mother-daughter relationships include Hirsch, *The Mother/Daughter Plot*, and Kaplan, *Motherhood and Representation*. In cinema studies, Jeanine Basinger's *A Woman's View: How Hollywood Spoke to Women, 1930–1960* (New York: Knopf, 1993), treats classical Hollywood's representation of women's relationships and friendships. Hollinger's *In the Company of Women* critically evaluates the progressive as well as politically conservative aspects of the so-called new woman's films of the 1970s and after. See Lucy Fischer, *Cinematernity: Film, Motherhood, Genre* (Princeton: Princeton University Press, 1996), for an overview of feminist film theory's treatment of motherhood in cinema. Fischer's article "Sisters: The Divided Self" is, of course, the exception to feminist film scholars' "amnesia" regarding sisters.

4. Barbara Mathias, *Between Sisters: Secret Rivals, Intimate Friends* (New York: Delacorte, 1992), x.

5. Carol Saline (with Sharon J. Wohlmuth, photographer), *Sisters* (Philadelphia: Running Press, 1994). *Sisters* spent more than a year on the *New York Times* bestseller list and features sisterly tales of sacrifice, devotion, and jealousy by Dixie Carter, Coretta Scott King, Chris Evert, and many others.

6. For an insightful discussion of *My Twentieth Century* and its treatment of technology and women's social roles, see Janet Lorenz, review of *My Twentieth Century* (Budapest Filmstudio/Mafilm movie), in *Magill's Cinema Annual 1991: A Survey of the Films of 1990* (Pasadena, Calif.: Salem, 1991), 271–74.

Index

Hide and Seek, 195n. 5
High Tide, 34
Hilary and Jackie, 178
Hirsch, Marianne, 130, 136
Hitchcock, Alfred, 156
Hoffman, Alice, 178
Hollander, Anne, 22, 23
Hour of the Wolf, 127, 156
How to Make an American Quilt, 16
Hui, Ann, 54
Hwang, David Henry, 87, 199n. 11

Ingmar Bergman: The Art of Confession
  (Cohen), 203n. 2
initiation, 18
Interiors, 124, 203n. 10, 205n. 21, 206–7n. 1,
  211n. 1
intersubjectivity, 11, 18, 176–77; and
  Bergman, 123; defined, 189 n. 22;
  dynamics of, 8–9, 189n. 22; and identity
  formation, 8, 176; and initiation, 18; and
  sister relationships, 176–78; and von
  Trotta, 148

Jackson, Peter, 59, 101, 103–4, 202n. 11
Jackson, Samuel L., 93
James, Henry, 22
Jane Eyre (Brontë), 25
Jones, Laura, 38, 42–43, 47
The Joy Luck Club (Tan), 199n. 6

Kaplan, E. Ann, 62, 151–52, 159–60, 165
Kaplan, Louise: on adolescence, 46, 52, 69,
  73, 100, 103
Kawin, Bruce, 4, 137, 139, 148, 210n. 27
Keller, Evelyn, 174–75
Kesselman, Wendy, 101, 111, 116
King, Coretta Scott, 211n. 5
Kingston, Maxine Hong, 85, 199n. 6
Klarwein, Eleonore, 64
Kristeva, Julia, 109, 115
Kristofovich, Vyacheslav, 54
Krueger, Lisa, 54
Künstlerroman, 13, 17, 190n. 6
Kurosawa, Akira, 119–20
Kurys, Diane, 57, 62; cinematic autobiogra-
  phies of, 63; negotiation of identities of
  women portrayed by, 9–10; on Pepper-
  mint Soda, 65, 66–68; Peppermint Soda as
  autobiography of, 68; Peppermint Soda
  dedicated to older sister by, 65; sisters

coauthoring family history in works of,
  178

Lacan, Jacques, 101, 170, 210n. 36
The Lagoon (Frame), 40
Laing, R. D., 44
Lampe, Jutta, 150, 160
The Last Days of Chez Nous, 3, 25–26, 33–35
The Last Picture Show, 197n. 24
Lee, Ang, 22, 33, 54, 87
Lee, Harper, 91
Lefkovitz, Lori Hope, 4–5, 8, 124, 188n. 11
Leigh, Jennifer Jason, 122
Leigh, Mike, 54
Leitch, Donovan, 74
Lemmons, Kasi, 3, 13, 58; on Eve's Bayou,
  94, 97, 99, 199n. 7, 200n. 17; and family
  relationships, 86; on folklore, 93; influ-
  ences on, 91; and Like Water for Chocolate,
  200n. 17; success of, 200n. 13
LeRoy, Mervyn, 23, 190n. 1
Lévi-Strauss, Claude, 84
Like Subjects, Love Objects (Benjamin), 9
Like Water for Chocolate, 188n. 11, 200n. 17
Lindblom, Gunnel, 131
Linville, Susan, 164, 167, 210n. 28; Marianne and Juliane critiqued by, 160, 209n.
  23; on the subjective flashback in Marianne and Juliane, 162, 210n. 27
Little Women (Alcott), 21, 27–29, 190–91n. 1
Little Women (Armstrong), 16–17; fantasy
  and self-exploration in, 26–27, 101, 192n.
  15; the female artist in, 12–13, 17–19,
  26–27, 122; feminist interpretation in, 22,
  27, 30, 191n. 4; idealized portrayal of a
  female utopian community in, 22–24; Jo
  March as mirror for contemporary
  women, 25, 27; linear construction of, 37,
  40; marriage treated in, 28–30; melodramatic structure of, 19; mentioned, 36, 41,
  57, 59; nineteenth-century gender roles
  portrayed in, 24–25, 191n. 12; relationship between Jo and Bhaer in, 32–33; sister relationships in, 12–13, 17–19, 30–31,
  33; sisters and identity formation of the
  artist in, 17–19; studio style of, 24, 191n.
  10; Victorian morality downplayed in, 22,
  27, 30, 192n. 18; windows in, 24, 176
Little Women (Cukor), 22–23
Little Women (LeRoy), 23
Litvak, Anatole, 188n. 15

search for identity in, 57, 64–65, 67–69; importance of female bonds in, 65, 67, 68, 196n. 14; mirrors used in, 65; older sister's sexuality in, 64–66, 70; photomontage structure of, 65, self-reflexivity of, 64; sisters' relationship in, 57, 65–67, 69, 89; triangulated bond between sisters and mother in, 57, 62–63, 67
Person, Ethel, 104, 192n. 15, 201n. 1
Persona, 127–28, 131, 134, 206n. 36; compared to von Trotta's work, 148, 156–57, 165
Picture Bride (Hatta), 199n. 6
Place, Mary Kay, 195n. 6
Pollock, George, 46
Porter, John D., 201n. 9
The Portrait of a Lady (James), 22
Portuges, Catherine, 7–8, 17, 120, 189n. 19, 195–96n. 2, 196n. 5
Potter, Sally, 10
Powers of Horror (Kristeva), 109
Practical Magic, 178
The Promise, 206–7n. 1
Psyche's Sisters (Downing), 16

Quart, Barbara, 53, 150, 152, 195n. 4

Rafferty, Terrence, 33
Rapper, Irving, 188n. 15
Rashomon, 120
Ray, Nicholas, 53
Rayson, Hannie, 121
Rebel Without a Cause 53
Reis, Irving, 188n. 15
Representing the Woman (Cowie), 7, 80–81, 188–89n. 17
Resnais, Alain, 10, 119
The Return, 206–7n. 1
Ribeiro, Luisa, 104, 110, 202n. 11
Rich, Adrienne, 137–38
Richardson, Joely, 112
Ripe, 54, 55, 152
rites-of-passage films. *See* coming-of-age films
Rohmer, Eric, 11
Romance and the "Yellow Peril" (Marchetti), 199n. 11
Romanticism, 11
"Rootedness: The Ancestor as Foundation" (Morrison), 92
Rosa Luxemburg, 206–7n. 1

Roüan, Brigitte, 120, 201n. 21
Rowe, Kathleen, 197n. 18, 202n. 10
Ryder, Winona, 22, 27, 31, 191n. 4

Saline, Carol, 178
Sandberg, Mark, 129, 204n. 9
Sandmaier, Marian, 56, 64, 79, 90, 117
Sarandon, Susan, 23
Sargeson, Frank, 40
Sartre, Jean-Paul, 101
Scacchi, Greta, 169
Schafer, Roy, 118, 190n. 3
Schlöndorff, Volker, 165
Schütte, Wolfram, 206–7n. 1
Schwartz, Stan, 78
The Second Awakening of Christa Klages, 206–7n. 1
Seiter, Ellen, 159, 209n. 23
Sense and Sensibility (Austen), 22, 33
The Seventh, 129
sex lies and videotape, 188n. 11
Shakespeare, William, 178
Shaw, George Bernard, 15
Sheer Madness, 206–7n. 1, 208n. 13, 210n. 37
Sherman, Bernard, 77
Sherman, Vincent, 188n. 15
Shum, Mina, 13, 58, 83
"Sibling Mysteries" (Rich), 137
siblings: familial and social worlds bridged by, 69; impact of loss of, 46; memories and renderings of the past of, 61, 62; in psychoanalytic theory, 16, 190n. 3
Sichel, Alex, 54
The Silence, 116, 123, 127, 143, 205n. 18; compared to *Cries and Whispers*, 128, 203n. 2; compared to von Trotta's work, 148, 166; deep focus shots of sisters in, 133–34; female subjectivity in, 128; influence of, 124; patriarchal logos criticized in, 129, 130, 135, 204n. 9; relationship between sisters in, 133, 134; sisters' relationship in, 3–4, 13, 132, 146; sisters' internalization of dead father in, 128, 131–32, 134–35; symbolic analysis of, 132
Silverman, Kaja, 111
Silverman, Marc, 164, 210n. 31
Sink or Swim (Friedrich), 195n. 5
sisterhood: feminist utopian views of, 16, 21, 177, 178; and intersubjectivity in identity formation, 176–77